Conversations with Paul Auster

Literary Conversations Series
Peggy Whitman Prenshaw
General Editor

Conversations
with Paul Auster

Edited by James M. Hutchisson

University Press of Mississippi   *Jackson*

www.upress.state.ms.us

The University Press of Mississippi is a member of the Association of American University Presses.

First printing 2013

∞

Library of Congress Cataloging-in-Publication Data

Auster, Paul, 1947–
  Conversations with Paul Auster / edited by James M. Hutchisson.
    p. cm.
  Includes index.
  ISBN 978-1-61703-736-8 (cloth : alk. paper) — ISBN 978-1-61703-737-5 (ebook) 1. Auster, Paul, 1947––Interviews. 2. Authors, American—20th century—Interviews. 3. Motion picture producers and directors—United States—Interviews. I. Hutchisson, James M.
  PS3551.U77Z46 2013
  813'.54—dc23   2012021648

British Library Cataloging-in-Publication Data available

Works by Paul Auster

Fiction

City of Glass (Los Angeles: Sun and Moon Press, 1985)
Ghosts (Los Angeles: Sun and Moon Press, 1986)
The Locked Room (Los Angeles: Sun and Moon Press, 1986)
(Republished in one volume as *The New York Trilogy* [London: Faber and
    Faber, 1987; NY: Penguin, 1990])
In the Country of Last Things (NY: Viking, 1987)
Moon Palace (NY: Viking, 1989)
The Music of Chance (NY: Viking, 1990)
Leviathan (NY: Viking, 1992)
Mr. Vertigo (NY: Viking, 1994)
Timbuktu (NY: Holt, 1999)
The Book of Illusions (NY: Holt, 2002)
Oracle Night (NY: Holt, 2003)
Auggie Wren's Christmas Story (NY: Holt, 2004)
The Brooklyn Follies (NY: Holt, 2005)
Travels in the Scriptorium (NY: Holt, 2006)
Man in the Dark (NY: Holt, 2008)
Invisible (NY: Holt, 2009)
Sunset Park (NY: Holt, 2010)

Poetry

Unearth (Weston, CT: *Living Hand 3*, Spring 1974)
Wall Writing (Berkeley, CA: The Figures, 1976)
Effigies (Paris: Orange Export Ltd., 1977)
Fragments from Cold (Brewster, NY: Parenthèse, 1977)
White Spaces (Barrytown, NY: Station Hill, 1980)
Facing the Music (Barrytown, NY: Station Hill, 1980)
Disappearances: Selected Poems (Woodstock, NY: Overlook Press, 1988)

Ground Work: Selected Poems and Essays 1970-1979 (London: Faber and Faber, 1991)
Autobiography of the Eye (Portland, OR: Beaverdam Press, 1993)
Collected Poems (Woodstock, NY: Overlook Press, 2004)

Essays, memoirs, and autobiographies

The Invention of Solitude (NY: SUN, 1982)
The Art of Hunger: Essays, Prefaces, Interviews (Los Angeles: Sun & Moon Press, 1992)
The Red Notebook and Other Writings (London: Faber and Faber, 1995)
Why Write? (Providence, RI: Burning Deck, 1995)
Hand to Mouth: A Chronicle of Early Failure (NY: Holt, 1997)
The Red Notebook: True Stories (NY: New Directions, 2002)
The Story of My Typewriter, with paintings and drawings by Sam Messer (NY: D.A.P., 2002)
Collected Prose: Autobiographical Writings, True Stories, Critical Essays, Prefaces, and Collaborations with Artists (NY: Picador, 2005; expanded second edition, 2010)
Winter Journal (NY: Holt, 2012)

Edited collections

The Random House Book of Twentieth-Century French Poetry: With Translations by American and British Poets (NY: Random House, 1982)
I Thought My Father Was God, and Other True Tales from NPR's National Story Project (NY: Holt, 2001); (British edition: *True Tales of American Life* [London: Faber and Faber, 2002])
Samuel Beckett: The Grove Centenary Edition (NY: Grove Press, 2006)

Selected Translations

A Little Anthology of Surrealist Poems (NY: Siamese Banana Press, 1972)
Fits and Starts: Selected Poems of Jacques Dupin (Weston, CT: Living Hand, 1973)
The Uninhabited: Selected Poems of André du Bouchet (NY: Living Hand, 1976)
Life/Situations: Essays Written and Spoken, by Jean-Paul Sartre (NY: Pantheon, 1977) (with Lydia Davis)

African Trio: Talatala, Tropic Moon, Aboard the Aquitaine, by Georges
 Simenon (NY: Harcourt, 1979) (with Lydia Davis)
A Tomb for Anatole, by Stéphane Mallarmé (San Francisco: North Point
 Press, 1983; rpt. NY: New Directions, 2005)
The Notebooks of Joseph Joubert (San Francisco: North Point Press, 1983;
 rpt. NY: New York Review Books, 2005)
Vicious Circles: Two Fictions and "After the Fact," by Maurice Blanchot
 (Barrytown, NY: Station Hill, 1985)
Joan Miro: Selected Writings and Interviews (Boston: G. K. Hall, 1986)
Chronicle of the Guayaki Indians by Pierre Clastres (NY: Zone Books,
 1998)

Filmography

Smoke (1995)
Blue in the Face (1995)
Lulu on the Bridge (1998)
[In *Three Films: Smoke, Blue in the Face, and Lulu on the Bridge* (NY: Pica-
 dor, 2003)]
The Inner Life of Martin Frost (NY: Picador, 2007)
Collected Screenplays (London: Faber and Faber, 2010)

Contents

Introduction

Paul Auster has granted a lot of interviews, more so perhaps than most contemporary writers and most writers like Auster, who seems to present a persona to the public of a brooding, philosophical artist, so devoted to his art as to be willingly cut off from the world. When one questioner in 2003 asked him if he'd prefer just to stay "locked away somewhere" and write, he responded that he would rather "not say a word to anybody" but that he felt an obligation to his publisher to "present [his] book[s] to the public." Yet by his own account he has been interviewed hundreds of times, and the number has risen sharply as he has advanced in his career and become one of the most prolific, critically acclaimed, and intensely studied of living American writers. In the words of one critic, he has "given the phrase 'experimental fiction' a good name" by fashioning bona fide literary works with all the rigor and intellect demanded of contemporary literature.[1]

Auster was born in Newark, New Jersey in 1947, attended Columbia University during the 1960s and graduated with both a bachelor's and master's degree in comparative literature. In the 1970s, Auster lived variously in Paris and southern France earning a meager living as a freelance reviewer and translator. His first major book, *The Invention of Solitude* (1982) was a memoir, an account of his relationship with his father, but he became known quickly as a novelist in 1985 when *City of Glass*—a book rejected by seventeen publishers before being accepted by Sun and Moon Press of Los Angeles—appeared to enthusiastic reviews. This grim and intellectually puzzling mystery belies its surface identity as a "detective novel" and goes on to become a profound meditation on transience and mortality, the inadequacy of language, and ontological isolation. One reviewer noted that it was as if "Kafka had gotten hooked on the gumshoe game and penned his own ever-spiraling version" of a "post-existentialist private eye" story.[2] Two other novels then appeared, *Ghosts* and *The Locked Room*, forming what Auster eventually entitled The New York Trilogy.

Auster followed that with a dystopian novel, *In the Country of Last Things* (1987), the chronicle of a woman's post-apocalyptic journey through a devastated urban landscape. *Moon Palace* (1989), his next major work, is a picaresque novel in the American tradition of Mark Twain and Jack Kerouac, about the interplay of freedom and chance. Eleven more novels have followed, as well as much nonfiction, several lengthy autobiographical pieces, and three film scripts. Indeed, Auster's large readership is due at least in part to the pleasing effect of his versatility. In Auster's ninth novel, *Timbuktu*, he stretches narrative conventions even further than in his earlier work by narrating the story from the point of view of a dog. His most recent book, *Sunset Park* (2010), addresses matters of maturity and family, broken homes and fractured lives. Running throughout all these varied books is an obsessive experimentation with narrative form, a weaving together of memoir and invented material, and the construction of an ultimately perplexing fictive universe in which characters try to find their way out of a labyrinth of ambiguity.

Auster's willingness to come out in public and talk about his books may also to some seem ironically at odds with his stubbornly Luddite approach to the mechanics of writing books: he does not use a computer to write, preferring the silence of the fountain pen or the mechanical pencil on the page. When he does need to generate a clean copy, he turns to an "archaic" industrial machine, a portable Olympia typewriter, which has become something of a talisman for him. The typewriter occupies such an important space in his creative mind that the artist Sam Messer became intrigued by its iconic significance. Messer produced some eighty to a hundred different paintings of the Olympia, and Auster was moved to write an essay to accompany Messer's exhibition, "The Story of My Typewriter." Yet Auster is just as decidedly not a technophobe. A unique feature of this collection shows how often Auster has been interviewed by online magazines (that is, periodicals with no print presence but available only on the Internet). He even participated in an online chat session with washingtonpost.com's book department. Here, readers from all around the world asked Auster questions online. Auster doesn't own a computer, so he responded to the questions via the telephone, and his answers were then typed up on a keyboard.

Auster's working methods are perhaps the most frequently recurring subject of these interviews. Indeed, a lengthy interview by Michel Contat in 1994 is devoted more or less entirely to this topic. He is an extraordinarily disciplined writer who, when he is engaged on the writing of a new book, rises each day and after a glass of orange juice, a pot of tea, and about forty-five minutes with the *New York Times*, leaves his house in the Park Slope neighborhood of Brooklyn to walk a few minutes to a small apartment nearby which he uses as a studio. In this spartan environment (there is a telephone, but only three people have the number), Auster works every day—even Sundays, unless there is a major family event taking place that day. Writing by hand in quadrille-lined notebooks, he proceeds a paragraph at a time—following the sequence of the story—revising heavily as he goes. He will type a clean copy of the paragraph at different points, to give him something fresh to work with, and then he takes it through several more rounds of revision. Auster admits that this is a very tedious way to write: "the pages pile up with excruciating slowness," he told one interviewer. On the other hand, the pen "is a much more primitive instrument [than a keyboard]. You feel that the words are coming out of your body and then you dig the words into the page. Writing has always had that tactile quality for me. It's a physical experience."[3] In his early years, he could manage, at best, one or two paragraphs a day, perhaps a page, until he had everything just right. This was usually six hours' work, and that was the end of his day. Now he works somewhat more quickly: his pattern has been to cogitate for a long time between projects, but he's written most of his recent books in as little as six months.

When he begins a novel, he has only the sketchiest idea of its plot, and he draws up only the barest of outlines—usually a series of around ten plot movements that say little more than, for example, "1. New York; 2. Pittsburgh," and so forth. Auster's characters have their own autonomy; like Henry James, he let's them do what they like, and he has no concrete sense of where they will take the story. An inveterate reviser (again like James) Auster does not work very closely with an editor. His editors usually make minor suggestions only. However, his first reader is always his wife, the novelist Siri Hustvedt. While at work on a novel, every couple of weeks, after twenty-five to thirty pages have been generated, he will read his work-in-progress to her in the evening. She is his most valuable sounding-board.

In these interviews, Auster is a low-key, unpretentious but serious and deeply thoughtful person. He freely admits that even he does not know all the meanings in his work and is not sure that he ever will. Auster believes that the true creative artist cannot know this. Speaking in a raspy voice that tells of many years smoking strong cigars, he tells one story of talking to Samuel Beckett—one of his early influences—about a 1946 novel (*Mercier and Camier*) published only in French.[4] At the time, Beckett had just translated the book into English but had cut more than a quarter of the original in the translation. Auster expressed surprise at this and told Beckett how good the deleted material was. Beckett responded with, "Do you really think so?"

Even Samuel Beckett could not, in Auster's view, objectively or empirically see value in something he had written.

Auster discusses some of the events in his own life that were catalysts for fiction. He often relates the incident that happened to him after the collapse of his first marriage and while living in a tiny New York apartment that led to the conceit of *City of Glass*—receiving a telephone call two nights running in which the wrong-number caller asked for Pinkerton's Detective Agency. Auster's consideration of what might have happened had he said he was in fact a detective led to the main narrative thread of *City of Glass*. We also learn about the gestation and composition of these early novels, especially The New York Trilogy: these books and the two subsequent ones, *In the Country of Last Things* and *Moon Palace*, were conceived much earlier, in the 1970s, then reworked after the completion of the Trilogy. Ideas from the Trilogy then remained with Auster as he continued to produce new books—hence the metatextual references in and among these five early novels.

More interesting, perhaps, are the differences that Auster cites between writing memoir and writing fiction. His first published books were poetry, followed by a work of nonfiction, *The Invention of Solitude*, in part a memoir of his father, which was written between 1979 and 1981. Auster claims that the effort involved in writing fiction versus writing autobiography is the same, but that an imaginative work "allows you a lot more freedom and maneuverability than a work of nonfiction." That wide a degree of imaginative latitude, however, can also be "scary": "What comes next? How do I know the next sentence I write isn't going to lead me off the edge of a cliff? With an autobiographical work, you know the story in advance, and your primary obligation is to tell the truth. But that doesn't make the job any easier."

The baseline question that perhaps every interviewer ever seeks an answer for when speaking with a writer is, of course, "Why do you write?" Auster has answered this question with solid consistency over the years that these documents span. He speaks insistently of writing as a way to relieve "some of the pressure" of "buried secrets"—"those inaccessible parts of ourselves." The sense of devotion to his art and dedication to writing is strong. Biographical details of his early career show a sort of starving artist ("The Art of Hunger" was the title of his M.A. thesis at Columbia University, and then of an early essay) but of absolutely loving what he was doing, even when eking out a meager living in Paris in the 1970s, translating, writing book reviews, and even manning the switchboard at the *New York Times* Paris bureau on the graveyard shift.

Early in his career, Auster spoke to one interviewer about the fact that he has had "no choice" in writing—that doing so was "a matter of survival" and that he could not get the stories out of his mind and onto the page fast enough. In more recent years, however—after an astonishingly productive fifteen- to twenty-year stint—he has confessed to periods of feeling "empty" of material and even in one videotaped question and answer session after a reading in New York joked that he may end up "moving to Florida and playing golf."[5]

Auster is intuitively wedded to the idea that writing is a solitary enterprise, as his work habits attest. And, as he's said numerous times, he is happy to be left alone to write, except where certain circumstances compel him to be a part of something else. Partly this disposition is an extension of his solitary childhood. In 2003, he described to an interviewer how ill he was as a small child: "I had all kinds of physical ailments, and I spent more time sitting in doctors' offices with my mother than running around outdoors with my friends." At age four or five, he became strong enough to do sports, and when he did, he threw himself into them "with a passion—as if making up for lost time." His sport of choice was baseball, for which he has held a lifelong interest. (Baseball figures into many of his novels, and as an out of work writer in the early 1970s, he even invented a card game based on the sport, "Action Baseball," much like the game in Robert Coover's novel, *The Universal Baseball Association*, which appeared in 1968. The rules of the game are reprinted in *Hand to Mouth: A Chronicle of Early Failure*.)

Perhaps this is why Auster has never been averse to, is indeed quite interested in, writing for the screen—as well as all other aspects of filmmaking—a "team sport" if there ever was one, with its dozens of supporting crew behind the writer, director, and producer as the work of art takes shape. Three interviews in this volume exclusively concern his filmmaking. Auster has four movies to his credit so far: *Smoke, Blue in the Face, Lulu on the Bridge*, and *The Inner Life of Martin Frost*. The first two, both of which appeared in 1995, were collaborations with director Wayne Wang, who talked Auster into working on the movies in the first place. Auster wrote and codirected *Smoke* and *Blue in the Face*. For *Lulu on the Bridge* (1998) and *The Inner Life of Martin Frost* (2007), he was sole writer and director. Auster likes the collaborative character of filmmaking and seems to welcome involvement in films as a break from his solitary routine of writing prose.

In these interviews, Auster explores all the variables that go into the mix of writing in different genres and for different audiences. He compares writing poetry to a still photograph and prose to the fluidity of a film camera—

or, what in a later television appearance in 2008 he called "narrative pro-pulsion."[6] Auster talks a great deal about the rhetorical strategies involved in writing for the page versus writing for the screen and about his under-standing of the audience's different expectations for a story absorbed via film versus that which is absorbed via written language. The culture of film-making also figures as a prominent theme in some of his novels. *The Book of Illusions* (2002) concerns a silent film star named Hector Mann thought to be dead, who is discovered by the protagonist to be leading an anonymous existence in the southwest, making private films for his own enjoyment. The reader experiences Mann's films within the pages of the novel. Auster later described this as "one of the most daunting tasks I've ever undertaken as a novelist . . . to try to make those films read on the page in such a way that the reader could experience them as films, not as descriptions of films. You needed the detail, but too much detail would have bogged it down."[7]

Auster's apprentice work in the 1970s also involved much translation work, from French into English (he would later go on to edit *The Random House Book of Twentieth-Century French Poetry* [1982]). He often speaks in praise of this type of creative work, asserting that the translator is as much a creative artist as a poet or novelist is. Finally, it should not be forgotten that Auster can be at times a very comic writer. He describes how humor can be used as a leavening agent in stories that are often not just tragic but cata-strophically so—some, like *The Book of Illusions*, for example, on the order of Shakespearean tragedy.

A major theme throughout his work is the interplay of chance and coin-cidence—how reality is often more bizarre than we want to give it credit for, hence the surrealistic or magical realism element in his works. The rational mind, Auster says, forces men and women to try to find an empirical cause for anything strange that happens, but what if strangeness and the bizarre are simply as "real" as everyday reality? Auster's detractors sometimes latch on to his preoccupation with the forces of coincidence as evidence that his art is forced or artificial—that is, "unrealistic." Responding to this point in a 1989 interview, Auster commented that, "in some perverse way," he thought such readers had "spent too much time reading books. They're so immersed in the conventions of so-called realistic fiction that their sense of reality has been distorted. Everything's been smoothed out in these novels, robbed of its singularity, boxed into a predictable world of cause and effect."[8] As if to lend credibility to his theory, Auster relates many incidents from his own life of "weird moments" where stories begin in one place, connect with oth-ers, then end back at the beginning, having come full circle in the process.

And that, Auster believes, also makes the important point that a culture is built on narrative; we cannot live without it. We struggle to make sense of our world through stories. To Auster, that makes the artist a figure of great importance, and art a high calling—no doubt the reason that in his early years he had made such large personal sacrifices in order to keep writing.

Moreover, he steadfastly maintains that he gathers evidence of the "mechanics of reality" and records it as faithfully as he can in his fiction: "It's not a method so much as an act of faith: to present things as they really happen, not as they're supposed to happen or as we'd like them to happen." Hence his passion for true tales from everyday life, some of them collected in *The Red Notebook* (1995)—"a kind of position paper on how I see the world. The bare-bones truth about the unpredictability of experience."[9] Auster built on this method when National Public Radio, where he had been interviewed several times, received such positive responses to his on-air presence that they cast about for a project he could do with them. Hence was born the National Story Project. His wife, Siri Hustvedt, suggested that listeners send in their own stories, which Auster selected and read on the air—true stories about their own lives. Over the course of one year, Auster ended up reading more than four thousand submissions, and the best were published in *I Thought My Father Was God and Other True Tales from NPR's National Story Project* (2001).

A pervasive influence has been the work of Nathaniel Hawthorne. Hawthorne's darkly brooding, obsessive characters would be right at home in the urban landscapes of Auster's tales, and his narrators' sometimes uncomfortably prurient interests in the characters also brings to mind the trend toward emotional voyeurism in Hawthorne. Hawthorne is most famous as an allegorist, as well; Auster's narratives, with their sometimes skeletal structures and tendentious details can be thought of as the next step beyond mere allegory—as fables of the mind. Consider, for instance, the characters Black and Blue in *Ghosts*—or Flower and Stone in *The Music of Chance*—or the unnervingly New York-like landscape of the dystopian *In the Country of Last Things*.[10] In a different vein, Hawthorne's historical terrain, seventeenth-century Puritan New England, figures prominently in one of the backstories of *City of Glass*. In *The Book of Illusions*, two characters engage in a lengthy analysis of a Hawthorne story, "The Birthmark"; the title of that author's early novel, *Fanshawe*, is the name of one of the characters in *The Locked Room*; and Hawthorne's story "Wakefield"—which concerns a man who decides to walk away from his home and family and lead a different existence somewhere else—becomes part of the structure of *Ghosts*.

Here Auster fuses his love for classic American literature with another impulse: that of creating cascading narratives, stories that generate other stories and that test the limits of conventional tale-telling. This is an impulse that makes him the direct heir to those metafictionists of the 1960s and 1970s that espoused the validity of a new "literature of exhaustion": John Barth, Richard Brautigan, Robert Coover, and others. More recent inventors in the Auster mold might be Jose Saramago, David Leavitt, Julia Alvarez, Thomas Pynchon, Don Delillo, Philip Roth, and Julian Barnes. "I was always drawn to books that doubled back on themselves, that brought you into the world of the book, even as the book was taking you into the world," Auster has said. "They posit the world as an illusion—which more traditional forms of narrative don't—and once you accept the 'unreality' of the enterprise, it paradoxically enhances the truth of the story." In this way, the reader also becomes complicit in the fictional enterprise, "not just a detached observer." This last trait locates Auster in the tradition of Kafka, Borges, and Poe, to whom his work has also frequently been compared. (In *City of Glass*, the pseudonym of the protagonist/author is "William Wilson.")

Auster most often locates the sources and influences on his work in fairy tales. When asked about who has influenced him the most, he has cited "the anonymous men and women who invented the fairy tales we still tell each other today . . . the whole oral tradition that started the moment men learned how to talk."[11] Such texts force the willing suspension of disbelief, but are also designed in such a way that crucial information, requisite in other forms of writing, is not only missing but is not sought out by the reader. In such works—again like the tales of Poe—we do not know anything of the background of the characters or the backstory of the plot. We don't know where the story is set, or what time in history it may be. These same traits can be seen in some of Auster's narratives.

Apropos of genre, a resentment that surfaces in some early interviews is Auster's annoyance at being labeled a "mystery writer"—largely because of the detective impulse underlying the Trilogy. As time went on, however, Auster shed the label as he tested new generic boundaries and struck out in new narrative directions. Over time, too, Auster has also become kinder to his critics. His work defies easy generic categorization and at times seems so implausibly imaginative that critics sometimes tend to discount the seriousness of his art. It is an illogical quirk of the reviewing establishment in America that if you give someone something delicious to eat but there's no name for it, it's pushed to the side of the plate in favor of things more recognizable.

In 2009, the *New Yorker* ran an overtly pugnacious piece by James Wood, a prominent literary reviewer, challenging Auster's claim to be a postmodernist. Wood's review drew hairline distinctions between postmodernism and realism, claiming that Auster was more the latter than the former. Auster's persistent and determined blurring of this line has created some disfavor for him with critics. Auster's response is that the imaginary can exist within the real, or, as the protagonist of *Man in the Dark*, August Brill, says, "the real and the imagined are one." As Auster has noted, "Thoughts are real, even thoughts of unreal things. It goes around and around. Once you accept the fact that the inside is also part of the outside, all bets are off. It's a bit like a flashback in a movie. Even if someone later says that it didn't really happen, you've seen it, and you are convinced by it."[12] Wood's thesis was so tenuous that perhaps that was why he concluded with a more direct and reliable line of attack—the anxiety of popularity: "The pleasing, slightly facile books come out almost every year, as tidy and punctual as postage stamps, and the applauding reviewers line up like eager stamp collectors to get the latest issue." Wood's views notwithstanding, Auster's critical reputation has always been relatively stronger in Europe than in the United States, especially in France and Spain. In fact, he has an unusually wide international readership. His books have been translated into forty-two languages and have found enthusiastic audiences in such countries as Turkey, Japan, Korea, Israel, and Iran. And, over time, Auster's reviews here have been far more positive than negative.

Within the U.S., it's notable that for most of his writing life, Auster's base of operations has been the borough of Brooklyn, and that the strong sense of place in his novels owes much to the comfortable allegiance he shows to that unique wedge of New York. Auster was living in Brooklyn long before it became fashionable for artists to do so, and now Brooklyn's eminence as a place with a long literary history has been much more widely acknowledged. Its literary residents have been many—beginning perhaps with Whitman and continuing on through the twentieth century with Norman Mailer and with many other great poets—among them, Louis Zukovsky, George Oppen, Charles Reznikoff. It is also the locus of probably one of the great twentieth-century poems, *The Bridge*, by Hart Crane. Brooklyn is now home to a new cadre of contemporary writers—Jonathan Lethem, Jonathan Ames, Colson Whitehead, and many others.

The great poetic tradition of Brooklyn can thus be numbered among the many elements of "the new" that we see in Auster's writing. In an early essay in *The Art of Hunger*, Auster quotes Samuel Beckett as saying that "There will be a new form." Perhaps it is more precise to say that Auster's fiction creates its own form—as it compels Auster to write it.

My thanks first to Paul Auster for generously allowing these interviews to be reprinted and for giving up a considerable amount of time to help me shape the final contents of the volume. I am grateful as well to Alisa Whittle for her assistance with transcriptions and other tasks. And finally, I appreciate the support for this project shown by my editor, Walter Biggins, and by Anne Stascavage, who oversaw the process of getting the manuscript into print.

JMH

Notes

1. Margaret Cannon, review of The New York Trilogy, *Toronto Globe and Mail*, 14 March 1987.

2. Review of *City of Glass*, *Washington Post Book World*, 5 December 1985.

3. "The Art of Fiction No. 178: Paul Auster," *Paris Review*, reprinted herein.

4. It later appeared in an English translation in 1974.

5. Video interview with John Freeman, *Granta* magazine, 20 May 2009.

6. Charlie Rose television show, 22 September 2008.

7. Mel Gussow, "Just Cuddle Up with a Film and Read a Good Novel," *New York Times*, 14 October. 2002.

8. Larry McCaffery and Sinda Gregory, "Interview with Paul Auster," reprinted herein.

9. "The Art of Fiction No. 178."

10. Auster's most extensive comments on Hawthorne can be found in his introduction to *20 Days with Julian and Little Bunny by Papa* (New York Review Books, 2003), a reprint of a self-contained children's story from one of Hawthorne's "American Notebooks" from 1851.

11. Ashton Applewhite, "An Interview with Paul Auster," reprinted herein.

12. Juliet Linderman, "A Connoisseur of Clouds, a Meteorologist of Whims: *The Rumpus* Interview with Paul Auster," reprinted herein.

Chronology

1947	3 February: born in Newark, New Jersey, to Samuel and Queenie (nee Bogat) Auster. With sister, grows up in New Jersey suburb. Sam is a landlord who owns several buildings with his brothers. Marriage is unhappy.
1954	Uncle Allen Mandelbaum, professor of comparative literature and prolific translator, leaves boxes of books in family home and Auster develops intense interest in writing and literature.
1965	Skips high school graduation and travels to Europe, visiting Italy, Spain, Paris, and Dublin. Enrolls at Columbia University, studying English and comparative literature.
1966	Spring: begins relationship with Lydia Davis.
1967–68	Goes to Paris for junior year abroad, but quits college after a little while there; lives in small hotel on the rue Clément; November 1967, returns to U.S.
1968	Reinstated at Columbia; participates in student strike (April) and is arrested and jailed with 700 others.
1969	June: graduates Columbia.
1970	Completes M.A. at Columbia. Contemplates further graduate school but instead takes job with the Census Bureau. Works for six months as seaman on tanker in Gulf of Mexico. Discovers among family papers that his grandmother murdered his grandfather when his father was seven years old.
1971	February, leaves for Paris; Lives in France working at odd jobs, including a telephone operator at the Paris bureau of the *New York Times*.
1973	Moves to Provence where he and Davis work as caretakers of a farmhouse.
1974	Returns to U.S., settling in New York, and on 6 October marries writer Lydia Davis; life is difficult with crumbling marriage and miniscule income from writing reviews, four slim volumes of poetry, and doing translations.

1976–77	Writes four one-act plays.
1977	Son, Daniel, is born.
1978	Writes first novel, *Squeeze Play* (published 1982) under pseudonym Paul Benjamin (his middle name; this "person" would later appear as a blocked writer in the film *Smoke*).
1979	14 January: Father dies and leaves Auster inheritance; begins fiction writing in earnest; writes *The Invention of Solitude*, in part about his father.
1980	Publishes *White Spaces*, "a little work of no identifiable genre," after attending rehearsal of dance performance; moves to apartment in Brooklyn—here receives two wrong-number phone calls, intended for the Pinkerton Detective Agency—that later lead to his writing *City of Glass*.
1981	After divorce from Davis, on 23 February meets writer Siri Hustvedt at a poetry reading.
1982	Marries Hustvedt on 16 June (Bloomsday); edits and writes introduction to *The Random House Book of Twentieth-Century French Poetry*, containing his translations of forty-two poems by various poets; also publishes *The Invention of Solitude*, a memoir.
1986	Takes position as lecturer at Princeton University, post he holds until 1990; eventually Auster and Hustvedt move to Park Slope neighborhood of Brooklyn; Edgar Award nominee for *City of Glass*.
1987	Daughter, Sophie, is born.
1989	Prix France Culture de Littérature Étrangère for *The New York Trilogy*.
1990	Morton Dauwen Zabel Award from the American Academy of Arts and Letters.
1991	PEN/Faulkner Award for Fiction finalist for *The Music of Chance*.
1992	Film version of *The Music of Chance*, with screenplay by Philip and Belinda Haas and cameo appearance by Auster.
1993	Prix Médicis Étranger for *Leviathan*.
1995	June: film *Smoke* (writer and uncredited co-director) is released; October: film *Blue in the Face* (writer and co-director).
1996	Bodil Awards—Best American Film: *Smoke*; John William Corrington Award for Literary Excellence; Independent Spirit Award for *Smoke*.

1999–2000	Participates in National Public Radio's National Story Project.
1998	*Lulu on the Bridge* (writer and director).
1999	Honorary Doctor of Letters from Williams College.
2001	*Timbuktu* wins Arcebispo Juan de Clemente prize for best foreign language novel.
2002	Narrates NPR's Peabody Award–winning "Sonic Memorial Project," about the 9/11 attacks.
2003	Fellow of the American Academy of Arts and Sciences; finalist for International IMPAC Dublin Literary Award for *The Book of Illusions.*
2004	Narrates "Ground Zero," audio guide produced by National Public Radio; wins Dalton Pen Award for Multimedia/Audio (2005) and is nominated for an Audie Award for best original work; Blue Metropolis Award (Montreal) for body of work.
2005	Vice-president of PEN American Center; Honorary Doctor of Letters from Pratt Institute.
2006	Prince of Asturias Award for Literature (received in previous years by Günter Grass, Arthur Miller, and Mario Vargas Llosa); elected to the American Academy of Arts and Letters for Literature.
2007	Honorary doctorate from the University of Liège; Commandeur de l'Ordre des Arts et des Lettres; *The Inner Life of Martin Frost* (writer and director); First Annual Best of Brooklyn Literary Award, presented by the Brooklyn Book Festival.
2007–08	Board of Trustees, PEN American Center; later, member of Advisory Council.
2008	Honorary Doctor of Humane Letters from Brooklyn College.
2010	Medaille Grand Vermeil de la Ville de Paris.
2011	November, Naples Prize for *Sunset Park.*
2012	April: First Annual NYC Literary Honors in the Category of Fiction; August: latest book of memoir, *Winter Journal*, released.

Conversations with Paul Auster

Translation

Stephen Rodefer/1985

Originally appearing in *The Archive Newsletter* (University of California, San Diego), this is reprinted from *The Art of Hunger* (1992) by permission of Paul Auster.

STEPHEN RODEFER: When did you begin doing translations?

PAUL AUSTER: Back when I was nineteen or twenty years old, as an undergraduate at Columbia. They gave us various poems to read in French class—Baudelaire, Rimbaud, Verlaine—and I found them terribly exciting, even if I didn't always understand them. The foreignness was daunting to me—as though works written in a foreign language were somehow not real—and it was only by trying to put them into English that I began to penetrate them. At that point, it was a strictly private activity for me, a method to help me understand what I was reading, and I had no thoughts about trying to publish what I did. I suppose you could say that I started doing translations because I was such a slow learner. I couldn't imagine a linguistic reality other than English, and I was driven by a need to appropriate these works, to make them part of my own world.

SR: Were you writing poetry of your own at that time, too?

PA: Yes. But like most young people, I had no idea what I was doing. One's ambitions at that stage are so enormous, but you don't necessarily have the tools to carry them out. It leads to frustration, a deep sense of your own inadequacy. I struggled along during those years to find my own way, and in the process I discovered that translation was an extremely helpful exercise. Pound recommends translation for young poets, and I think that shows great understanding on his part. You have to begin slowly. Translation allows you to work on the nuts and bolts of your craft, to learn how to live intimately with words, to see more clearly what you are actually doing. That is the positive benefit, but there is also a negative one. Working on translations removes the pressure of composition. There is no need to be brilliant

3

and original, no need to attempt things that you are finally not capable of doing. You learn how to feel more comfortable with yourself in the act of writing, and that is probably the most crucial thing for a young person. You submit yourself to someone else's work—someone who is necessarily more accomplished than you are—and you begin to read more profoundly and intelligently than you ever have before. Scholarly analysis of poetry serves an important function, but this kind of practical experience is irreplaceable. A young poet will learn more about how Rilke wrote sonnets by trying to translate one than by writing an essay about it.

SR: How does translation relate to your own work now?

PA: At this point hardly at all. In the beginning, it occupied a central place for me, but then, as time went on, it became more and more marginal. My first translations years ago of modern French poets were real acts of discovery, labors of love. Then I went through a long period when I earned my living by doing translations. That was a completely different matter. I had nothing to do with choosing the texts. The publishers would tell me that they needed a translation of such and such a book, and I would do it. It was very draining work and had nothing to do with literature or my own writing. History books, anthropology books, art books. You grind out so many pages a day, and it puts bread on the table. Eventually, I stopped doing it to save my sanity. For the past five or six years, I've tried to limit myself to things that I am passionately interested in—works that I have discovered and want to share with other people. Joubert's notebooks, for example, or the Anatole fragments by Mallarmé. I find both those works extraordinary, unlike anything I have ever read. The same with the book about high-wire walking by Philippe Petit, which was published last summer. I did it because Philippe is a friend and because he is one of the most remarkable artists I know. If those books are not exactly connected to my writing, they still belong to my inner world. But the act of translating in itself is no longer the adventure for me that it once was. There are sublimely talented translators out there in America today—Manheim, Rabassa, Wilbur, Mandelbaum, to name just a few. But I don't think of myself as belonging to the fraternity of translators. I'm just someone who likes to follow his nose, and more often than not this leads me into some odd corners. Occasionally, I will stumble onto something that excites me enough to want to translate it, but these generally seem to be eccentric and peculiar works—works that correspond to my own eccentric and peculiar tastes!

Interview with Paul Auster

Joseph Mallia/1987

Originally commissioned by, edited, and published in *BOMB Magazine*, from *BOMB Magazine* Issue 23, Spring 1988, pp. 24–27. Copyright Bomb Magazine, New Art Publications, and its Contributors. All rights reserved. The BOMB Digital Archive can be viewed at www .bombsite.com.

MALLIA: In your book of essays *The Art of Hunger* you cite Samuel Beckett as saying, "There will be a new form:" Is your work an example of that new form?

AUSTER: It seems that everything comes out a little strangely and my books don't quite resemble other books, but whether they're "new" in any sense, I really can't say. It's not my ambition to think about it. So I suppose the answer is yes and no. At this point I'm not even thinking about anything beyond doing the books themselves. They impose themselves on me, so it's not my choice. The only thing that really matters, it seems to me, is saying the thing that has to be said. If it really has to be said, it will create its own form.

MALLIA: All of your early work, from the 1970s, is poetry. What brought about this switch in genres, what made you want to write prose?

AUSTER: Starting from a very early age, writing novels was always my ambition. When I was a student in college, in fact, I spent a great deal more time writing prose than poetry. But the projects and ideas that I took on were too large for me, too ambitious, and I could never get a grip on them. By concentrating on a smaller form, I felt that I was able to make more progress. Years went by, and writing poetry became such an obsession that I stopped thinking about anything else. I wrote very short, compact lyrical poems that usually took me months to complete. They were very dense, especially in the beginning—coiled in on themselves like fists—but over the years they gradually began to open up, until I finally felt that they were heading in the

5

direction of narrative. I don't think of myself as having made a break from poetry. All my work is of a piece, and the move into prose was the last step in a slow and natural evolution.

MALLIA: As a younger writer, who were the modern writers you were interested in?
AUSTER: Of prose writers, unquestionably Kafka and Beckett. They both had a tremendous hold over me. In some sense, the influence of Beckett was so strong that I couldn't see my way beyond it. Among poets, I was very attracted to contemporary French poetry and the American Objectivists, particularly George Oppen, who became a close friend. And the German poet Paul Celan, who in my opinion is the finest postwar poet in any language. Of older writers, there were Hölderlin and Leopardi, the essays of Montaigne, and Cervantes' *Don Quixote*, which has remained a great source for me.

MALLIA: But in the '70s you also wrote a great number of articles and essays about other writers.
AUSTER: Yes, that's true. There was a period in the middle '70s in particular when I found myself eager to test my own ideas about writers in print. It's one thing to read and admire somebody's work, but it's quite another to marshal your thoughts about that writer into something coherent. The people I wrote about—Laura Riding, Edmond Jabès, Louis Wolfson, Knut Hamsun, and others—were writers I felt a need to respond to. I never considered myself a reviewer, but simply one writer trying to talk about others. Having to write prose for publication disciplined me, I think, and convinced me that ultimately I was able to write prose. So in some sense those little pieces of literary journalism were the training ground for the novels.

MALLIA: Your first prose book was *The Invention of Solitude*, which was an autobiographical book.
AUSTER: I don't think of it as an autobiography so much as a meditation about certain questions, using myself as the central character. The book is divided into two sections, which were written separately, with a gap of about a year between the two. The first, *Portrait of an Invisible Man*, was written in response to my father's death. He simply dropped dead one day, unexpectedly, after being in perfect health, and the shock of it left me with so many unanswered questions about him that I felt I had no choice but to sit down and try to put something on paper. In the act of trying to write about him, I began to realize how problematical it is to presume to know anything about

anyone else. While that piece is filled with specific details, it still seems to me not so much an attempt at biography but an exploration of how one might begin to speak about another person, and whether or not it is even possible.

The second part grew out of the first and was a response to it. It gave me a great deal of trouble, especially in terms of organization. I began writing it in the first person, as the first part had been written, but couldn't make any headway with it. This part was even more personal than the first, but the more deeply I descended into the material, the more distanced I became from it. In order to write about myself, I had to treat myself as though I were someone else. It was only when I started all over again in the third person that I began to see my way out of the impasse. The astonishing thing, I think, is that at the moment when you are most truly alone, when you truly enter a state of solitude, that is the moment when you are not alone anymore, when you start to feel your connection with others. I believe I even quote Rimbaud in that book, "Je est un autre"—I is another—and I take that sentence quite literally. In the process of writing or thinking about yourself, you actually become someone else.

MALLIA: Not only is the narrative voice of *The Book of Memory* different, but the structure is different as well.

AUSTER: The central question in the second part was memory. So in some sense everything that happens in it is simultaneous. But writing is sequential, it unfolds over time. So my greatest problem was in trying to put things in the correct order.

The point was to be as honest as possible in every sentence. I wanted to write a work that was completely exposed. I didn't want to hide anything. I wanted to break down for myself the boundary between living and writing as much as I could. That's not to say that a lot of literary effort didn't go into the book, but the impulses are all very immediate and pressing. With everything I do, it seems that I just get so inside it, I can't think about anything else. And writing the book becomes real for me. I was talking about myself in *The Book of Memory*, but by tracking specific instances of my own mental process, perhaps I was doing something that other people could understand as well.

MALLIA: Yes, that's how it worked for me. *The Book of Memory* dwells on coincidences, strange intersections of events in the world. This is also true in the novels of The New York Trilogy.

AUSTER: Yes, I believe the world is filled with strange events. Reality is a great deal more mysterious than we ever give it credit for. In that sense, the Trilogy grows directly out of *The Invention of Solitude*. On the most personal level, I think of *City of Glass* as an homage to my wife. It's a kind of fictitious subterranean autobiography, an attempt to imagine what my life would have been like if I hadn't met her. That's why I had to appear in the book as myself, but at the same time Auster is also Quinn, but in a different universe. . . .

MALLIA: Reviews of the book seem to emphasize the mystery elements of The New York Trilogy, making it out to be a gloss on the mystery genre. Did you feel that you were writing a mystery novel?

AUSTER: Not at all. Of course I used certain elements of detective fiction. Quinn, after all, writes detective novels, and takes on the identity of someone he thinks is a detective. But I felt I was using those elements for such different ends, for things that had so little to do with detective stories, and I was somewhat disappointed by the emphasis that was put on them. That's not to say that I have anything against the genre. The mystery, after all, is one of the oldest and most compelling forms of storytelling, and any number of works can be placed in that category: *Oedipus Rex*, *Crime and Punishment*, a whole range of twentieth-century novels. In America, there's no question that people like Raymond Chandler and James M. Cain are legitimate writers, writers who have contributed something important to the language. It's a mistake to look down on the popular forms. You have to be open to everything, to be willing to take inspiration from any and all sources. In the same way that Cervantes used chivalric romances as the starting point for *Don Quixote*, or the way that Beckett used the standard vaudeville routine as the framework for *Waiting for Godot*, I tried to use certain genre conventions to get to another place, another place altogether.

MALLIA: The problem of identity, right?

AUSTER: Exactly. The question of who is who and whether or not we are who we think we are. The whole process that Quinn undergoes in that book—and the characters in the other two, as well—is one of stripping away to some barer condition in which we have to face up to who we are. Or who we aren't. It finally comes to the same thing.

MALLIA: And the detective is somebody who's supposed to deal with the problems we have in maintaining a conventional identity. He deals with the messy edges of reality. Like, "My wife, she's not doing what she's supposed to—"

AUSTER: Right, exactly—or, "Somebody's missing." So the detective really is a very compelling figure, a figure we all understand. He's the seeker after the truth, the problem-solver, the one who tries to figure things out. But what if, in the course of trying to figure it out, you just unveil more mysteries? I suppose maybe that's what happens in the books.

The books have to do with the idea of mystery in several ways. We're surrounded by things we don't understand, by mysteries, and in the books these are people who suddenly come face to face with them. It becomes more apparent that they're surrounded by things they don't know or understand. So in that sense there might be some psychological resonance. Even though the situations aren't strictly realistic, they might follow some realistic psychology. These are things that we all feel—that confusion, that lack of knowing what it is that surrounds us.

MALLIA: I saw the protagonists dropping into a kind of necessity, suddenly, and putting personal life aside, driven by some extraordinary hunger. It has almost religious undertones to it. I remember reading a review by Fanny Howe in the *Boston Globe*, and she said that the book is about a kind of gnosis—"grace among the fallen."

AUSTER: "Religious" might not be the word I would use, but I agree that these books are mostly concerned with spiritual questions, the search for spiritual grace. At some point or another, all three characters undergo a form of humiliation, of degradation, and perhaps that is a necessary stage in discovering who we are.

Each novel in the Trilogy, I suppose, is about a kind of passionate excess. Quinn's story in *City of Glass* alludes to *Don Quixote*, and the questions raised in the two books are very similar: what is the line between madness and creativity, what is the line between the real and the imaginary, is Quinn crazy to do what he does or not? For a time, I toyed with the idea of using an epigraph at the beginning of *City of Glass*. It comes from Wittgenstein: "And it also means something to talk of 'living in the pages of a book.'"

In *Ghosts*, the spirit of Thoreau is dominant—another kind of passionate excess. The idea of living a solitary life, of living with a kind of monastic intensity—and all the dangers that entails. Walden Pond in the heart of the city. In his *American Notebooks*, Hawthorne wrote an extraordinary and luminous sentence about Thoreau that has never left me. "I think he means to live like an Indian among us." That sums up the project better than anything else I've read. The determination to reject everyday American life, to go against the grain, to discover a more solid foundation for oneself. In *The Locked Room*, by the way, the name Fanshawe is a direct reference to Hawthorne. *Fanshawe* was the title of Hawthorne's first novel. He wrote it when he was very young, and not long after it was published, he turned against it in revulsion and tried to destroy every copy he could get his hands on. Fortunately, a few of them survived . . .

MALLIA: In *Ghosts*, Blue, in effect, loses his whole life in taking the case, and the narrator in *The Locked Room* goes through that terrible experience in Paris—

AUSTER: But in the end, he manages to resolve the question for himself—more or less. He finally comes to accept his own life, to understand that no matter how bewitched or haunted he is, he has to accept reality as it is, to tolerate the presence of ambiguities within himself. That's what happens to him with relation to Fanshawe. He hasn't slain the dragon, he's let the dragon move into the house with him. That's why he destroys the notebook in the last scene.

MALLIA: And the reader feels it. We're inside him.

AUSTER: The one thing I try to do in all my books is to leave enough room in the prose for the reader to inhabit it. Because I finally believe it's the reader who writes the book and not the writer. In my own case as a reader (and I've certainly read more books than I've written!), I find that I almost invariably appropriate scenes and situations from a book and graft them onto my own experiences—or vice versa. In reading a book like *Pride and Prejudice*, for example, I realized at a certain point that all events were set in the house I grew up in as a child. No matter how specific a writer's description of a place might be, I always seem to twist it into something I'm familiar with. I've asked a number of my friends if this happens to them when they read fiction as well. For some yes, for others no. I think this probably has a lot to do with one's relation to language, how one responds to words printed on a page. Whether the words are just symbols, or whether they are passageways into our unconscious.

There's a way in which a writer can do too much, overwhelming the reader with so many details that he no longer has any air to breathe. Think of a typical passage in a novel. A character walks into a room. As a writer, how much of that room do you want to talk about? The possibilities are infinite. You can give the color of the curtains, the wallpaper pattern, the objects on the coffee table, the reflection of the light in the mirror. But how much of this is really necessary? Is the novelist's job simply to reproduce physical sensations for their own sake? When I write, the story is always uppermost in my mind, and I feel that everything must be sacrificed to it. All the elegant passages, all the curious details, all the so-called beautiful writing—if they are not truly relevant to what I am trying to say, then they have to go. It's all in the voice. You're telling a story, after all, and your job is to make people want to go on listening to your tale. The slightest distraction or wandering leads to boredom, and if there's one thing we all hate in books, it's losing interest, feeling bored, not caring about the next sentence. In the end, you don't only write the books you need to write, but you write the books you would like to read yourself.

MALLIA: Is there a method to it?

AUSTER: No. The deeper I get into my own work, the less engaging theoretical problems have become. When you look back on the works that have moved you, you find that they have always been written out of some kind of necessity. There's something calling out to you, some human call, that makes you want to listen to the work. In the end, it probably has very little to do with literature.

Georges Bataille wrote about this in his preface to *Le Bleu du Ciel*. I refer to it in *The Art of Hunger*, in an essay on the schizophrenic Wolfson. He said that every real book comes from a moment of rage, and then he asked: "How can we read works that we don't feel compelled to read?" I believe he's absolutely correct: there's always some indefinable something that makes you attend to a writer's work—you can never put your finger on it, but that something is what makes all the difference.

MALLIA: In other words, the writer has to be haunted by his story before he can write it.

AUSTER: In my own experience I've often lived for years with the ideas for books before I could manage to write them. In *The Country of Last Things* is a novel I started writing back in the days when I was a college student. The idea of an unknowable place . . . it got under my skin and I couldn't let go of it. I would pick up the manuscript, work on it for a while, and then put it down. The essential thing was to capture her voice, and when I couldn't hear it anymore, I would have to stop. I must have started the book thirty times. Each time it was somewhat different than the time before, but the essential situation was always the same.

MALLIA: In the same way that some reviewers classified The New York Trilogy as a mystery, there were many articles about this book that classified it as apocalyptic science fiction.

AUSTER: That was the farthest thing from my mind while I was writing it. In fact, my private, working subtitle for the book was "Anna Blume Walks through the 20th Century." I feel that it's very much a book about our own moment, our own era, and many of the incidents are things that have actually happened. For example, the pivotal scene in which Anna is lured into a human slaughterhouse is based on something I read about the siege of Leningrad during World War II. These things actually happened. And in many cases, reality is far more terrible than anything we can imagine. Even the garbage system that I describe at such length was inspired by an article I once read about the present-day garbage system in Cairo. Admittedly, the book takes on these things from a somewhat oblique angle, and the country Anna goes to might not be immediately recognizable, but I feel that this is where we live. It could be that we've become so accustomed to it that we no longer see it.

MALLIA: What are you working on now?

AUSTER: I'm coming close to the end of a novel called *Moon Palace*. It's the longest book I've ever written and probably the one most rooted in a specific time and place. The action begins in 1969 and doesn't get much beyond 1971. At bottom, I suppose it's a story about families and generations, a kind of *David Copperfield* novel, and it's something that I've been wanting to write for a long time. As with the last book, it's gone through many changes. The pages pile up, but God knows what it will look like when it's finished. . . . Whenever I complete a book, I'm filled with a feeling of immense disgust and disappointment. It's almost a physical collapse. I'm so disappointed by my feeble efforts that I can't believe I've actually spent so much time and accomplished so little. It takes years before I'm able to accept what I've done—to realize that this was the best I could do. But I never like to look at the things I've written. The past is the past, and there's nothing I can do about it any more. The only thing that counts is the project I'm working on now.

MALLIA: Beckett once said in one of his stories, "No sooner is the ink dry than it revolts me."

AUSTER: You can't say it any better than that.

An Interview with Paul Auster

Larry McCaffery and Sinda Gregory/1989

From *The Art of Hunger*. Reproduced with permission of Larry McCaffery and Sinda Gregory.

LARRY McCAFFERY: At one point in *Moon Palace*, Marco Fogg says that art's purpose is "penetrating the world and finding one's place in it." Is that what writing does for you?

PAUL AUSTER: Sometimes. I often wonder why I write. It's not simply to create beautiful objects or entertaining stories. It's an activity I seem to need in order to stay alive. I feel terrible when I'm not doing it. It's not that writing brings me a lot of pleasure—but not doing it is worse.

SINDA GREGORY: Your books have always relied more on chance and synchronicity to move their plots forward than the sorts of causality found in most fiction: this is even more apparent in your two new novels, *Moon Palace* and *The Music of Chance*. Is this foregrounding of chance a result of your own sense of how life operates (your "personal philosophy")? Or does it have more to do with your sense that this approach has interesting aesthetic applications?

PA: From an aesthetic point of view, the introduction of chance elements in fiction probably creates as many problems as it solves. I've come in for a lot of abuse from critics because of it. In the strictest sense of the word, I consider myself a realist. Chance is a part of reality: we are continually shaped by the forces of coincidence, the unexpected occurs with almost numbing regularity in all our lives. And yet there's a widely held notion that novels shouldn't stretch the imagination too far. Anything that appears "implausible" is necessarily taken to be forced, artificial, "unrealistic." I don't know what reality these people have been living in, but it certainly isn't my reality. In some perverse way, I believe they've spent too much time reading books. They're so immersed in the conventions of so-called realistic fiction that their sense of reality has been distorted. Everything's been smoothed out in these novels, robbed of its singularity, boxed into a predictable world of cause and effect. Anyone with the wit to get his nose out of his book and study what's actually in front of him will understand that this realism is a complete sham. To put it another way: truth is stranger than fiction. What I am after, I suppose, is to write fiction as strange as the world I live in.

LM: I'd say your books don't use coincidence in an effort to "smooth things over" or to create the usual realist's manipulated illusion that everything can be explained. Your books seem more fundamentally "about" mystery and coincidence, so that these operate almost as governing principles that are constantly clashing with causality and rationality.

PA: Precisely. When I talk about coincidence, I'm not referring to a desire to manipulate. There's a good deal of that in bad eighteenth- and nineteenth-century fiction: mechanical plot devices, the urge to tie everything up, the happy endings in which everyone turns out to be related to everyone else. No, what I'm talking about is the presence of the unpredictable, the utterly bewildering nature of human experience. From one moment to the next, anything can happen. Our lifelong certainties about the world can he demolished in a single second. In philosophical terms, I'm talking about the powers of contingency. Our lives don't really belong to us, you see, they belong to the world, and in spite of our efforts to make sense of it, the world is a place beyond our understanding. We brush up against these mysteries all the time. The result can be truly terrifying—but it can also be comical.

SG: What sorts of things are you thinking of—a small thing, like someone getting a phone call to the wrong number (which sets the plot of *City of Glass* in motion)? Or something more outlandish, like meeting your long-lost father by accident in *Moon Palace*?

PA: I'm thinking of both small things and large things. Meeting three people named George on the same day. Or checking into a hotel and being given a room with the same number as your address at home. Seven or eight years ago, my wife and I were invited to a dinner party in New York, and there was an exceedingly charming man at the table—very urbane, full of intelligence and humor, a dazzling talker who had all the guests captivated with his stories. My wife had grown up in a small town in Minnesota, and at one point she actually said to herself: this is why I moved to New York, to meet people like this. Later on in the evening, we all started talking about our childhoods and where we had grown up. As it turned out, the man who had so enthralled her, the man who had struck her as the very embodiment of New York sophistication, came from the same little town in Minnesota that she did. The same town! It was astonishing—like something straight out of an O. Henry story.

These are coincidences, and it's impossible to know what to make of them. You think of a long-lost friend, someone you haven't seen in ten years, and two hours later you run into him on the street. Things like that happen to me all the time. Just two or three years ago, a woman who had been reading my books wrote to me to say that she was going to be in New York and would like to meet me. We had been corresponding for some time, and I welcomed the chance to talk to her in person. Unfortunately, there was a conflict. I already had an appointment with someone else for that day, and I couldn't make it. I was supposed to meet my friend at three or four o'clock in a delicatessen in midtown Manhattan. So I went to the restaurant—which was rather empty at that hour, since it was neither lunchtime nor dinnertime—and not fifteen minutes after we sat down, a woman with an absolutely startled expression on her face walked up to me and asked if I was Paul Auster. It turned out to be the same woman from Iowa who had written me those letters, the same woman I hadn't been able to meet with because I was going to this restaurant. And so I wound up meeting her anyway—in the very place where I hadn't been able to meet her!

Chance? Destiny? Or simple mathematics, an example of probability theory at work? It doesn't matter what you call it. Life is full of such events. And yet there are critics who would fault a writer for using that episode in a novel. Too bad for them. As a writer of novels, I feel morally obligated to incorporate such events into my books, to write about the world as I experience it, not as someone else tells me it's supposed to be. The unknown is rushing in on top of us at every moment. As I see it, my job is to keep myself open to these collisions, to watch out for all these mysterious goings-on in the world.

LM: When you say that your job as a writer is to open yourself to these collisions that are really occurring around you, does this imply that your works are usually inspired in some fairly direct way from the mysteries you've actually experienced or is the autobiographical basis of your work less literal?
PA: Essentially, I'm a very intuitive writer, which makes it difficult for me to talk about my work in any coherent way. There's no question that my books are full of references to my own life, but more often than not, I don't become aware of these references until after the fact. *Moon Palace* is a good case in

point. It sounds more like an autobiography than any of my other novels, but the truth is that it's probably the least autobiographical novel I've ever written. Still, there are a number of private allusions buried in the story, but it was only after the book was finished that I began to see them.

The business about the boxes of books in the beginning, for example. Fogg receives these boxes from his Uncle Victor, and after his uncle dies, Fogg sells off the books to keep himself afloat. Well, it turns out that the image of those boxes must have been planted in my head way back in my early childhood. My mother's sister is married to Allen Mandelbaum, who is widely known now as the translator of Virgil and Dante. When I was five or six, my aunt and uncle went off to live in Italy and wound up staying there for twelve years. My uncle had an enormous library, and since we lived in a large house, he left his books with us for all the years he was gone. At first, they were stored in boxes in the attic, but after a while (I must have been nine or ten at that point), my mother began to worry that the books might get damaged up there. So one fine day she and I carried the boxes downstairs, opened them up, and put the books on shelves in the living room. Until then, our household had been largely devoid of books. Neither of my parents had gone to college, and neither of them was particularly interested in reading. Now, quite suddenly, literally overnight, I had a magnificent library at my disposal: all the classics, all the great poets, all the major novels. It opened up a whole new world to me. When I think back on it now, I realize that these boxes of books probably changed my life. Without them, I doubt I ever would have dreamed of becoming a writer.

The Edison material has deep roots in my past as well. Our house wasn't far from the Seton Hall University campus, and every two weeks I would go for a haircut at Rocco's Barbershop, which did a brisk business with the college students and the boys from the town. This was the late fifties and everyone walked around in crewcuts then, which meant that you wound up going to the barbershop quite often. Anyway, it so happened that Rocco had been Thomas Edison's barber for many years, and hanging on a wall of the shop was a large framed portrait of Edison, along with a handwritten message from the great man himself. "To my good friend Rocco," it said. "Genius is 1% inspiration, 99% perspiration. Thomas A. Edison." I found it tremendously exciting that my barber was the same man who had once cut the hair of the inventor of the lightbulb. It was ennobling, somehow—to imagine that the hands touching my head had once touched the head of America's greatest genius. I used to think that ideas from Edison's brain had been transferred to Rocco's fingers—which meant that those ideas were now going into my brain! Edison became the hero of childhood, and each time I went for a hair-cut, I'd stare at his portrait and feel as though I were worshipping at a shrine.

Some years later, this beautiful myth of my boyhood shattered to pieces. It turned out that my father had once worked as an assistant in Edison's lab at Menlo Park. He had been hired straight out of high school in 1929, but just a few weeks after he started the job, Edison discovered that he was Jewish and fired him. My idol turned out to be a vicious anti-Semite, a scoundrel who had done my father a terrible injustice. None of this is mentioned in *Moon Palace*, of course, but the unflattering references to Edison no doubt come from the personal animosity I developed for him. I won't bore you by citing other examples, but in some way the whole book is impregnated with subliminal connections of this sort. There's nothing unusual about that. All writers draw on their own lives to write their books; to a greater or lesser degree, every novel is autobiographical. What is interesting, however, is how the work of the imagination intersects with reality.

SG: Do you mean that eerie sense that Borges kept writing about—the author who begins to find evidence of his writing somehow finding its way into the world? A big responsibility . . .

PA: It can become quite disturbing at times, utterly uncanny. The very day I finished writing *The Music of Chance*—which is a book about walls and slavery and freedom—the Berlin Wall came down. There's no conclusion to be drawn from this, but every time I think of it, I start to shake.

Back in 1984, when I was in the middle of writing *The Locked Room*, I had to go to Boston for a few days. I already knew that the final scene in the book was going to take place in a house in Boston, at 9 Columbus Square, which happens to be a real address. The house is owned by good friends of mine, and I have slept there on many occasions over the past fifteen years or so. That's where I was going to stay this time as well, and I remember thinking how odd it would be to visit this house again now that I had fictionalized it for myself, had appropriated it into the realm of the imagination. I took the train to Boston, and when I arrived at South Station, I climbed into a cab and asked the driver to take me to 9 Columbus Square. The moment I gave him the address, he started to laugh. It turned out that he had once lived there himself—back in the 1940s, at a time when the building had been used as a boarding house. Not only that, but he had lived in the very room where my friend now had his study. For the rest of the ride, he told me stories about the people who had lived there, the woman who had owned it, and all the mischief that had gone on in the rooms I knew so well. Prostitution, pornographic films, drugs, crimes of every sort. It was all so odd, so mysterious. Even today, it's hard for me not to feel that I invented this cab driver myself, that he didn't materialize out of the pages of my own book. It was as if I had met the spirit of the place I was writing about. The ghost of 9 Columbus Square!

LM: You told me once that in a certain way you felt all of your books were really "the same book." What book is that?

PA: The story of my obsessions, I suppose. The saga of the things that haunt me. Like it or not, all my books seem to revolve around the same set of questions, the same human dilemmas. Writing is no longer an act of free will for me, it's a matter of survival. An image surges up inside me, and after a time I begin to feel cornered by it, to feel that I have no choice but to embrace it. A book starts to take shape after a series of such encounters.

SG: Have you tried to figure out the specific source of these encounters?

PA: Frankly, I'm never really certain where any of it comes from. I'm sure there are deep psychological explanations for most of it, but I'm not terribly interested in trying to track down the source of my ideas. Writing, in some sense, is an activity that helps me to relieve some of the pressure caused by these buried secrets. Hidden memories, traumas, childhood scars—there's no question that novels emerge from those inaccessible parts of ourselves.

Every once in a while, however, I'll have a glimmer or a sudden intuition about where something came from. But, as I said before, it always happens after the fact, after the book is finished, at a moment when the book no longer belongs to me. Just recently, as I was going through the manuscript of *The Music of Chance* for typographical errors, I had a revelation about one of the scenes that takes place toward the end of the novel: the moment when Nashe opens the door of the trailer and discovers Pozzi lying on the ground. As I read that passage—which goes on to describe how Nashe bends over the body and examines Pozzi to see if he is alive or dead—I understood that I was writing about something that had happened to me many years before. It was one of the most terrible moments of my life, an episode that has stayed with me ever since, and yet I wasn't aware of it at the time I composed that scene.

I was fourteen years old and had been sent to a summer camp in upstate New York. One day, a group of about twenty of us went for a hike in the woods, accompanied by one or two counselors. We trekked for several miles, I remember, all of us in good spirits, when it suddenly began to rain.

A moment later, the sky opened up, and we found ourselves in the middle of a ferocious downpour, a summer lightning storm punctuated by tremendous claps of thunder. It wasn't just some passing cloud. It was an out-and-out tempest, a monumental attack from the heavens. Lightning bolts were shooting down all around us, and there we were, stuck in the woods, with no shelter in sight. It became very terrifying, as though we had suddenly been caught in an aerial bombardment. One of the boys said that we would be safer if we got away from the trees, and so we began to scramble back toward a clearing we had passed a little while before. He was right, of course. In a lightning storm, you have to protect yourself by going to open ground. The problem in this case was that in order to enter the clearing, we had to crawl under a barbed wire fence. So, one by one, we crawled under the fence and made our way to what we thought would be safety. I was somewhere in the middle of the line, behind a boy named Ralph. Just as he was crawling under the fence, an enormous bolt of lightning struck the wire. I couldn't have been more than two feet away from him. He stopped, apparently stunned by the lightning, and I remember that I crawled under the fence at that point, inching under the wire to Ralph's left. Once I got through, I turned around and dragged him into the meadow to make room for the other boys. It didn't occur to me that he was seriously hurt. I figured that he had received a shock and would soon recover from it. Once we were all in the clearing, the lightning attack continued; the bolts were dancing around us like spears. Several of the boys were hit, and they lay there weeping and moaning on the ground. It was an awful scene, truly awful. Another boy and I stayed with Ralph the whole time, rubbing his hands to keep him warm, holding his tongue to make sure he didn't swallow it. His lips were turning blue, his skin was turning cold, but still, I kept thinking he would start coming around at any moment. He was dead, of course. He had been killed the instant the lightning hit the fence—electrocuted, with an eight-inch burn across his back. But I didn't learn that until afterward, until after the storm had stopped.

LM: That's the kind of experience you never leave behind completely.
PA: No, never. I can't tell you how deeply it affected me. Not just the tragedy of a young boy losing his life like that—but the absolute suddenness of it, the fact that I could easily have been the one crawling under the fence when the lightning struck. Speaking about it now, I understand how crucial it was to me. In some sense, my entire attitude toward life was formed in those woods in upstate New York.

SG: In retrospect, is that why *Moon Palace* winds up having those two critical scenes involving lightning?

PA: There's no question that those storms refer to the storm I lived through, I'm certain of it. And there are other traces of that event in *Moon Palace*. The passage when Effing watches over Byrne's body in the Utah desert. Clearly I was reliving the experience of watching over the dead boy's body in the woods . . .

What I am trying to say, I suppose, is that the material that haunts me, the material that I feel compelled to write about, is dredged up from the depths of my own memories. But even after that material is given to me, I can't always be sure where it comes from.

LM: How do you balance this sense of feeling *compelled* to write about these things, your desire to leave yourself open, creatively, to these powerful resonances, versus your goal as an artist to *control* them, to shape them into an aesthetic arrangement?

PA: I don't mean to imply that my books are nothing but an outpouring of my unconscious. There's art involved as well, and effort, and a very precise sense of the kinds of feelings I am trying to convey. To say that "all my books are the same book" is probably too simple. What I mean is that all my books are connected by their common source, by the preoccupations they share. But each book belongs to its central character: Quinn, Blue, the narrator of *The Locked Room*, Anna Blume, Fogg, Nashe. Each one of these people thinks differently, speaks differently, writes differently from all the others. But each one is also a part of myself—which probably goes without saying. If all these books were put together in one volume, they would form the book of my life so far, a multifaceted picture of who I am. But there's still more to come, I hope. If you think of the imagination as a continent, then each book would be an individual country. The map is still quite sketchy at this point, with many gaps and unexplored territories. But if I'm able to keep going long enough, perhaps all the blanks will eventually be filled in.

SG: On the other hand, you frequently seem to return to the same "terrain," even if it's located on different literary continents. For example, there's a recurrent motif in several of your books (I'm thinking of *City of Glass*, *Moon Palace*, and *The Music of Chance*) of the windfall or inheritance that creates a suspension of the daily routine for the main character, followed by a gradual dissipation of the money until the character is left with nothing. This sounds almost like a starving artist's fantasy, but since the process is described so vividly and convincingly, I wonder if it might have a basis in your autobiography . . .

PA: As a matter of fact, I did receive an inheritance after my father died eleven years ago. It wasn't a tremendous amount of money as far as inheritances go, but it made a huge difference, it was enough to change my life entirely. I was pushing thirty-two at the time, and in the ten years since graduating from college I had been scraping along as best I could, often in very miserable circumstances. There were long stretches of time when I had nothing, when I was literally on the brink of catastrophe. The year before my father died was a particularly bad period. I had a small child, a crumbling marriage, and a minuscule income that amounted to no more than a fraction of what we needed. I became desperate, and for more than a year I wrote almost nothing. I couldn't think about anything but money. Half-crazed by the pressure of it all, I began devising various get-rich-quick schemes. I invented a game (a card baseball game—which was actually quite good) and spent close to six months trying to sell it. When that failed, I sat down and wrote a pseudonymous detective novel in record time, about three months. It was eventually published, but it only brought in about two thousand dollars, which was hardly the kind of money I had been hoping for.

At another point, I made some inquiries about getting a job as a sports writer, but nothing came of that either. As a last resort, I even broke down and applied for a job as a teacher. A full load of freshman composition courses at Dutchess Community College for $8,000 a year. This was the worst thing I could imagine, but I swallowed my pride and took the plunge. I thought my credentials were decent. I had an M.A. from Columbia, I had published two or three books of poetry, I had translated quite a bit, had written articles for the *New York Review of Books*, *Harpers*, and so on. But it turned out that there were three hundred applicants for that miserable job, and without any prior experience, I didn't have a chance. I was rejected on the spot. I don't think I've ever been closer to feeling that I was at the end of my rope. Then, out of nowhere, with absolutely no warning at all, my father dropped dead of a heart attack and I inherited some money. That money changed everything for me; it set my life on an entirely different course.

LM: Your early published creative works were nearly all poems. Wasn't it just after the death of your father that you first started writing prose—the materials that eventually became *The Invention of Solitude*?

PA: Not exactly. Although you might say that it was only then that I began to think of myself as a prose writer. But the fact is that I had always dreamed of writing novels. My first published works were poems, and for ten years or so I published only poems, but all along I spent nearly as much time writing prose. I wrote hundred and hundreds of pages, I filled up dozens of notebooks. It's just that I wasn't satisfied with it, and I never showed it to anyone. But the ideas for several of the novels I eventually published—at least in some kind of preliminary form—came to me back then, as far back as 1969 and 1970. I'm thinking particularly of *In the Country of Last Things* and *Moon Palace*, but also certain parts of *City of Glass*. The crazy speech about *Don Quixote*, the maps of Stillman's footsteps, the crackpot theories about America and the Tower Of Babel—all that was cooked up when I was still in my early twenties.

SG: But at some point you fairly consciously decided to shift your focus away from prose to poetry. What was behind this decision?
PA: It was like someone trying to will himself to break a bad habit. By about the mid-seventies, I stopped writing fiction altogether. I felt that I was wasting my time, that I would never get anywhere with it, and so I decided to restrict myself exclusively to poetry.

LM: Was it really so exclusive, though? Wasn't this about the time your first critical essays began appearing?
PA: Yes, I suppose I failed to break the habit. I continued writing prose anyway, quite a bit of it, in fact. Critical prose, articles, book reviews. Between 1974 and 1979, I must have written twenty-five or thirty pieces. It started right after I returned to New York. I had just spent four years living in France, and right before I left, an American friend of mine in Paris who knew Bob Silvers of the *New York Review of Books* suggested that I contact him once I returned. I eventually did, and when I proposed writing an article about Louis Wolfson's book *Le Schizo et les Langues*, he said go ahead. He made no promises, of course, but I remember that he offered to pay me something even if they didn't publish it, which I found very generous and uncalled-for. It turned out that he liked the article, and I wound up writing a number of others for him. They were mostly on poets—Laura Riding, Jabès, Ungaretti, and so on. Bob Silvers was an excellent editor—tough, respectful, very businesslike, and very enthusiastic—and I'm still grateful to him for having given me a chance.
LM: Did you find any of the same kinds of pleasures writing those critical articles that you received from your creative work?

PA: I never thought of myself as a critic or literary journalist, even when I was doing a lot of critical pieces. Eventually, I started doing articles for other magazines as well. *Harper's, Saturday Review, Parnassus*, the *San Francisco Review of Books*, I can't remember all of them. I never accepted assignments or did pieces to order. I only wrote about writers who interested me, and in nearly every case I was the one who suggested the article to the editor, not the other way around. I looked on those pieces as an opportunity to articulate some of my ideas about writing and literature, to map out some kind of aesthetic position. In effect, I could have accomplished the same thing by keeping a journal, but I felt it was more interesting and challenging to throw my thoughts out into a public arena. I wasn't able to cheat. Everything had to be stated with absolute clarity: there was no room for vague impressions. All in all, I feel it was a useful apprenticeship. I wasn't writing fiction, but I was writing prose, and the experience of working on those articles proved to me that I was gradually learning how to express myself.

SG: How was your poetry evolving during this period?
PA: It was beginning to change, beginning to open up. I had started out by writing poems that resembled clenched fists; they were short and dense and obscure, as compact and hermetic as Delphic oracles. But by the mid-seventies I could feel them taking on a new direction. The breath became somewhat longer, the propositions became somewhat more discursive. At times, a certain prose tonality began to creep in. In 1976 and 1977, I wrote four one-act plays, wondering if this wouldn't be the proper medium for these new urges that were growing inside me. One of them, to my everlasting regret, was even performed. There's no point in talking about that now—except to say that the memory of that performance still pains me. But another of those plays eventually came to life again. Six years later, I went back to it and reworked it into a piece of prose fiction. That was where *Ghosts* came from, the second novel of The New York Trilogy.

LM: Was there any particular breakthrough moment for you in terms of your prose—something that made you realize you could work in this form? Or was it more a matter of one thing leading to another—the essays, the plays, and so on—until you felt comfortable with it?
PA: It was both, I think, if such a thing is possible. But first came all the emotional and financial hardships I mentioned before. I barely wrote anything for close to a year. My wife and I were grinding out translations to put food on the table, and the rest of the time I was pursuing my half-baked

money schemes. There were moments when I thought I was finished, when I thought I would never write another word. Then, in December of 1978, I happened to go to an open rehearsal of a dance piece choreographed by the friend of a friend, and something happened to me. A revelation, an epiphany—I don't know what to call it. Something happened, and a whole world of possibilities suddenly opened up to me. I think it was the absolute fluidity of what I was seeing, the continual motion of the dancers as they moved around the floor. It filled me with immense happiness. The simple fact of watching men and women moving through space filled me with something close to euphoria. The very next day, I sat down and started writing *White Spaces*, a little work of no identifiable genre which was an attempt on my part to translate the experience of that dance performance into words. It was a liberation for me, a tremendous letting go, and I look back on it now as the bridge between writing poetry and writing prose. That was the piece that convinced me I still had it in me to be a writer. But everything was going to be different now. A whole new period of my life was about to begin.

It's very strange, but I remember finishing that piece on January 14. I went to sleep very late that night, around two or three in the morning. At eight o'clock the phone rang, and there was one of my uncles on the other end of the line, telling me that my father had died during the night. . . .

LM: And along with that news came the inheritance.

PA: Yes, then came the inheritance. The money gave me a cushion, and for the first time in my life I had the time to write, to take on long projects without worrying about how I was going to pay the rent. In some sense, all the novels I've written have come out of that money my father left me. It gave me two or three years, and that was enough to get me on my feet again. It's impossible to sit down and write without thinking about it. It's a terrible equation, finally. To think that my father's death saved my life.

SG: The way you describe this movement from initially writing prose, to abandoning it in favor of poetry when you felt you had failed at prose, to returning to it almost triumphantly during this moment of conversion—it almost sounds as if all along you had strong personal and aesthetic preferences for prose forms. If that's the case, how do you feel about the poetry you wrote during that period?

PA: What it boils down to, I think, is a question of scope. It was a gradual process, but at the same time there was also a leap, a last little jump right at the end.

I remain very attached to the poetry I wrote, I still stand by it. In the final analysis, it could even be the best work I've ever done. But there's a fundamental difference between the two activities, at least in the way I've approached them. In some sense, poetry is like taking still photographs, whereas prose is like filming with a movie camera. Film is the medium for both those arts—but the results are totally different. In the same way, words are the medium for both poetry and prose, but they create entirely different experiences, both for the writer and the reader.

SG: In other words, prose is able to encompass a lot more for you.

PA: That's essentially it. My poems were a quest for what I would call a uni-vocal expression. They expressed what I felt at any given moment, as if I'd never felt anything before and would never feel anything again. They were concerned with essences, with bedrock beliefs, and their aim was always to achieve a purity and consistency of language. Prose, on the other hand, gives me a chance to articulate my conflicts and contradictions. Like everyone else, I am a multiple being, and I embody a whole range of attitudes and re-sponses to the world. Depending on my mood, the same event can make me laugh or make me cry; it can inspire anger or compassion or indifference. Writing prose allows me to include all of these responses. I no longer have to choose among them.

LM: That sounds like Bakhtin's notion of "the dialogic imagination," with the novel arising out of this welter of conflicting but dynamic voices and opinions. Heteroglossia . . .

PA: Exactly. Of all the theories of the novel, Bakhtin's strikes me as the most brilliant, the one that comes closest to understanding the complexity and the magic of the form.

It probably also explains why it's so rare for a young person to write a good novel. You have to grow into yourself before you can take on the de-mands of fiction. I've been talking about it in theoretical and literary terms, but there's also the simple fact of growing older, of acquiring a better sense of who you are.

SG: I know you had started other books before *City of Glass*, but one thing that struck me in reading that book was how fully formed this literary sensibility seemed to be for somebody just publishing his first novel. Were there some private, personal factors at work, beyond the death of your father, that helped you mature as a writer and as an individual, so that you were in fact ready to write that first novel?

PA: I'm certain that having children has had a lot to do with it. Becoming a parent connects you to a world beyond yourself, to the continuum of generations, to the inevitability of your own death. You understand that you exist in time, and after that you can no longer look at yourself in the same way. It's impossible to take yourself as seriously as you once did. You begin to let go, and in that letting go—at least in my case—you find yourself wanting to tell stories.

When my son was born twelve years ago, Charlie Simic, who's been a close friend for a long time, wrote me a letter of congratulations in which he said, "Children are wonderful. If I didn't have kids, I'd walk around thinking I was Rimbaud all the time." He put his finger right on the heart of the experience.

This past summer, something funny happened to me that threw this whole question of children and writing into very sharp focus. We rented a house in Vermont for two months, old fallen-down place in the middle of nowhere, a wonderful refuge. I was still writing *The Music of Chance* then, and every morning I'd walk over to a little outbuilding on the property to work on the book. It was about twenty or thirty yards from the house, and the kids and their friends would often play in the area between the two buildings. Right at the end of the summer, I was coming to the end of the first draft. As it happened, I finished on the day before we were supposed to head back to New York. I wrote the last sentence at about twelve or twelve-thirty in the afternoon, and I remember standing up from the table and saying to myself: "You've finally done it, old man. For once in your life, you've written something halfway decent." I felt good, really very good—which is something that almost never happens to me when I think about my work. I lit a cigar and opened the door to step out into the sun, wanting to savor the triumph for a few minutes before I returned to the house. So there I was, standing on the steps of my little shack, telling myself what a genius I was, when all of sudden I looked up and saw my two-year old daughter in front of the house. She was stark naked (she scarcely wore any clothes all summer) and at that moment she was squatting over some stones and taking a shit. She saw me looking at her and began shouting very happily: "Look at me, Daddy! Look at what I'm doing!" So, rather than being able to bask in my own brilliance, I had to clean up my daughter's mess. That was the first thing I did after finishing my book [Laughs]. Thirty seconds of glory, and then right back to earth. I can't be sure if Sophie was offering me a not-so-subtle form of literary criticism, or if she was simply making a philosophical statement about the equality of all creative acts. One way or the other, she knocked me off my cloud, and I was very grateful to her for it.

LM: You mentioned earlier that all of your books are finally about yourself, that they are all exploring parts of your inner terrain. *City of Glass* supplies a lot of hints that it is in fact very much a book about you: not only do "you" literally appear by name in the book, but everyone Quinn meets—all these doubles and mirrors of his lost wife and family—seems to reflect back to us Quinn's psychic dilemmas. And presumably yours. Had the experience of writing about yourself so prismatically in *The Invention of Solitude* helped prepare you, in a sense, for writing about yourself in the way you did in your novel?

PA: I think so. Yes, most definitely. In some sense, *City of Glass* was a direct response to *The Invention of Solitude*, particularly the second part, the section called "The Book of Memory." But, in spite of the evidence, I wouldn't actually say that I was "writing about myself" in either book. *The Invention of Solitude* is autobiographical, of course, but I don't feel that I was telling the story of my life so much as using myself to explore certain questions that are common to us all: how we think, how we remember, how we carry our pasts around with us at every moment. I was looking at myself in the same way a scientist studies a laboratory animal. I was no more than a little gray rat, a guinea pig stuck in the cage of my own consciousness. The book wasn't written as a form of therapy; it was an attempt to turn myself inside out and examine what I was made of. Myself, yes—but myself as anyone, myself as everyone. Even the first part, which is ostensibly about my father, is finally concerned with something larger than one man's life. It's about the question of biography, about whether it's in fact possible for one person to talk about another person. *The Locked Room* picks up this problem again and approaches it from a somewhat different angle.

SG: Given what you've just said, I would have assumed you would have tried to prevent your audience from reading *City of Glass* as a disguised autobiography. Instead you introduce this possibility, and play with it in various ways. Why?

PA: I think it stemmed from a desire to implicate myself in the machinery of the book. I don't mean my autobiographical self, I mean my author self, that mysterious other who lives inside me and puts my name on the covers of books. What I was hoping to do, in effect, was to take my name off the cover and put it inside the story. I wanted to open up the process, to break down walls, to expose the plumbing. There's a strange kind of trickery involved in the writing and reading of novels, after all. You see Leo Tolstoy's name on the cover of *War and Peace*, but once you open the book, Leo Tolstoy disappears. It's as though no one has really written the words you're reading. I find this "no one" terribly fascinating—for there's finally a profound truth to it. On the one hand, it's an illusion; on the other hand, it has everything to do with how stories are written. For the author of a novel can never be sure where any of it comes from. The self that exists in the world—the self whose name appears on the covers of books—is finally not the same self who writes the book.

SG: And of course it turns out that the "Paul Auster" whom Quinn visits in the novel isn't the author of the book we've been reading—which literalizes this idea.

PA: Right. Paul Auster appears as a character in *City of Glass*, but in the end the reader learns that he is not the author. It's someone else, an anonymous narrator who comes in on the last page and walks off with Quinn's red notebook. So the Auster on the cover and the Auster in the story are not the same person. They're the same and yet not the same. Just as the author of *War and Peace* is both Tolstoy and not Tolstoy.

LM: Was there a specific incident or impulse that started *City of Glass*?

PA: About a year after my first marriage broke up, I moved to an apartment in Brooklyn. It was early 1980, and I was working on "The Book of Memory" then—and also editing an anthology of twentieth-century French poetry for Random House. One day, a couple of months after I moved in, the telephone rang, and the person on the other end asked if he had reached the Pinkerton Agency. I said no, you've got the wrong number, and hung up. I probably would have forgotten all about it, but the very next day another person called and asked the same question. "Is this the Pinkerton Agency?" Again I said no, told him he'd dialed the wrong number, and hung up. But the instant after I hung up, I began to wonder what would have happened if I had said yes. Would it have been possible for me to pose as a Pinkerton agent? And if so, how far could I have taken it? The book grew out of those telephone calls, but more than a year went by before I actually began to write it. The wrong numbers were the starting point, but there's no question that they influenced some of the other elements of the book as well—the private detective element, for example, and the idea of involving myself in the action of the story.

LM: There's a scene in *City of Glass* where Quinn says that writing his Max Work mystery novels under the pen name of William Wilson made him feel he was writing these books at one step removed, so that "Wilson served as a kind of ventriloquist. Quinn himself was the dummy, and Work was the ani-mated voice that gave purpose to the enterprise." Since I know that you also wrote a detective novel under a pseudonym, I was wondering if you shared some of Quinn's feelings about this process.

PA: It was exactly the same. All through the months I worked on that book, I felt as though I were writing with a mask on my face. It was an odd expe-rience, but I can't say that it was unenjoyable. Posing as someone else was quite a bit of fun, in fact—but at the same time disturbing and provocative. If I hadn't gone through that experience of pseudonymity myself, I never would have been able to develop Quinn in the way I did.

SG: You must have had mixed feelings about finding yourself labeled so of-ten (at least initially) as a "detective writer."

PA: Yes, I must say I've found it rather galling at times. Not that I have any-thing against detective fiction—it's just that my work has very little to do with it. I refer to it in the three novels of the Trilogy, of course, but only as a means to an end, as a way to get somewhere else entirely. If a true follower of detective fiction ever tried to read one of those books, I'm sure he would be bitterly disappointed. Mystery novels always give answers; my work is about asking questions.

In the long run, it probably doesn't matter. People can say whatever they want; they're entitled to misread books in any way they choose. It takes time for the dust to settle, and every writer has to be prepared to listen to a lot of stupidities when his work is discussed. The reviewing situation is particu-larly bad here, after all. Not only do we have the worst infant mortality rate in the Western world, but we probably have the lowest standard of literary journalism anywhere. Some of the people who review books strike me as quasi-illiterate, out-and-out morons. And theirs are the opinions that circu-late, at least at the beginning of a book's life.

SG: And yet, there are certain aspects about detective writing that are enormously attractive and compelling—things you point to in *City of Glass* about nothing being wasted in a good mystery novel, that "the center of the book shifts with each event that propels it forward," its potential for having everything come to life, seething with possibilities.

PA: Of course. At its best, detective fiction can be one of the purest and most engaging forms of story-telling. The idea that every sentence counts, that every word can make a difference—it creates a tremendous narrative propulsion. It's on that level that the form has been most interesting to me.

In the end, though, I would say that the greatest influence on my work has been fairy tales, the oral tradition of story telling. The Brothers Grimm, the Thousand and One Nights—the kinds of stories you read out loud to children. These are bare-bones narratives, narratives largely devoid of details, yet enormous amounts of information are communicated in a very short space, with very few words. What fairy tales prove, I think, is that it's the reader—or the listener—who actually tells the story to himself. The text is no more than a springboard for the imagination. "Once upon a time there was a girl who lived with her mother in a house at the edge of a large wood." You don't know what the girl looks like, you don't know what color the house is, you don't know if the mother is tall or short, fat or thin, you know next to nothing. But the mind won't allow these things to remain blank; it fills in the details itself, it creates images based on its own memories and experiences—which is why these stories resonate so deeply inside us. The listener becomes an active participant in the story.

LM: A lot of the contemporary writers who have also acknowledged a fascination with fairy tales (I'm thinking of people like Barth, Coover, Calvino, Borges) seem to share the sense that the fairy tale offers a method of communicating with readers that the novel basically ignores because it wants to provide all the details, the background, the explanation.

PA: I'd certainly agree that novel-writing has strayed very far from these open-ended structures—and from oral traditions as well. The typical novel of the past two hundred years has been crammed full of details, descriptive passages, local color—things that might be excellent in themselves, but which often have little to do with the heart of the story being told, that can actually block the reader's access to that story. I want my books to be all heart, all center, to say what they have to say in as few words as possible. This ambition seems so contrary to what most novelists are trying to accomplish that I often have trouble thinking of myself as a novelist at all.

SG: In "The Book of Memory" you described your reaction to the breakup of your first marriage and your separation from your son by saying, "Each day would drag a little more of the pain out into the open." Was writing *City of Glass* one way for you to work through or (or at least get at) that pain?

PA: That was the emotional source of the book, yes. My first wife and I split up in late 1978, and for a year-and-a-half after that I lived in a kind of limbo—first on Varick Street in Manhattan, then in that apartment in Brooklyn. But once the arrangements were worked out, my son was with me half the time. He was just three back then, and we lived together like a couple of old bachelors. It was a strange existence, I suppose, but not without its pleasures, and I assumed that life would go on like that for a long time. Then, early in 1981 (February 23, to be exact, it's impossible for me to forget the date) I met Siri Hustvedt, the person I'm married to now. We took each other by storm, and nothing has ever been the same since. For the past nine years, she's meant everything to me, absolutely everything . . .

So, by the time I started writing *City of Glass*, my life had undergone a dramatic improvement. I was in love with an extraordinary woman; we were living together in a new apartment; my inner world had been utterly transformed. In many ways, I think of *City of Glass* as an homage to Siri, as a love letter in the form of a novel. I tried to imagine what would have happened to me if I hadn't met her, and what I came up with was Quinn. Perhaps my life would have been something like his. . . .

SG: Let's talk a bit about the question of "solitude." It's a word that comes up often in your works—and of course it appears in the title of your first book of prose, *The Invention of Solitude*. It's a concept that seems to contain a lot of different resonances for you, both personal and aesthetic.

PA: Yes, I suppose there's no getting rid of it. But solitude is a rather complex term for me; it's not just a synonym for loneliness or isolation. Most people tend to think of solitude as a rather gloomy idea, but I don't attach any negative connotations to it. It's simply a fact, one of the conditions of being human, and even if we're surrounded by others, we essentially live our lives alone: real life takes place inside us. We're not dogs, after all. We're not driven solely by instincts and habits; we can think, and because we think, we're always in two places at the same time. Even in the throes of physical passion, thoughts come pouring through our head. At the very height of sexual arousal, a person can be thinking about an unanswered letter on the dining room table or about standing on a street in a foreign city twenty years ago—or anything, anything at all . . .

What it boils down to is the old mind-body problem. Descartes. Solipsism. Self and other, all the old philosophical questions. In the end, we know who we are because we can think about who we are. Our sense of self is formed by the pulse of consciousness within us—the endless monologue, the lifelong conversation we have with our selves. And this takes place in absolute solitude. It's impossible to know what someone else is thinking. We can only see the surfaces: the eyes, the face, the body. But we can't see another person's thoughts, can we? We can't hear them or touch them; they're utterly walled off from us.

Oliver Sacks, the neurologist, has made some astute observations about such things. Every whole person, he says, every person with a coherent identity, is in effect narrating the story of his life to himself at every moment—following the thread of his own story. For brain-damaged people, however, this thread has been snapped. And once that happens, it's no longer possible to hold yourself together.

But there's more to it than that. We live alone, yes, but at the same time everything we are comes from the fact that we have been made by others. I'm not just referring to biology—mothers and fathers, uterine birth, and so on. I'm thinking about psychology and the formation of the human personality. The infant feeding at the mother's breast looks up into the mother's eyes and sees her looking at him, and from that experience of being seen, the baby begins to learn that he is separate from his mother, that he is a person in his own right. We literally acquire a self from this process. Lacan calls it the "mirror-stage," which strikes me as a beautiful way of putting it. Self-consciousness in adulthood is merely an extension of those early experiences. It's no longer the mother who's looking at us then—we're looking at ourselves. But we can only see ourselves because someone else has seen us first. In other words, we learn our solitude from others. In the same way that we learn language from others.

LM: "Solitude," then, is the essential condition of being locked inside one's own head—but also something that only comes into our awareness because of other people. This sounds like a paradox . . .

PA: It does, but I don't know how else to express it. What is so startling to me, finally, is that you don't begin to understand your connection to others until you are alone. And the more intensely you are alone, the more deeply you plunge into a state of solitude, the more deeply you feel that connection. It isn't possible for a person to isolate himself from other people. No matter how apart you might find yourself in a physical sense—whether you've been marooned on a desert island or locked up in solitary confinement—you discover that you are inhabited by others. Your language, your memories, even your sense of isolation—every thought in your head has been born from your connection with others. This is what I was trying to explore in "The Book of Memory," to examine both sides of the word "solitude." I felt as though I were looking down to the bottom of myself, and what I found there was more than just myself—I found the world. That's why that book is filled with so many references and quotations, in order to pay homage to all the others inside me. On the one hand, it's a work about being alone; on the other hand, it's about community. That book has dozens of authors, and I wanted them all to speak through me. In the final analysis, "The Book of Memory" is a collective work.

SG: Earlier, when we were talking about your pseudonymous mystery novel, you said you felt like you were "wearing a mask" while writing that book. Could you talk a bit about the different relationships you have with your characters when you're writing a book from the first-person, as opposed to a third-person perspective? For example, do you feel less that you're wearing this mask when you're writing in the first person? Or do you feel a more abstract relationship to all your characters?

PA: This is a fundamental question for me. Some of my books have been written in the first person, others have been written in the third, and in each case the entire story has developed out of the particular narrative voice I've chosen. Yes, obviously a novel written in the first person is going to sound more intimate than one written in the third person. But there's a vast range within those two categories, and it's possible to bring the boundaries of first person and third person so close to each other that they touch, even overlap.

SG: How does this overlap work in your own books? Do you mean by confusing the distinction between who the reader thinks the narrator is and who finally is revealed to actually be telling the story, as you did in *City of Glass*?

PA: That's probably where the overlap is most obvious, because in *City of Glass* you have a book written in the third person throughout, and then, right at the end, the narrator appears and announces himself in the first person which colors the book in retrospect somehow, turning the whole story into a kind of oblique, first-person narrative. But I've been interested in pursuing different ranges of effects that can be produced with this sort of thing in most of my books. Even in *Ghosts*, which reads something like a fable, you feel the presence of the narrator lurking behind each sentence. The storyteller is a part of the story, even though he never uses the word "I." In the few places where he breaks in, he always refers to himself in the plural—as if addressing the reader directly, including him in what is finally a very personal "we." *The Locked Room* is written in the first person, but so much of it is about trying to understand someone else that certain sections of it are actually written in the third person. The same holds true for *In the Country of Last Things*. The little phrases that appear a few times at the beginning—"she wrote" or "her letter continued"—put the whole book in a third-person perspective. Someone has read Anna Blume's notebook; somehow or other, her letter has arrived. *Moon Palace* functions a bit like *The Locked Room* in that it's an intimate, first-person narrative that veers off into the third person. There are long passages in that book where Fogg literally disappears. When it comes right down to it, *The Music of Chance* is the only one of my novels that doesn't combine first- and third-person narration. It's written strictly in the third person.

LM: Your handling of the narrative perspective in *The Music of Chance* reminded me of what we find in several of Kafka's best works—your narrator is "outside" the character but somehow manages to convey very directly Nashe's intensely subjective, emotionally charged "inner" life. It's a delicate balance: the seemingly objective representation of an emotionally charged, psychological landscape.

PA: Yes, that third person is so close to the first person, is so deeply imagined from Nashe's point of view, that there's hardly any difference at all. It was a very wrenching experience to write that book—utterly grueling and exhausting. For weeks after I finished it, I felt like a dead man.

LM: You chose to present the two sections of *The Invention of Solitude* through two different narrative perspectives, with "Portrait of an Invisible Man" being written in the first person, while "The Book of Memory" is in the third person. What was involved in that choice?

PA: The opening part was written very naturally in the first person. I didn't question it; it just came to me that way, and I went with it. When I started the next section, I assumed it would be written in the first person as well. I worked on it for six or eight months in that form, but something about it disturbed me, something wasn't right. Eventually, after groping in the dark with it for a long time, I understood that the book could only be written in the third person. Rimbaud: "Je est un autre." It opened a door for me, and after that I worked in a kind of fever, as though my brain had caught fire.

What it came down to was creating a distance between myself and myself. If you're too close to the thing you're trying to write about, the perspective vanishes, and you begin to smother. I had to objectify myself in order to explore my own subjectivity—which gets us back to what we were talking about before: the multiplicity of the singular. The moment I think about the fact that I'm saying "I," I'm actually saying "he." It's the mirror of self-consciousness, a way of watching yourself think.

SG: Were there any particular difficulties in writing from a woman's perspective, as you did with Anna in *In the Country of Last Things*?
PA: Not really. But something in me resisted it for a long time. In many ways, writing that book was like taking dictation. I heard her voice speaking to me—and that voice was utterly distinct from my own. In that sense, there was almost no difficulty at all.

But when you consider that I first heard that voice in 1970 and didn't finish the book until 1985, it's safe to conclude that it was a very difficult book to write. I didn't want to do it. I felt it was presumptuous to write from the viewpoint of a woman, and so every time I started working on it again, I'd stop. I'd cross my fingers and hope that the voice had talked itself out, that at last I'd he free of it. A year or two would go by, and then I'd start hearing her again. I'd write for a while, then stop again. This went on for years and years. Finally, some time in the early eighties, right when I was in the middle of The New York Trilogy (I think I was between the second and third books), she came back to me in full force, and I wrote the first thirty or forty pages as they stand now. Still not sure of myself, I showed them to Siri and asked her what she thought. She said those pages were the best work I had ever done and that I had to finish the book. I had to finish the book as a present to her. "It's my book," she said, and she's continued to refer to it in that way ever since.

Still, there was a pause after writing those initial pages. I wanted to finish the Trilogy first, so more time went by before I returned to it. But in that interval, I published what I had already written in the *Paris Review*. It's the only time I've ever published a piece of a novel, but in this case it seemed to make sense. I did it as a kind of promise to myself, as a guarantee that I would actually finish it.

LM: There's an obvious way that *In the Country of Last Things* is grounded in the dystopian or post-holocaust tradition of science fiction. But I was mostly struck with how palpably real this urban nightmare scene is. It seems not too different, in fact, from what you can find right here in New York.

PA: As far as I'm concerned, the book has nothing to do with science fiction. It's quite fantastical at times, of course, but that doesn't mean it's not firmly anchored in historical realities. It's a novel about the present and the immediate past, not about the future. "Anna Blume walks through the twentieth century." That's the phrase I carried around in my head while I was working on the book.

LM: What sorts of historical realities do you mean—the massive devastations caused in the two world wars?

PA: Among other things, yes. There are specific references to the Warsaw ghetto and the siege of Leningrad, but also to events taking place in the Third World today—not to speak of New York, which is rapidly turning into a Third World city before our eyes. The garbage system, which I describe at such great length in the novel, is loosely based on the present-day garbage system in Cairo. All in all, there's very little invented material in the book. The characters, yes, but not the circumstances. Even the pivotal event in the story—when Anna, hoping to buy a pair of shoes, is lured into a human slaughterhouse—even that scene is based on historical fact. Precisely that kind of thing happened in Leningrad in World War II. The city was surrounded by the Germans for two and a half years, and in that time 500,000 people lost their lives. 500,000 people in one city. Just stop for a moment and try to imagine what it must have been like. Once you begin to think about such things, it's difficult to think about anything else.

I realize that many people found this book depressing, but there's nothing I can do about that. In the end, I find it the most hopeful book I've ever written. Anna Blume survives, at least to the extent that her words survive. Even in the midst of the most brutal realities, the most terrible social conditions, she struggles to remain a human being, to keep her humanity intact. I can't imagine anything more noble and courageous than that. It's a struggle that millions of people have had to face in our time, and not many of them have been as tenacious as she is. I think of Anna Blume as a true heroine.

SG: Earlier in the interview you referred to yourself as basically an "intuitive writer" in terms of the way your writing process operates. Maybe we could have you discuss the relationship between your conscious intentionality versus your intuition by having you discuss the way a specific image in your work develops. For instance, the moon image in *Moon Palace* appears in dozens of different contexts that occasionally dovetail or coalesce into groupings—Barber's legends of the Indians (with their origins on the

moon), the way the Utah desert is described as a lunar landscape, the fortune cookie that says, "The sun is the past, the earth is the present, the moon
is the future" (and which turns out to be a quote from Tesla), the restaurant
named "Moon Palace," and so on. Is the unfolding of these connections and
resonances the product of conscious design or happy accident?

PA: If you think about any one thing long enough or hard enough, it's going
to begin to reverberate for you. Once that happens, waves are emitted, and
those waves travel through space and bounce off other things, which in turn
emit their own waves. It's an associative process, and if you stick with it con-
scientiously enough, large portions of the world will eventually be touched
by your thoughts. It's not really a question of accident or design. This is the
way the mind works. It just happens, but you have to be watching attentively
for it to go on happening. Pick any object in front of you—a coffee cup, or a
box of cigars, or a telephone—and try to think about where it comes from.
Within ten minutes, you're onto any number of other things—geology, history, labor problems, biology, God knows what—a whole range of subjects.
"To see the world in a grain of sand." If you're capable of doing that, imagine
how much can be seen in the moon!

LM: There's also a certain sense in which those elaborate connections and
metaphorical associations being developed grow naturally out of the kind of
sensibility you project for Fogg.

PA: Precisely. Fogg is a bookish young man, an intellectual, and he has a
penchant for this kind of thing. It's something he inherits from his Uncle
Victor, a man who is constantly searching the world for hidden connections.
The moon imagery comes from Fogg—I wasn't trying to impose it on him.
At the same time, remember, he's telling the story of his youth from the
distance of middle age, and he often pokes fun at himself. He's looking back
on the way he used to think, the way he *used* to interpret the world. It's one
of the many follies of his adolescence, a symptom of the madness of those
times. But Fogg is a unique case. Other characters I've written about have
none of these tendencies; they don't indulge in such elaborate mental gym-
nastics. Nashe, for example, the hero of *The Music of Chance*, has nothing in
common with Fogg. He's a much more straightforward kind of person, and
consequently the book he appears in is a much simpler story.

LM: Let's go back for a second to your comment about seeing the world in
a grain of sand. What made it seem so much a part of what you were doing
in the novel? And how did this fit in with the "follies" of Fogg's adolescence?

PA: The moon is many things all at once, a touchstone. It's the moon as myth, as "radiant Diana, image of all that is dark within us"; the imagination, love, madness. At the same time, it's the moon as object, as celestial body, as lifeless stone hovering in the sky. But it's also the longing for what is not, the unattainable, the human desire for transcendence. And yet it's history as well, particularly American history. First there's Columbus, then there was the discovery of the West, then finally there is outer space: the moon as the last frontier. But Columbus had no idea that he'd discovered America. He thought he had sailed to India, to China. In some sense, *Moon Palace* is the embodiment of that misconception, an attempt to think of America as China. But the moon is also repetition, the cyclical nature of human experience. There are three stories in the book, after all, and each one is finally the same. Each generation repeats the mistakes of the previous generation. So it's also a critique of the notion of progress. And if America is the land of progress, what are we to make of ourselves then? And so on and so on and so on. Fogg wends his way among all these ideas, this pinball machine of associations, struggling to find a place for himself. By the end of the book I think he manages to get somewhere. But he only reaches the beginning, the brink of his adult life. And that's where we leave him—getting ready to begin.

SG: You've described how emotionally exhausting it was for you to write your latest novel, *The Music of Chance*. Did you realize when you started it that it was going to be such a wrenching book to write?
PA: It's never possible to predict what it's going to be like. With my other books, I've usually known the general shape of the story before beginning to write it, but in this case a number of crucial elements were altered as I went along. I began with a different ending in mind, but at a certain point I realized that I had been wrong, that the book was heading for a much darker conclusion than I had originally planned. This revelation came as a shock to me, it stopped me cold in my tracks. But there was no getting around it, and after thinking it over for several days, I understood that I had no choice.

SG: Do you recall what the origins of the book were?
PA: At the end of *Moon Palace*, Fogg is driving out west in a car. The car is stolen, and he winds up continuing the journey on foot. I realized that I wanted to get back inside that car, to give myself a chance to go on driving around America. So there was that very immediate and visceral impulse, which is how *The Music of Chance* begins—with Nashe sitting behind the wheel of a car.

At the same time, I wanted to explore the implications of the windfall I had received after my father's death—which is something we discussed before. This led me to start thinking about the question of freedom, which is ultimately the true subject of the book.

As for the wall—those stones had been standing inside me for years. The play that I mentioned earlier, the one that was performed in the seventies, was about two men building a wall. The whole play consists of them lugging stones around the stage, and by the end they're completely blocked off from the audience. I was never satisfied with it, but at the same time I couldn't get rid of the idea. It plagued me and haunted me for all those years. So this was my attempt to improve on what I had done with it the first time. Those are three elements of the novel that I was able to think about before I wrote it. The conscious material, so to speak. Everything else is shrouded in obscurity.

When I was about two-thirds of the way through the first draft, it occurred to me that the story had the same structure as a fairy tale. Up until then, I had only thought about the book in concrete terms, the reality of the action. But if you reduce the book to its skeleton, then you wind up with something that resembles a typical story by the Brothers Grimm, don't you? A wanderer stumbles onto an opportunity to make his fortune; he travels to the ogre's castle to test his luck, is tricked into staying there, and can win his freedom only by performing a series of absurd tasks that the ogre invents for him. I don't know if I want to make too much out of this, but it was an interesting discovery anyway. Another example of how elusive the whole activity of writing is. Yet another testimony to my own ignorance.

Memory's Escape—Inventing the Music of Chance: An Interview with Paul Auster

Mark Irwin/1992

From *Denver Quarterly* 28.3 (Winter 1994), 111–22. Reproduced with permission of Mark Irwin.

IRWIN: There is a wonderful obsession with space in your work which begins with early prose writings about Sir Walter Raleigh and the arctic explorer, Peter Freuchen, continues through your most recent novels, and seems to have distinguished you from many of your contemporaries. Your characters vacillate from boxed-in extremes to expansive, often vagrant wanderings. I'm reminded of Pascal's quote, "All the unhappiness of man stems from one thing only, that he is incapable of staying quietly in his room."

AUSTER: I've never made a conscious decision to write about space in those terms, but looking back over the body of my work now, I can see that it does shuttle between these two extremes: confinement and vagabondage—open space and hermetic space. At the same time, there's a curious paradox embedded in all this: when the characters in my books are most confined, they seem to be most free. And when they are free to wander, they are most lost and confused. So, in some funny way, there's a reversal of expectations about these two conditions. In my first prose book, *The Invention of Solitude*, there's a long passage about my friend the composer, the man I call "S." He lived in the tiniest, most minimal space I've ever been in. And yet, he probably had the biggest mind of any person I've ever known, and he managed to inhabit that space as if he were utterly free. More recently, a character like Nashe in *The Music of Chance* is a wanderer. He crisscrosses America for an entire year, and yet, in some sense, he's a prisoner. He's imprisoned in his own desire for what he construes to be a notion of freedom. But freedom isn't possible for him until he stops and plants himself somewhere and takes on responsibility for something, for some other person. It's a paradoxical shuttling between the two, but neither one stands for what you might think it would. I think what excites me about this is not the idea of traveling to a destination that one has picked out in advance—but thrashing out into the unknown. In the way that Cabeza de Vaca did, for example, the first white man to set foot on this continent. It's a story of being lost, of immense wanderings, of never knowing what's going to happen next. Just like writing, I suppose, or at least writing as I practice it. Every day, I set off on a journey into the unknown, and yet the whole time I'm just sitting there in my room. The door is locked, I never budge, and yet that confinement offers me absolute freedom—to be whoever I want to be, to go wherever my thoughts take me.

IRWIN: But would you say that you find some comfort in shuttling between two extremes? For example, *Moon Palace* begins with Marco Stanley Fogg, who inherits box upon box of books from his uncle and creates a sort of modular prison, a bed, a desk, out of the boxes. Slowly he reads the books and then begins a trek, which is a sort of escape *to freedom*. Whereas *The Music of Chance* begins with Jim Nashe, who drives randomly across the country, accidentally meets Jack Pozzi, enters a card game, and then agrees to build a wall out of fifteenth-century stones in the middle of a meadow. His is an escape *from freedom.* Do you find some particular freedom in this shuttling back and forth between extremes?

AUSTER: In some sense, *Moon Palace* and *The Music of Chance* are opposite books, mirror reflections of each other. Toward the end of *Moon Palace*, if you remember, Fogg and Barber begin traveling out west in a red car. Barber dies along the way, and Fogg continues the journey by himself. He gets as far as Utah, at which point the car is stolen and he has to finish the trip on foot. After I completed the book, I realized that I wanted to get back in the car. This was the first step toward writing *The Music of Chance.* I wanted to get back in the car. I felt I hadn't been in there long enough. There was something I wanted to explore about this idea. And, logically enough, *The Music of Chance* begins with a man in a red car. It was red in both cases. Driving around the country with no definite purpose. This idea of contrasts, contradictions, paradox, I think, gets very much to the heart of what novel writing is for me. It's a way for me to express my contradictions. Unlike poetry, which for me was always a univocal act—a way of trying to ground myself in the very substance of my being and to express, in as articulate, lyrical, and intense a form as possible, what I believed at any given moment. But novel writing is different. Novel writing is a way of speaking out of both sides of your mouth at once. It's multi-voiced. And I think this suits me better. I can go back and forth, explore different parts of myself and the world in a single work. Freedom, confinement: those are the two sides of a single thought, and the one couldn't exist without the other.

IRWIN: If poetry summons a certain freedom by imposing a form, would you say that fiction summons this freedom through a poly-vocalness?
AUSTER: I think so. I think it's helped me to unleash all the different sides of myself, which I was never able to accomplish as a poet. Novel-writing seems to be more generative for me. One book seems to give birth to another. The farther I go, the more it seems I have to tell. It's very surprising. When I began as a novelist, I thought I had one or two books in me, and yet, here I am, ten years later, still doing it. Beckett compared himself to Joyce by saying: "The more Joyce knew, the more he could. The more I know, the less I can." As far as I'm concerned, there's an altogether different equation: The less I know, the more I can.

IRWIN: Let's talk for a minute about memory and chance. Your characters seem propelled both by chance and memory, buffeted from one to the other. In *The Invention of Solitude*, you say, "For the story would not have occurred to him unless whatever summoned its memory had not already been making itself felt." Then you narrate the story of M., who writes his father from a "chambre de bonne" in Paris, only to find that his father had hidden out in that same room, many years before, from the Nazis.
AUSTER: I believe that the world is filled with stories, that our lives are filled with stories, but it's only at certain moments that we are able to see them or to understand them. You have to be ready to make sense of what's happening to you. Most of us, myself included, walk through life not paying much attention. Suddenly, a crisis occurs when everything about ourselves is called into question, when the ground drops out from under us. I think it's at those moments when memory becomes a powerful force in our lives. You begin to explore the past, and invariably you come up with a new reading of the past, a new understanding, and because of that you're able to encounter the present in a new way.

IRWIN: Continuing on with this notion of chance. . . . In *The Music of*

Chance there is a great sense of allegory, perhaps "architectural closure" is the phrase, in which a nonsensical, expanding universe contracts to a mansion of terrifying and deductive logic, a mansion owned by two characters, Stone and Flower (the inorganic, and the organic). The castle-like house, with its black-and-white checkered floor, contains Stone's model, "The City of the World," the card game, victory, loss, the building of a wall. It all collapses to a terrifying certainty in which Nashe, having obsessively escaped from freedom, now must escape to it. I guess we're back to this shuttling from one to another. So could you speak a little bit about allegory in the sense that it pertains to this idea of chance?

AUSTER: Allegory seems to imply a specific intention on the author's part, a plan. I myself never have one. From day to day, I scarcely know what I'm doing. I begin blindly with a few images, a few buzzes in my head—the sound of the voice of a character, a gesture. The story then begins to develop within me, and often it takes years for the thing to form itself to the point that I'm able to begin writing. But allegory, symbolism, and so on—those are words that don't even enter my head. Nothing in any of my books means anything, as far as I know, except what I'm putting down on the page. There are no hidden meanings. On the other hand, if you're able to tell a story that resonates with the same power it has inside you, it's almost as if it's coming out of your dreams. It comes from a place so dark and inaccessible if it's done well that it will resonate with the same power for the reader. . . . Writing isn't mathematics, after all. This doesn't equal that, one thing can't be substituted for another. A book is composed of irreducible elements, and I would almost say that to the degree the writer does *not* understand them, that is the degree to which the book is allowed to become itself, to become a human and not just a literary exercise. . . . We were talking about Beckett earlier, which reminds me of something that happened the first time I met him—back in 1972 or 1973. He told me that he had just finished a translation of *Mercier and Camier*, his first French novel, which had been written a good twenty-five years earlier. I had read the book in French and liked it very much, "A wonderful book," I said. I was just a kid, after all, and I couldn't suppress my enthusiasm. Beckett shook his head and said, "Oh no, no, not very good. In fact, I've cut out about twenty-five percent of the original. The English version is going to be quite a bit shorter than the French." And I said, "Why would you do such a thing? It's a wonderful book, you shouldn't have taken anything out." And he shook his head, "No, no, not very good, not very good." And then we went on to talk about other things. Then, out of the blue, ten minutes later, he turns to me and says, "You really liked it, huh?

You really thought it was good?" This was Samuel Beckett, remember, and not even he had any grasp of his work. Good or bad, meaningful or not—no writer ever knows, not even the best ones.

IRWIN: When I was speaking about the wonderful closure in *The Music of Chance*: the castle-like house, the black-and-white checkered floor, Stone's model of "the city of the world," the card game, victory, loss, the building of a wall—this incredible vortex of closure reminds me of something Camus said about the novel. He talks about a "metaphysical principle of unity," a great density, where suddenly things become inevitable. Did you feel that was beginning to happen at that point in *The Music of Chance*?

AUSTER: There's no question that the book took over and had its own life independent of my will or judgment about what should or shouldn't go into it. There was an interesting example during the poker game. Nashe leaves the table and goes upstairs to look at "The City of the World" again. He stays for an hour and winds up stealing the two little figures of Flower and Stone. I had no idea he was going to do this until I wrote the passage. It was as though Nashe had become entirely real for me and was doing it on his own. I still don't understand why he did it, and yet it was right that he did it. It had to be that way. Another example would be the ending of the book. When I first started writing, I had altogether different end in mind. And yet, as I began to grapple with the material—when I had a good part of it behind me already—I began to understand things that I hadn't even guessed in the beginning. I realized that the book had to end in the car, the same place where it had begun. The book had to end before the end, so to speak. I mean, there is no conclusion—something is about to happen, but you don't know what the result is going to be. Whether Nashe lives or dies is almost unimportant. The important thing is that he has triumphed. By the end of the book, he has transcended everything he had been—he has become, I think, a great figure—a truly powerful human being who understands himself and what he's capable of (which was not the case in the beginning) and what this means is that he's willing to take the world as it comes to him. If death is what's coming, he's willing to face that, too. He's not afraid anymore, he's not afraid of anything. So whether the car crashes or whether he manages to elude the on-coming headlights, whether he dies or whether he lives is much less important than the inner victory he's won at that moment.

IRWIN: The scene where Nashe gets up from the poker table after his partner Pozzi begins winning—it's really one of my favorite scenes in the entire novel. I love the "punitive whims" in your work. At times they seem wonderfully mischievous and boyish, which seems to make them more American. Are you aware of this? Often, there seems to be a sense of caricature, a "making fun." For instance, when Pozzi and Nashe show up at the mansion, and they expect to have a lavish dinner, but they're served hamburgers with potato chips—is this to you a sense of caricature? Or is this just you having fun, discovering where the novel will go?

AUSTER: Well, no. It's the characters. It's the characters, Flower and Stone, and it's also the unexpected. If my work is about anything, I think it's about the unexpected, the idea that anything can happen. You never know what's looming up ahead. Nashe and Pozzi walk into this mansion, they expect to have a lavish dinner, and they're given a crazy little meal, a kiddie banquet. Flower and Stone are eccentrics, latter-day versions of Laurel and Hardy. And if there's one thing that distinguishes Laurel and Hardy, it's their infantilism, the way these grown men in their suits and ties can suddenly turn around and act like seven-year-old boys. The scene in the book is quite surprising, I suppose. Strange. But it's strange for me too. As strange for me as it is for Nashe.

IRWIN: Again, we seem to be getting back to closure and freedom. We're in this castle-like mansion and we're having a kiddie banquet. Both John Ashbery and Marshall McLuhan have said that part of the American-ness of poetry and the novel is "to let everything in" as opposed to the more European notion "to control it." So you seem very much at one with this idea of letting the world in. You've already talked about Tesla, fairy tales, and Laurel and Hardy. There's great range to your work. So you would agree with that, letting the world in, in the sort of discovering sense?

AUSTER: Absolutely. What's interesting about fiction is that it can encompass everything. There's nothing in the world that is not material for a novel. I think that's been the glory of American writing, as opposed to, say, European writing: the fact that we've allowed things in. It gives a kind of flexibility and questioning force to a lot of the American fiction that I admire. I feel that I want to stay open to everything, that there's nothing that can't be an influence. Everything from the most banal elements of popular culture to the most rigorous, demanding philosophical works. It's all part of the world we live in, and once you begin to draw lines and exclude things, you're turning your back on reality—a fatal mistake for a novelist.

IRWIN: Perhaps for me, one of the most original aspects of your work is the notion that chance, memory, and the act of writing itself, all seek to violate space, both in a physical and in a metaphysical sense. As an example, let me quote a letter from Nadezhda Mandelstam to Osip Mandelstam, in October, 1938, the same letter you quote at the end of *The Invention of Solitude.* "I have no words, my darling, to write this letter. I am writing it into empty space. Perhaps you will come back and not find me here." Does it haunt you, this writing into *empty space*, the terror and grace of the eternal?

AUSTER: At bottom, I think, my work has come out of a position of intense personal despair, a very deep nihilism and hopelessness about the world, the fact of our own transience and mortality, the inadequacy of language, the isolation of one person from another. And yet, at the same time, I've wanted to express the beauty and extraordinary happiness of feeling yourself alive, of breathing in the air, the joy of being alive in your own skin. To manage to wrench words out of all of this, no matter how inadequate they might be, is at the core of everything I've ever done. What I mean to say is that it matters. And the people in my books are engaged in struggles that matter to them. I've never really been able to write about what most novelists seem to concentrate on—what we might call the sociological moment, the world of things around us, the world of tastes and fads. It's simpler than that, it's deeper than that, it's probably a lot more naive than that. It's about living and dying and trying to make sense of what we're doing here. All the basic questions you ask yourself when you're fifteen years old, trying to come to terms with the fact that you are on this planet, figuring out some reason for being here. These are the questions that are driving all my characters. In some ways, I think this is the element in my novels that links them to the work I did as a poet and why I think of my work as a continuous whole rather than two distinct movements. It's also why I often have trouble thinking of myself as a novelist. When I read other novelists, admiring as I might be of their work, impressed as I might be by what they're able to articulate and express, I'm struck by how different it is from what I'm trying to do. In the long run, I suppose, I tend to think of myself more as a storyteller than a novelist. I believe that stories are the fundamental food for the soul. We can't live without stories. In one form or another, everybody is living on them from the age of two until their death. People don't necessarily have to read novels to satisfy their need for stories. They watch television or read comic books or go to the movies. In whatever form they get them, these stories are crucial. It's through stories that we struggle to make sense of the world. This is what keeps me going—the justification for spending my life locked up in a little room, putting words on paper. The world won't collapse if I never write another book. But in the end, I don't think of it as an entirely useless activity. I'm part of the great human enterprise of trying to make sense of what we're doing here in the world. There are so many moments of questioning why you do it and what the purpose of it is—it's important to remember sometimes that it's not for nothing. This is about the only thing I've ever come up with that makes any sense.

IRWIN: This deep sense of despair that you said your novels are *birthed from*, reminds me of your quoting Faulkner in *The Music of Chance*. "Until some day in very disgust, he risks everything in the blind turn of a card." So this sense of nihilism, is that the origin of this personal despair, the break in the narrative thread that fascinates you, that compels you and makes us human in a way?
AUSTER: Perhaps. It's interesting about the quote from Faulkner. I came across it as I was writing the book—purely by chance—and I couldn't ignore it. There it was. That sentence seemed to articulate the entire book for me, and so I felt compelled to put it in. You can't turn your back on what you're given. . . . Nashe is a good example of the despair I was talking about, the despair that leads to a terrible kind of nihilism—an impulse to chuck everything at the drop of a hat. It's a very scary position to be in.

IRWIN: Is that American? Is that distinctly American to chuck everything at the blind turn of a card? It seems American somehow . . .
AUSTER: I don't know. I tend to think of it as human. But since we're a country without a long past, a place in which most people have obliterated their connection to the past, maybe it's easier for Americans to do such a thing than it is for people from other countries. I wouldn't want to insist on that idea, though. It's dangerous to talk in generalities, to make assumptions about national characteristics. On the other hand, we're all products of a particular place. I've grown up here, I've spent my entire life here, and undoubtedly America has settled into my very bones.

IRWIN: Your work resembles, or at least shares an obsession with the nomadic road films of the great German filmmaker Wim Wenders, with whom you now work. How do you feel about this relationship and its coincidental nature?
AUSTER: A little over two years ago, I got a letter from Wim Wenders. I'd had no contact with him before. A letter out of the blue, written from Australia where he was shooting his last film. It was such a beautiful and

kind and generous letter that my heart melted. He simply said, Dear Mr. Auster, I've read all your books, I love them deeply, and I'm very sad that there are no more to read. I make movies. I don't know if you know who I am. I've made X, Y, and Z. I have no plan, nothing to propose to you, simply the idea that someday, if you would be willing, I would like to make a movie with you. And that was it. A letter that dropped out of nowhere. We eventually met and became friends. Now we're about to begin a project together. I'm going to write something that we hope will one day be turned into a film. I admire his work a great deal. It might prove to be an interesting collaboration. Only time will tell. But there's an interesting story in all this, which somehow connects with the other things we've been talking about. . . . About six months before I received the letter from Wim Wenders, I was in Paris. I ran into someone in a bookstore who said some nice things about my work. One of his remarks stuck with me for the rest of the day. "You're the first writer I've read since Peter Handke who's made a real difference to me," he said. It was a flattering thing to say. Peter Handke is an excellent writer, but I'd never thought of my work as having any connection with his, and so for the next few hours I walked around thinking about him. Then, as I was rushing back to my hotel at around eight o'clock to see some friends, I saw Peter Handke on the street. It was unmistakably him, I recognized him from photographs. It was one of those weird moments. You start thinking about someone—an absolute stranger—and then, after a few hours, he materializes before your eyes. Several months later, I went to Vermont with my family for the summer. About two weeks before Wenders's letter turned up in the mail, my agent called. She'd just received a message from *Elle* magazine in France. They were planning to do a series of articles of conversations between men and women, and they wanted me to participate in one of them. "The question is," my agent said, "what French woman do you want to meet?" I thought it was a joke. I burst out laughing and said, "Well, if you put it that way—Jeanne Moreau, of course," and then promptly forgot about the whole thing. Two weeks later, Wenders's letter arrived. A couple of days after that, my agent called back. "Jeanne Moreau was out of the country," she said, "so it took them a while to track her down. She says yes, *Elle* magazine says yes, and it's on. You're going to meet her in Paris in October." So in October I went to Europe—first of all to Germany, where I met Wenders for the first time. We got together on October 3, the day of German unification—an historic moment. While we were eating dinner, I mentioned that I was going to go to Paris to meet Jeanne Moreau. He found that very amusing, since it turned out that she had just played a major part in his last film. Another strange twist. At the moment I mentioned Jeanne Moreau's name to my agent, she was in Australia with Wim, who was just sitting down to write a letter to me. And neither one of them knew what the other was up to. So—back to the dinner in Germany—Wim wrote out a short letter to Jeanne Moreau, put it in an envelope, and asked me to give it to her in Paris. When I saw her a few days later, the first thing I did was hand her the letter. "Here's a note from Wim Wenders," I said. She opened it up, read it, and broke into a big smile. "Do you want to read it?" she said. What Wim had written was this: "Dear Jeanne, It's no accident that you're meeting Paul Auster today. There is no such thing as chance. Love, Wim." A perfect little note. So we started talking, she and I. And I found her remarkable in every way, an extremely intelligent, well-read person who has many interests in life besides her own career. Naturally enough, we talked about Wim for a little while. That led to something about Peter Handke (who's worked with Wenders on some film projects), and I mentioned that I had seen Handke on the street earlier that year. "Oh yes," she said, "Peter Handke had just moved to France then. As a matter of fact, he was staying as a guest in my apartment." I felt as if I'd been hit on the head with a hammer. The story had come full circle, a chain of unlikely coincidences that had traveled around the entire globe. It seems that things like this are happening to me all the time. You think about someone and he suddenly appears. Then, months later, you meet someone else who can tell you what he was doing on that street at that particular moment. And on and on it goes.

IRWIN: I like this music of chance. Two days ago, after I had finished writing these interview questions (there were seven of them, I believe, at 8:00 in the morning), I walked upstairs to dial your number and the phone rang, and you in fact gave me the time that you would arrive in Denver. (Laughter). And I think, we all feel like Wim Wenders, that there's a certain sadness . . . there are not enough Paul Auster novels.

The Making of *Smoke*

Annette Insdorf/1994

From *Smoke and Blue in the Face: Two Films* by Paul Auster (Hyperion, 1995), 3–16. Interview conducted November 22, 1994. Reprinted with permission of Paul Auster.

ANNETTE INSDORF: I gather that *Smoke* began with a Christmas story you wrote for the *New York Times.*

PAUL AUSTER: Yes, it all started with that little story. Mike Levitas, the editor of the Op-Ed page, called me out of the blue one morning in November of 1990. I didn't know him, but he had apparently read some of my books. In his friendly, matter-of-fact way he told me that he'd been toying with the idea of commissioning a work of fiction for the Op-Ed page on Christmas Day. What did I think? Would I be willing to write it? It was an interesting proposal, I thought—putting a piece of make-believe in a newspaper, the paper of record, no less. A rather subversive notion when you get right down to it. But the fact was that I had never written a short story, and I wasn't sure I'd be able to come up with an idea. "Give me a few days," I said. "If I think of something, I'll let you know." So a few days went by, and just when I was about to give up, I opened a tin of my beloved Schimmelpennincks—the little cigars I like to smoke—and started thinking about the man who sells them to me in Brooklyn. That led to some thoughts about the kinds of encounters you have in New York with people you see every day but don't really know. And little by little, the story began to take shape inside me. It literally came out of that tin of cigars.

AI: It's not what I would call your typical Christmas story.

PA: I hope not. Everything gets turned upside down in "Auggie Wren." What's stealing? What's giving? What's lying? What's telling the truth? All these questions are reshuffled in rather odd and unorthodox ways.

AI: When did Wayne Wang enter the picture?

PA: Wayne called me from San Francisco a few weeks after the story was published.

AI: Did you know him?
PA: No. But I knew of him and had seen one of his films, *Dim Sum*, which I had greatly admired. It turned out that he'd read the story in the *Times* and felt it would make a good premise for a movie. I was flattered by his interest, but at that point I didn't want to write the script myself. I was hard at work on a novel [*Leviathan*] and couldn't think about anything else. But if Wayne wanted to use the story to make a movie, that was fine by me. He was a good filmmaker, and I knew that something good would come of it.

AI: How was it, then, that you wound up writing the screenplay?
PA: Wayne came to New York that spring. It was May, I think, and the first afternoon we spent together we just walked around Brooklyn. It was a beautiful day, I remember, and I showed him the different spots around town where I had imagined the story taking place. We got along very well. Wayne is a terrific person, a man of great sensitivity, generosity, and humor, and unlike most artists, he doesn't make art to gratify his ego. He has a genuine calling, which means that he never feels obligated to defend himself or beat his own drum. After that first day in Brooklyn, it became clear to both of us that we were going to become friends.

AI: Were any ideas for the film discussed that day?
PA: Rashid, the central figure of the story, was born during that preliminary talk. And also the conviction that the movie would be about Brooklyn. . . . Wayne went back to San Francisco and started working with a screenwriter friend of his on a treatment. He sent it to me in August, a story outline of ten or twelve pages. I was with my family in Vermont just then, and I remember feeling that the outline was good, but not good enough. I gave it to my wife Siri to read, and that night we lay awake in bed talking through another story, a different approach altogether. I called Wayne the next day, and he agreed that this new story was better than the one he'd sent me. As a small favor to him, he asked me if I wouldn't mind writing up the treatment of this new story. I figured I owed him that much, and so I did it.

AI: And suddenly, so to speak, your foot was in the door.
PA: It's funny how these things work, isn't it? A few weeks later, Wayne went to Japan on other business. He met with Saturn Iseki of NDF [Nippon Film

Development] about his project, and just in passing, in a casual sort of way, he mentioned the treatment I had written. Mr. Iseki was very interested. He'd like to produce our film, he said, but only if "Auster writes the script." My books are published in Japan, and it seemed that he knew who I was. But he would need an American partner, he said, someone to split the costs and oversee production. When Wayne called me from Tokyo to report what had happened, I laughed. The chances of Mr. Iseki ever finding an American partner seemed so slim, so utterly beyond the realm of possibility, that I said yes, I'll do the screenplay if there's money to make the film. And then I immediately went back to writing my novel.

AI: But they did find a partner, didn't they?

PA: Sort of. Tom Luddy, a good friend of Wayne's in San Francisco, wanted to do it at Zoetrope. When Wayne told me the news, I was stunned, absolutely caught off guard. But I couldn't back out. Morally speaking, I was committed to writing the script. I had given my word, and so once I finished *Leviathan* [at the end of '91], I started writing *Smoke*. A few months later, the deal between NDF and Zoetrope fell apart. But I was too far into it by then to want to stop. I had already written a first draft, and once you start something, it's only natural to want to see it through to the end.

AI: Had you ever written a screenplay before?

PA: Not really. When I was very young, nineteen or twenty years old, I wrote a couple of scripts for silent movies. They were very long and very detailed, seventy or eighty pages of elaborate and meticulous movements, every gesture spelled out in words. Weird, deadpan slapstick. Buster Keaton revisited. Those scripts are lost now. I wish to hell I knew where they were. I'd love to see what they looked like.

AI: Did you do any sort of special preparation? Did you read scripts? Did you start watching movies with a different eye toward construction?

PA: I looked at some scripts, just to make sure of the format. How to number the scenes, moving from interiors to exteriors, that kind of thing. But no real preparation—except a lifetime of watching movies. I've always been drawn to them, ever since I was a boy. It's the rare person in this world who isn't, I suppose. But at the same time, I also have certain problems with them. Not just with this or that particular movie, but with movies in general, the medium itself.

AI: In what way?

PA: The two-dimensionality, first of all. People think of movies as "real," but they're not. They're flat pictures projected against a wall, a simulacrum of reality, not the real thing. And then there's the question of the images. We tend to watch them passively, and in the end they wash right through us. We're captivated and intrigued and delighted for two hours, and then we walk out of the theater and can barely remember what we've seen. Novels are totally different. To read a book, you have to be actively involved in what the words are saying. You have to work, you have to use your imagination. And once your imagination has been fully awakened, you enter into the world of the book as if it were your own life. You smell things, you touch things, you have complex thoughts and insights, you find yourself in a three-dimensional world.

AI: The novelist speaks.

PA: Well, needless to say, I'm always going to come down on the side of books. But that doesn't mean movies can't be wonderful. It's another way of telling stories, that's all, and I suppose it's important to remember what each medium can and can't do . . . I'm particularly attracted to directors who emphasize telling stories over technique, who take the time to allow their characters to unfold before your eyes, to exist as full-fledged human beings.

AI: Who would you put in that category?

PA: Renoir, for one. Ozu for another. Bresson . . . Satyajit Ray . . . a whole range, finally. These directors don't bombard you with pictures, they're not in love with the image for its own sake. They tell their stories with all the care and patience of the best novelists. Wayne is that kind of director. Someone who has sympathy for the inner lives of his characters, who doesn't rush things. That was why I was happy to be working with him——to be working *for* him. A screenplay is no more than a blue print, after all. It's not the finished product. I didn't write the script in a vacuum. I wrote it for Wayne, for a movie that he was going to direct, and I very consciously tried to write something that would be compatible with his strengths as a director.

AI: How long did it take you to write it?

PA: The first draft took about three weeks, maybe a month. Then the negotiations between NDF and Zoetrope broke down, and suddenly the whole project was left dangling. It was probably dumb of me to start without a signed contract, but I hadn't yet understood how iffy and unstable the movie business is. At that point, however, NDF decided to go ahead and "develop" the script anyway while they searched for another American partner. That meant that I'd be given a little money to continue writing, and so I kept at it. Wayne and I discussed the first draft, I tinkered with it a little more, and then we both moved on to other things. Wayne went into preproduction for *The Joy Luck Club*, and I began writing a new novel [*Mr. Vertigo*]. But we stayed in close touch, and every once in a while over the next year and a half we'd talk on the phone or get together somewhere to discuss new ideas about the script.

I did about three more versions, and each time that entailed a week or two of work—adding elements, discarding elements, rethinking the structure. There's a big difference between the first draft and the final draft, but the changes happened slowly, by increments, and I never felt that I was changing the essence of the story. Gradually finding it is probably more like it. At some point in all this, Peter Newman came in as our American producer, but the money to make the movie still had to be found. Meanwhile, I kept working on *Mr. Vertigo*, and by the time I finished it, Wayne's movie was about to be released. And so there we were, ready to tackle *Smoke* again.

By some twist of good luck, Wayne decided to show the script to Robert Altman. Altman had very nice things to say about it, but he felt it lagged a bit in the middle and probably needed one more little something before it found its definitive shape. Robert Altman is not someone whose opinion should be discounted, and so I went back and reread the script with his comments in mind, and lo and behold, he was right. I sat down to work again, and this time everything seemed to fit. The story was rounder, fuller, more integrated. It was no longer a collection of fragments. It finally had some coherence to it.

AI: A very different process from writing a novel, then. Did you enjoy it?

PA: Yes, completely different. Writing a novel is an organic process, and most of it happens unconsciously. It's long and slow and very grueling. A screenplay is more like a jigsaw puzzle. Writing the actual words might not be very time-consuming, but putting the pieces together can drive you crazy. But yes, I did enjoy it. I found it a challenge to write dialogue, to think in dramatic terms rather than narrative terms, to do something I had never done before.

AI: And then Miramax stepped in and decided to back the film.

PA: *The Joy Luck Club* turned out to be a big success, the screenplay was finished, and Peter Newman happens to be a very droll and persuasive man. I was out of the country for a couple of weeks last fall, and when I came home, it seemed that we were in business. All the arrangements were in place.

AI: And that's when the screenwriter is supposed to disappear.
PA: So they say. But Wayne and I forgot to pay attention to the rules. It never occurred to either one of us to part company then. I was the writer, Wayne was the director, but it was *our* film, and all along we had considered ourselves equal partners in the project. I understand now what an unusual arrangement this was. Writers and directors aren't supposed to like each other, and no one had ever heard of a director treating a writer as Wayne treated me. But I was naive and stupid, and I took it for granted that I was still involved.

AI: Not all that naive, though. You'd been involved in another film once before—*The Music of Chance.*
PA: Yes, but that was completely different. Philip Haas adapted a novel of mine and turned that adaptation into a movie. A different story altogether. He and his wife wrote the script, and he directed it. He had a free hand to interpret the book as he chose, to present his particular reading of the book I had written. But my work was already finished before he started.

AI: Yes, but you also wound up playing a role in that film, didn't you? As an actor, I mean.
PA: True, true. My thirty-second cameo appearance in the final scene. Never again! If nothing else, I emerged from that experience with a new respect for what actors can do. I mean trained, professional actors. There's nothing like a little taste of the real thing to teach you humility.

AI: Back to *Smoke*, then. Were you involved in the casting, for example?
PA: To some degree, yes. And Wayne and I discussed every decision very thoroughly. We had some disappointments along the way, and also some very hard decisions to make. One actor I made a very intense plea for was Giancarlo Esposito. His role is very small. He plays Tommy, the OTB Man, and appears only peripherally in two scenes. But his character gets to speak the first lines in the movie, and I knew that if he accepted, things would get off to a flying start. It was a great moment for me when he said yes. The same with Forest Whitaker. I couldn't imagine any other actor playing Cyrus, and I can't tell you how thrilled I was when he agreed to do the part. . . . Other

than that, I sat in on a lot of the auditions. What a heart-breaking spectacle that can be. So many talented people marching in with their high hopes and tough skins. It takes courage to court rejection on a daily basis, and I must say that I was moved by all this. . . .

Looking back on it now, though, I would say that the single most memorable experience connected with the casting was an open call organized by Heidi Levitt and Billy Hopkins. A bitter cold Saturday in late January, snow on the ground, howling winds, and three thousand people showed up at a high school in Manhattan to try out for bit parts in *Smoke*. Three thousand people! The line went all the way down the block. What a motley collection of humanity. The large and the small, the fat and the thin, the young and the old, the white, the black, the brown, the yellow . . . everyone from a former Miss Nigeria to an ex-middleweight boxing champion, and every last one of them wanted to be in the movies. I was astonished.

AI: Well, you wound up with an extraordinary cast. Harvey Keitel, William Hurt, Stockard Channing, Forest Whitaker, Ashley Judd . . . and Harold Perrineau in his first role. It's a great line-up.

PA: They were good people to work with, too. None of the actors made a lot of money, but they all seemed enthusiastic about being in the film. That made for a good working atmosphere all around. . . . About two months before shooting began, Wayne and I started meeting with the actors to discuss their roles and examine the nuances of the script. I wound up writing "Character Notes" for many of the parts, exhaustive lists and comments to help fill in the background of each character's life. Not just biographies and family histories, but the music they listened to, the foods they ate, the books they read—anything and everything that might help the actor get a handle on his role.

AI: Marguerite Duras used precisely that approach when she wrote her script for *Hiroshima Mon Amour*, one of my favorite films of all time. There is a sense of texture about the characters, even though we aren't told very much about their backgrounds.

PA: The more you know, the more helpful it is. It's not easy pretending to be someone else, after all. The more you have to hold on to, the richer your performance is going to be.

AI: I take it there were rehearsals for *Smoke*—something for which there isn't always time with movies.

PA: It seemed essential in this case, given that there's so much talk in the film and so little action! Rehearsals went on for several weeks in a church near Washington Square. Harvey, Bill, Harold, Stockard, Ashley . . . they all worked very hard.

AI: Were there any other aspects of preproduction that you were involved with?

PA: Involved might be too strong a word, but I did have numerous conversations with Kalina Ivanov, the production designer. Particularly about the apartment that Bill Hurt's character lives in. That was the only set constructed for the movie—on a sound stage in Long Island City. Everything else was filmed in real places. Considering that the apartment is lived in by a novelist, it made sense that Kalina should want to consult with me. We talked about everything: the books on the shelves, the pictures on the walls, the precise contents of the clutter on the desk. I think she did a remarkable job. For once, there's an authentic-looking New York apartment in a movie. Have you ever noticed how many supposedly ordinary people in Hollywood films manage to live in three-million-dollar TriBeCa lofts? The apartment that Kalina designed rings true, and a lot of work and thought went into what she did, things that often aren't even visible on screen. The little coffee-cup rings on the table, the postcard of Herman Melville over the desk, the unused word processor sitting in the corner, a thousand and one minute details. . . . Philosophically speaking, production design is a fascinating discipline. There's a real spiritual component to it. Because what it entails is looking very closely at the world, seeing things as they really are and not as you want them to be, and then re-creating them for wholly imaginary and fictitious purposes. Any job that requires you to look that carefully at the world has to be good job, a job that's good for the soul.

AI: You're beginning to sound like Auggie Wren!

PA: (Laughs) Well, Auggie didn't come out of nowhere. He's a part of me—just as much as I'm a part of him.

AI: Once the shooting started, did you go to the set?

PA: Occasionally. Every now and then I'd stop by to see how things were going, especially when they were filming the cigar store scenes, since that set was within walking distance of my house. And I was up in Peekskill for the last three or four days of shooting. But in general I kept myself at a distance. The set was Wayne's territory, and I didn't want to get in his way. He didn't sit in my room with me while I wrote the script, so it seemed only right to do the same for him. . . . What I did do, however, was attend the dailies every evening at the DuArt Building on West 55th Street. That proved to be indispensable. I saw every inch of footage, and when we went into the cutting room in mid-July, I had a pretty good understanding of what the options were. . . . The dailies were also instructive in teaching me how to cope with disappointment. Every time an actor blew a line or strayed from the script, it was like a knife going through my heart. But that's what happens when you collaborate with other people, it's something you have to learn to live with. I'm talking about the smallest deviations from what I wrote, things that only I would notice, probably. But still, you work hard to get the words to scan in a certain way, and it's painful to see them come out in another way. . . . And yet, there's another side to it, too. Sometimes the actors improvised or threw in extra lines, and a number of these additions definitely improved the film. For example, Harvey yelling at the irate customer in the cigar store: "Take it on the arches, you fat fuck!" I'd never heard that expression before, and I found it hilarious. Just the kind of thing Auggie would say. . . .

AI: So, even if you didn't go to the set every day, you were prepared to contribute after the shooting was finished.

PA: I hadn't really planned to get so involved in the editing, but like so many other things connected with *Smoke*, it just seemed to happen on its own. Maysie Hoy had worked with Wayne on his last movie, Wayne and I already knew each other well, and it turned out that Maysie and I hit it off—as if we'd been friends in some previous incarnation. It was an excellent three-way relationship. We all felt free to express our opinions, to talk through every little problem that arose, and each one of us listened carefully to what the other two had to say. The atmosphere was one of respect and equality. No hierarchies, no intellectual terrorism. We worked together for weeks and months, and there was rarely any tension. Hard work, yes, but also a lot of jokes and laughter.

AI: When it comes down to it, that's where every movie is really made. In the cutting room.

PA: It's like starting all over again. You begin with the script, which establishes a certain idea of what the film should be, and then you shoot the script, and things begin to change. The actors' performances bring out different meanings, different shadings, things are lost, other things are found. Then you go into the cutting room and try to marry the script to the performances. At times, the two mesh very harmoniously. At other times, they don't, and that can be maddening. You're stuck with the footage you have, and that limits the possibilities. You're like a novelist trying to revise his book, but fifty percent of the words in the dictionary are not available to you. You're not allowed to use them. . . . So you fiddle and shape and juggle, you search for a rhythm, a musical flow to carry you from one scene to the next, and you have to be willing to discard material, to think in terms of the whole, of what is essential to the overall good of the film. . . . Then, on top of these considerations, there's the question of time. A novel can be ninety pages or nine hundred pages, and no one thinks twice about it. But a movie has to be a certain length, two hours or less. It's a fixed form, like a sonnet, and you have to get everything into that limited space. As it happened, the script I wrote was too long. I cut things from it before we started shooting, but even so, it was still too long. The first assemblage that Maysie put together was two hours and fifty minutes, which meant that we had to cut out almost a third of the story. To tell the truth, I didn't see how it could be done. From what I understand, nearly everyone who makes a movie has to face this problem. That's why it always takes longer to cut a film than to shoot it.

AI: What was the biggest surprise that turned up in the cutting room?

PA: There were many surprises, but the biggest one would have to be the last scene, when Auggie tells Paul the Christmas story. As originally written, the story was supposed to be intercut with black-and-white footage that would illustrate what Auggie was saying. The idea was to go back and forth between the restaurant and Granny Ethel's apartment, and when we weren't watching Auggie tell the story, we would hear his voice over the black-and-white material. When we put it together that way, however, it didn't work. The words and the images clashed. You'd settle into listening to Auggie, and then, when the black-and-white pictures started to roll, you'd get so caught up in the visual information that you'd stop listening to the words. By the time you went back to Auggie's face, you'd have missed a couple of sentences and lost the thread of the story.

We had to think through the whole business from scratch, and what we finally decided to do was keep the two elements separate. Auggie tells his story in the restaurant, and then, as a kind of coda, we see a close-up of Paul's typewriter typing out the last words of the title page of the story Auggie has given him, which then dissolves into the black-and-white footage with the Tom Waits song playing over it. This was the only plausible solution, and I feel it works well. It's a rare thing in movies to watch someone tell a story for ten minutes. The camera is on Harvey's face for almost the whole time, and because Harvey is such a powerful and believable actor, he manages to pull it off. When all is said and done, it's probably the best scene in the film.

AI: The camera moves in very close in that scene, right up against Harvey's mouth. I wasn't expecting that at all.
PA: Wayne worked out the visual language of the film in a very bold and interesting way. All the early scenes are done in wide shots and masters. Then, very gradually, as the disparate characters become more involved with each other, there are more and more close shots and singles. Ninety-nine percent of the people who see the film probably won't notice this. It works in a highly subliminal way, but in relation to the material in the film, to the kind of story we were trying to tell, it was the right approach. By the time we get to the last scene in the restaurant, the camera has apparently moved in on the actors as close as it ever will. A limit has been established, the rules have been defined—and then, suddenly, the camera pushes in even closer, as close as it can get. The viewer is not at all prepared for it. It's as if the camera is bulldozing through a brick wall, breaking down the last barrier against genuine human intimacy. In some way, the emotional resolution of the entire film is contained in that shot.

AI: I like the title of the film, *Smoke*. It's catchy and evocative. Would you care to elaborate?
PA: On the word "smoke"? I'd say it's many things all at once. It refers to the cigar store, of course, but also to the way smoke can obscure things and make them illegible. Smoke is something that is never fixed, that is constantly changing shape. In the same way that the characters in the film keep changing as their lives intersect. Smoke signals . . . smoke screens . . . smoke drifting through the air. In small ways and large ways, each character is continually changed by the other characters around him.

AI: It's hard to pin down the tone of the film. Would you call it a comedy? A drama? Perhaps the French category "dramatic comedy" is more appropriate?
PA: You're probably onto something there. I've always thought of it as a comedy—but in the classical sense of the term, meaning that all the characters in the story are a little better off at the end than they were in the beginning. Not to get too high-flown about it, but when you think about the

difference between Shakespeare's comedies and tragedies, it's not so much in the material of the plays as in how the conflicts are resolved. The same kinds of human problems exist in both. With the tragedies, everyone winds up dead on the stage. With the comedies, everyone is still standing and life goes on. That's how I think of *Smoke*. Good things happen, bad things happen, but life goes on. Therefore, it's a comedy. Or, if you prefer, a dramatic comedy.

AI: With some dark spots.

PA: Definitely. That goes without saying. It's not farce or slapstick, but at bottom it takes a fairly optimistic view of the human condition. In many ways, I think the screenplay is the most optimistic thing I've ever written.

AI: It's also one of the very few American films of recent years in which the characters take pleasure in smoking. And there's no one walking into the frame telling them not to do it.

PA: Well, the fact is that people smoke. If I'm not mistaken, more than a billion people light up around the world every day. I know the antismoking lobby in this country has grown very strong in the last few years, but Puritanism has always been with us. In one way or another, the teetotalers and zealots have always been a force in American life. I'm not saying that smoking is good for you, but compared to the political and social and ecological outrages committed every day, tobacco is a minor issue. People smoke. That's a fact. People smoke, and they enjoy it, even if it isn't good for them.

AI: You won't get an argument from me.

PA: I'm just guessing now, but maybe all this is connected to the way the characters act in the film . . . to what you might call an undogmatic view of human behavior. Does this sound too farfetched? I mean, no one is simply one thing or the other. They're all filled with contradictions, and they don't live in a world that breaks down neatly into good guys and bad guys. Each person in the story has his strengths and weaknesses. At his best, for example, Auggie is close to being a Zen master. But he's also an operator, a wise guy, and a downright grumpy son-of-a-bitch. Rashid is essentially a good and very bright kid, but he's also a liar, a thief, and an impudent little prick. Do you see what I'm driving at?

AI: Absolutely. As I said before, you won't get an argument from me.

PA: That's the spirit.

AI: Another question—about Brooklyn. I'd like you to tell me why the film is set there. I know you live in Brooklyn, but was there any special reason—other than familiarity?

PA: I've been living there for fifteen years now, and I must say I'm fond of my neighborhood, Park Slope. It has to be one of the most democratic and tolerant places on the planet. Everyone lives there, every race and religion and economic class, and everyone pretty much gets along. Given the climate in the country today, I would say that qualifies as a miracle. I also know that terrible things go on in Brooklyn, not to speak of New York as a whole. Wrenching things, unbearable things—but by and large the city works. In spite of everything, in spite of all the potential for hatred and violence, most people make an effort to get along with each other most of the time. The rest of the country perceives New York as a hellhole, but that's only one part of the story. I wanted to explore the other side of things in *Smoke*, to work against some of the stereotypes that people carry around about this place.

AI: I'm curious why the novelist in *Smoke* is named Paul. Is there an auto-biographical element in the film?

PA: No, not really. The name Paul is a holdover from the Christmas story published in the *Times*. Because the story was going to appear in a newspaper, I wanted to bring reality and fiction as close together as possible, to leave some doubt in the reader's mind as to whether the story was true or not. So I put in my own name to add to the confusion—but only my first name. The writer that Bill Hurt plays in *Smoke* has nothing to do with me. He's an invented character.

AI: Tell me a little about *Blue in the Face*. Not only did you and Wayne make this other film after *Smoke*, but you wound up as co-director.

PA: Weird but true. It's a crazy project that was filmed in a total of six days. We're still in the process of putting it together, so I don't want to say too much about it, but I can give you the rough outline.

AI: Please.

PA: It all started during the rehearsals for *Smoke*. Harvey came in to work on some of the cigar store scenes with the OTB Men—Giancarlo Esposito, José Zuniga, and Steve Gevedon. As a way of warming up and getting to know each other, they launched into a few short improvisations. It turned out to be very funny. Wayne and I just about fell on the floor, and in a burst of enthusiasm he announced: "I think we should make another film with you guys after *Smoke* is finished. Let's go back into the cigar store for a few days and see what happens."

AI: It might have started out with those four, but the cast certainly grew. You had some of the other actors from *Smoke*—Jared Harris, Mel Gorham, Victor Argo, and Malik Yoba—but also Lily Tomlin, Michael J. Fox, Roseanne, Lou Reed, Jim Jarmusch, Mira Sorvino, Keith David, and Madonna. Not too shabby.

PA: No, not too shabby. Everyone worked for scale—with the best spirit in the world. They were all troupers, every last one of them.

AI: And you did it with no script?

PA: No script—and no rehearsals. I wrote out notes for all the scenes and situations, so each actor more or less knew what had to be done, but there was no script per se, no written dialogue. . . . It was shot in two stages: three days in mid-July and three days in late October. It was wild, let me tell you, pure chaos from start to finish.

AI: And fun.

PA: Oh yes, lots of fun. I enjoyed myself immensely. The finished film is sure to be one of the oddest films ever made: wall-to-wall wackiness, a lighter-than-air creampuff, an hour and a half of singing, dancing, and loopy shenanigans. It's a hymn to the great People's Republic of Brooklyn, and a cruder, more vulgar piece of work would be hard to imagine. Strangely enough, it appears to work well with *Smoke.* They're opposite sides of the same coin, I guess, and the two films seem to complement each other in mysterious ways.

AI: Now that you've caught the bug, do you have any desire to direct again?

PA: No, I can't say that I do. Working on these films has been a terrific experience, and I'm glad it happened, I'm glad I got caught up in it as fully as I did. But enough is enough. It's time for me to crawl back into my hole and begin writing again. There's a new novel calling out to be written, and I can't wait to lock myself in my room and get started.

The Manuscript in the Book: A Conversation

Michel Contat/1994

Originally appearing in *Yale French Studies*, this is reprinted from *Portraits and Recontres* (2005) by permission of Michel Contat.

Michel Contat: Have you ever looked at or even studied the manuscripts of a work you were particularly fond of?

Paul Auster: I don't think I ever have. I've looked at manuscripts in books, facsimiles, and they have always attracted me. I've always been fascinated to see how any particular writer, especially a writer I admire, went about composing his work. But I have never studied a manuscript, no.

MC: So if you have a very strong relationship to one particular work, you wouldn't like to know how it was composed?

PA: Well, I suppose this shows a certain mental laziness on my part [laughter]. But I somehow always treated the finished text as the choice of the author. This is what he wanted me to see. And I've been satisfied with that, I suppose. I haven't had much of a scholarly approach to reading. There was a poet I was very interested in when I was a student, Christopher Smart, a minor eighteenth-century poet who was locked up in Bedlam for a long time, and he wrote some extraordinary, very wild poems. I remember writing an essay about him for the student newspaper at Columbia, years and years ago. There was another student I was friendly with, and he got very interested in this poet because of me. He had never heard of him before, but he, like a true scholar, went to England the next year and started examining all of Christopher Smart's manuscripts and eventually wrote a big study of them. I remember when he came back and told me about them, how amazed I was that you could actually do this. But at the same time I realized that I had no desire to do it myself and that I was satisfied with the printed book.

MC: But you don't think that it is wrong for you or anybody to go and scrutinize the manuscripts?

PA: No, I think if I were a literary critic or scholar, I would be doing that all the time.

MC: Can you think of one work that you would be very curious about the making of?

PA: I suppose I would love to see the manuscript of *Ulysses*, such a large, complex book. I'm sure there was lots of material that was discarded, so it would be interesting to see what didn't get into the book and see how certain passages evolved. Something like *The Trial* by Kafka, on the other hand, was written in about six weeks. I think the manuscript was sold recently . . .

MC: And it was supposed to be burned by Kafka's literary executor, Max Brod . . .

PA: Yes, that's right. But I think that it is probably a rather clean manuscript. He probably just sat down and wrote it, without much revision, which is extraordinary. And that would be interesting to see, for a completely different reason. I have a friend, a poet, William Bronk (I wrote about him in my book of essays). He's not young anymore, well into his seventies. A few years ago, another writer and I went to his house in upstate New York, and we interviewed him for a magazine. He showed us his manuscripts, and it turned out that he never revised anything. It was absolutely appalling—because it was so impressive. He never revised anything! Every poem he had ever published just came out straight. He showed us the notebooks he wrote in, and there were the poems—perfect, first try.

MC: Do you think he composed them in his head before writing them down?

PA: Absolutely. He would walk around with the poems in his head. He works in a very erratic way. He writes when he's ready to write and doesn't feel compelled to sit down every day and do it. So that's extraordinary.

MC: Are they short pieces?

PA: Mostly short, yes. The late George Oppen, another poet—I never actually saw his manuscripts—was a very good friend and, I think, a great American poet. He told me that the way he wrote was to type out a draft of the poem, and then, as he revised and changed it, he would take lines and paste them on top of the old lines, so that each manuscript was a palimpsest, and he could peel back the layers—four, five, six drafts—down to an earlier version and rearrange the lines and sometimes combine bits of the different drafts before he had the finished poem.

MC: Was that the state in which he wanted them to be read? Like Queneau's *Cent mille milliards de poèmes*?
PA: No, that was his working method. To have all the drafts in layers, so he could come up with his final version.

MC: A kind of kinetic manuscript?
PA: Yes. It's strange, isn't it? I've never heard of anyone working like that before.

MC: What is, for you, the status of the manuscript, generally speaking? You said you were interested in the final, published version. Do you think that an author can be mistaken, and that the version he chooses to publish might not be the most interesting one?
PA: I think that's possible. One often has the sense, with certain writers, that they revise too much, that they work too hard, and that, if a story or a book has gone through eight drafts, maybe the fifth one is the one they should have published, and not the eighth. But, I don't know, sometimes it's hard for a writer to let go of what he's doing. I think of a manuscript as very private material. It's still attached to you, it belongs to you. The book, on the other hand, is a public object. This is what you are willing to show the world. And so, even though I'm involved in my manuscripts as I work on them, they are always just a stage toward making the book. I have never kept a diary, for example, I have never been able to. I have always felt a very strange sense of self-consciousness about trying to write a diary. I tried it when I was younger.

MC: You mean a diary of the work itself, like Gide's *Journal des faux-monnayeurs*?
PA: No, just a journal, a daily journal, as many writers do, as many people do who aren't writers. "Journal intime." And so there must be something in me that feels that sitting down to write my thoughts about something is somehow public property. A letter is something else again. That's really just a private communication between two people. But manuscripts for me have always been a stage along the way, a step toward a published work. It's a bit like a butterfly, from the caterpillar to the butterfly, going through different stages of metamorphosis. You shed one skin and become who you are going

to be. At that point the manuscripts lose all interest for me. I never look at them, I don't think about them, they just vanish into unimportance.

MC: Why don't you just destroy them?

PA: Well, I don't know why. That's a very good question, isn't it? What I've done in almost every case—there are things that are lost and that I wish I had, in fact—was just put them away. I didn't really want to throw them away. They represented too much effort, too much time.

MC: As if they were the testimony of the work done?

PA: Something like that. Each notebook that I have written in might represent months of my life, and it just doesn't seem right to throw it in the garbage. They represented something. So I would just put them in boxes and shut them away in my closet. And never look at them.

MC: Didn't you try, before closing them in the boxes, to organize them? That is a question I was led to, looking at those boxes in the Berg Collection. It seems that sometimes the drafts are arranged in some order, and sometimes the order seems arbitrary.

PA: Yes. When I was writing poetry only, nothing was very organized. I would just slip drafts in folders and put them away. But when I started publishing prose books, what I tended to do was this: all the material that went into writing a book would be put in a big folder or a box, everything together, in no particular order. The way these manuscripts got sold to the Library was by chance. Again, I wasn't thinking about it at all. If I ever did think about it, I would say to myself: "Well, I have all these things, I haven't thrown them away, they represent all the work I've done, someday my children will have them, and maybe they'll be valuable, maybe they'll produce some money for my children or grandchildren." And I never thought much about it beyond that. Several years ago, though, somebody called me up, a dealer in manuscripts, and he said to me: "Are you interested in selling your manuscripts and letters?" And I thought about it a moment and said: "Why not? They're taking up space here, I never look at these things." And in fact my little studio was just inundated with paper. I thought it would be a good idea to get rid of them, and a good way to raise some money too. I'm still relatively young, it's not as though I'm giving away my entire life. And I knew about the interest in manuscripts from friends of mine. There is a very good collection, for example, at the University in La Jolla, mostly of contemporary poets. It just so happened that a poet friend of mine was the head of that archive for a number of years and he would tell me about it, and once when I was out there to give a reading, he gave me a tour of the archive. And in fact I had the odd experience of coming upon letters I had written to other people in that archive. It was a shocking thing, and after the shock wore off I was actually pleased that these letters were there. For example, letters to George Oppen. All his papers were sold to San Diego, and there he was for anybody who wanted to study his work in a serious way, all there neatly arranged in files, alphabetical, chronological. It seemed good.

MC: Good that there had been work done by professionals?

PA: Yes. And a number of other people I know had sold manuscripts. So it wasn't as though it was an idea that had come from Mars. I knew about these things, it's just that I had never thought about selling my own papers. So the dealer came, and every week he would come, for about two months, to my studio, and he organized everything. He wanted to make an inventory, because this is what he had to do. So we put everything in different bundles. Eventually he made the inventory, and then he put a price on it. He had to know what was there before he could approach anyone. He didn't know how long it would take. But the first place he approached was the Berg Collection, and they wanted the papers. So it wound up happening very quickly.

MC: Did you take this as a kind of consecration?

PA: Not really, no. I was very flattered. I thought that it showed real interest in this work, and that touched me, it made me feel good, but not as a consecration. I think of it rather as a bet that they were making, a gamble. They thought: "Well, maybe this writer will last, and maybe he won't. But if he does last, then it will be good to have this material."

MC: Has it something to do with the City of New York? I mean, the fact that you are working in New York and writing about New York?

PA: I really have no idea. The Berg Collection is subsidized entirely by private money. It's in the New York Public Library and they use space there, but they don't have money from the city, which, as you know, is just about bankrupt. They have contributions from different sources, donors. The collection has all kinds of amazing material. They had a manuscript exhibition last summer and some of my manuscripts were on display, as well as work by Nabokov, Dickens, Melville, Twain, Jack Kerouac. It's an extraordinarily rich collection.

MC: Any writer of your generation?

PA: There are some living writers who are there—the names escape me. It is an extraordinary collection and an extraordinary place too: a strange twilight world.

MC: At this moment the manuscript itself has an undecided status: in between fetishism and aesthetic object. Of course, manuscripts are also used for publishing purposes, for "scientific" or scholarly editions of great writers. This has come out of the very old philological tradition from Germany. The Germans started these national editions of Goethe, Schiller, etc. So, to come back to your own work, maybe it is too early for this question, but would you consider having an annotated edition of your work done at this stage, or do you think it would be premature?

PA: Oh, it's premature in the extreme. I wouldn't even begin to think about it. There were two reasons why I think I was happy to have those papers go to the Library. One: they would be taken care of. Because they were very sloppily kept, and they could have burned up, they could have been stolen, and that would have been sad somehow, for all the reasons I expressed before. Two: I know that there are people writing about my work, all over the world. I get letters from them, and it was beginning to become a burden. "Where can I find this critical study? Where can I find your manuscripts? Can I come and see you?" Now all I have to do is write back and say: "Go to the New York Public Library." [Laughter] So it was relieving me of a burden, something that was becoming difficult to deal with.

MC: Did you actually work with this dealer who organized your manuscripts?

PA: Yes.

MC: So there is an order that has been thought of?

PA: I don't know exactly. What I sold to the Library was, on the one hand, manuscripts and, on the other hands, letters, literary letters. I went through the letters very carefully to make sure that there was nothing personal in there, nothing that would compromise anyone. Just literary talk and literary business. And then we put them all in different folders by name. With the manuscripts it wasn't very difficult. It's not as though I've written so many books.

MC: But for each one there is a lot of material. And the question of course for scholars is to know the exact genetic progression.

PA: Yes. And it's not clear, I'm sure.

MC: Not always. I'll tell you more about *The Invention of Solitude.* There are problems. But to come back to a previous question, you said something interesting about not writing a diary. Did I understand you correctly, that maybe you have the feeling that some parts of very private thoughts and feelings go into the bulk of the unpublished work and are there to be pried out or just known?

PA: I don't think there is anything too private in that collection, except the work that I was trying to do with the idea of eventually publishing it.

MC: That is exactly the meaning of my question: when you write you have the public in mind, you don't write out of some personal compulsion—especially speaking of the "Portrait of an Invisible Man," which is in between autobiography and let's not say fiction . . .

PA: No, meditation . . .

MC: It has nothing to do with confession. In a way it involves people, and I was wondering if you started writing it without knowing exactly what you would keep at the end but that there were some things that you wanted to get on paper for your own sake . . .

PA: That book is different from the novels I have written since. I think when you start to write a novel, you know automatically that you want other people to see it. I didn't know, when I started writing *The Invention of Solitude,* especially the first part, the one you're talking about, what would happen. I didn't know whether it was a book. If I was able to give it up later, it was because it did become a book. If it hadn't, I think I would have just held on to the manuscript.

MC: So, I seem to be the first one to have gone to see the manuscript, and I'm not a specialist of your work.

PA: Well, there's at least one person who's spent some time at the Library. Bill Drentell has done a bibliography of my work, which is about to be published. He went every week for about a year to the Berg Collection. He told me that they haven't even begun to organize the material yet.

MC: They know it's going to be difficult, and they asked me for some advice or help. I said: "I can give you my hypotheses about the order of composi-

tion, but they are to be confirmed by closer examination." And they asked me: "Do you think that the author would be helpful?" I said: "Helpful certainly. But would he want to help, to take time, I don't know."
PA: I don't know, that's a good question. Maybe one day I could go in and sift through the material a little bit . . .

MC: I told them that for the author to be useful in that kind of work, the librarians have to have their own hypotheses first, their own ideas about the order, so you can contradict them or confirm them. Because if they just ask you what came first, you might not remember accurately.
PA: No, I could probably put it together by seeing the papers. At least I think so.

MC: As a student were you ever "exposed" to literary manuscripts? [Laughter.]
PA: It would probably have been possible if I had been interested. There were no courses. I could be wrong, but I think that in graduate schools, in PhD programs, there might be courses now about how to study manuscripts.

MC: I ask the question because sometimes you have the feeling, when you examine the different stages Flaubert goes through, that these stages offer a guide to someone who wants to write. For instance, Flaubert starts with a synopsis, an outline. Then he takes notes in his notebooks, writes a first draft, it sometimes goes up to thirteen drafts, he has a copy made, makes revisions, etc. And just seeing what he does is a kind of lesson in writing.
PA: But, you see, everyone has to find his own method. That's the problem. There are no rules to any of this. That's why I don't think you can teach anyone how to write. You just have to find what works for you.

MC: What we actually are doing in the study of manuscripts is first setting up a typology of the procedures and then seeing if any generalizations can be drawn. As far as general ideas are concerned, our findings remain rather poor, if we have to expose them to the layman. For instance, we come up with something that is quite obvious: that there are two different tendencies in writing, one that we call "écriture à programme," and Zola would be the best example of this (he has a complete knowledge of the scenario, and complete documentation, and when he has this, he starts writing, it is a textualization of something that is already worked out), and the other we call "écriture à processus," and maybe the best example would be Aragon (he starts with the first line and doesn't really know where he's going, and the first line calls for the second line and it goes on and on that way).

PA: And most people fall in between. I, for one, am in between. I mean, I have an idea of what I want to do, but it's constantly changing the whole time I'm doing it.

MC: So that's what I would like to ask you about now. Your writing method. Has it changed through the years? Can you first describe it and tell what changes it has undergone?

PA: Actually, it's an interesting history. Because I think that the reason I was unable to write fiction as a younger person, even though I tried—and I know in the Library there are a lot of manuscripts of things that weren't published—was the result of being a student and taking literature seriously, of being intoxicated by a certain kind of modernism, which made me feel that in order to write a novel you had to know everything in advance about what you were going to do. I thought that you had to analyze everything and see all the consequences of every idea and every turn of phrase, not only aesthetic, but moral, philosophical, religious, political, everything to do with the text you were writing. So by the time I sat down to write, I was so freighted, so loaded down with so much baggage that I couldn't breathe. I worked with a degree of self-consciousness that made it impossible to produce anything. Later on, after many chapters in the story that I'll skip over, I simply didn't care anymore, and the idea that a book is written in order to be studied no longer interested me. You just do what you have to do and let the results fall where they may. Knowing too much in advance is a hindrance, not a help. Every book I've written, every novel in any case, is something I've lived with for a long time. I've often spent years thinking about the story and the characters, and I don't start to write it until I feel absolutely compelled to write it. I have a pretty good idea of what I would call the shape of the story and who the characters are, but not everything is worked out. Every day is an adventure. Every day, you discover something about yourself and about the work you are trying to do. If you had it all worked out, if you knew the answers already, why would you bother to do it? This is what I've learned over the years. It's a very stupid way to live your life, you know, stuck in a little room writing. If it's not going to be an adventure, I don't see how you can do it. Just transcribing earlier conclusions and fleshing them out would be very stultifying, a very unhappy way to live your life.

MC: And this sense of an adventure is an art of improvising on a prepared scheme?

PA: I suppose "scheme" would be even too big a word for it. I never take notes for a book. At most, I jot down little things, mostly to do with shape. I don't know if you looked at these manuscripts, but I often do a very rough outline of the book I'm writing in the vaguest terms imaginable. Like: 1. New York. So and so goes home. 2. Pittsburgh, Something about . . . Just little signposts that will remind me of all the thoughts I've had about a particular subject. But I rarely write them out in advance.

MC: So maybe the few plans we find in those papers come at a later stage, as a reminder?

PA: Yes.

MC: One thing that struck me is the presence of titles for future works. And I was wondering when the title comes in and what importance the title has.

PA: This is an interesting little sideline about work methods. For some reason, I have a fascination for titles. Titles as an art form in themselves. But I have discovered over the years that in order to write a novel, I need relief from the work. If I think about it all the time, I get mentally exhausted, and the work doesn't go well. So, as much as possible—because one becomes obsessed with this, you dream about the book you're working on—as much as possible I try to keep a pact with myself, which is that when I leave my room, my studio around the corner, I won't think about the book I'm working on. But I will allow myself to think about the next book. So I wind up dreaming about the next book in a very idle, formless kind of way, letting ideas come to me. This means that I'm always working on two, or even three, books at the same time. As for the book I am actually writing, I think it's healthier to let your unconscious do the work when you're not sitting at your desk.

MC: And the title helps to coagulate the idea?

PA: Yes. But, you see, those titles are just little signposts for me. I know what they mean, but they wouldn't make sense to anyone else. A whole world is embedded in that title, a universe of ideas and thoughts and plans.

MC: Do you use the Hemingway method, which is to stop only when you know how to continue?

PA: Often that is helpful. I remember reading about that when I was very young, and I thought that was one of the best ideas I ever heard about how to write. So I try to do that, because it really helps you the next day, if you know the first sentence or two. It gets you off to a better start. Usually when I'm working on a novel, two paragraphs is about all I can do during a day. One or two. A page. It takes me about six hours.

MC: Which means you can write ten or more drafts of the same paragraph.
PA: Yes. Over and over and over again.

MC: So at the end of the day you want to have the paragraph as it should finally be? Or do you think you could go back and rewrite it?
PA: It happens like this: I build up the manuscript, I write in the notebook, and I go over and over the paragraph. I really move by paragraphs, that's how I write a book, and I don't go on to the next paragraph until I'm satisfied with the paragraph I'm writing, and I go over and over it by hand. And even when I'm making changes I keep writing it over again from the start, from scratch, to make it so familiar and so organic that it begins to feel indestructible. Again, I don't know how to put it. I write out the paragraph, and then I look it over and start crossing out words and making changes. Then it becomes hard to read. So I copy it out again, and then I go through the same thing all over again.

MC: The paragraph itself, of course you know how it is going to take its place in a whole?
PA: Yes. I always have the whole in mind. And this is the mysterious thing about writing a novel—and why it is so hard. Because you spend anywhere from one to five years working on a book, and it's often easy to lose sight of the whole project. And that mysterious balance of how you know whether something is right or wrong in relation to the whole is something I can't even begin to articulate. But I know that I'm always thinking about the overall book. Sometimes you get off track, you say too much about a particular thing, you lose your way a little bit. But then of course you take it out, you go back to where you should be. So everyday I write and rewrite that paragraph, and then I type it up. If there is still time left in the day, I do a second paragraph, perhaps even a third. From the notebook to the typewriter and then back to the notebook. Strange.

MC: Which means that you will have something like ten or more type-scripts?

PA: No. Because I've already written it ten times in the notebook. It's only when I think it's done that I type it up. But of course it rarely is. And so I begin revising on the typescript.

MC: This is exactly what we see in your files. I just wondered how it is that you decide the book is done, and do you get it typed?

PA: I type it myself.

MC: So you have the whole book and you can reread and see it from a distance and see what doesn't work?

PA: Right. But I have been revising all along. Every time I have another page, I look through it again and start making changes on the page. So by the time the first draft is finished in typescript, it's already marked up. Then I go back and fiddle with the manuscript again, typing up each page as I complete it. So I guess each book is typed three times. There is that first time, then there is a second time with a cleaner draft that embodies all the changes that I've been making, and then I go through it again. And this was the discovery I made with my last book, *Mr. Vertigo.* I remember this very well. I finished the second typescript and I said to myself: "This book is done. I can't do anything more with it." And there were three hundred and something pages that I had to type on my little manual typewriter. All that typing gives me a sore neck, and I find it very unpleasant. I said: "Why don't I have a computer? Now I could just push a button and everything could come out and I wouldn't have to spend three weeks doing this." So I said to myself: "This is the last time I'm ever going to type up a final draft of a book. I'm going to buy a computer." So I sat down to start doing the clean copy. And on almost every page I made changes, and I understood that living with a book had a different rhythm now: there is a certain speed that comes from typing this final draft and you feel the music of the book in your fingers, it's almost like playing the piano. And each sentence, each paragraph, each section of the book has its own rhythm and shape, and I can feel it in my fingers. I understood that the changes came out of this new relationship with the text, and that this last typing was essential to finishing the book and that if I had a button to push I would have missed everything. You have to live with the book once more, in order to see how to finish it.

MC: Now, what about what we call "les incipit," the first sentences of a book, the starting sentences? When do you know that you have found the right beginning?

PA: It's impossible to write a novel until you have the first sentence. You can live with an idea for years. Then, once you have the first sentence, you have a way to propel yourself into the work. The first sentence defines the entire novel you're proposing to write. I've always needed a title, and I've always needed a first sentence, before this formless idea could take shape. *Moon Palace* was a book I started when I was very young and it had many different titles. But it wasn't until I had the definitive title that I actually began writing the book as it exists now. The same thing with *In the Country of Last Things*. In both cases the title made it possible for me to write the book. The story with *The Music of Chance* was a little different. I had a working title, and it wasn't until I was halfway into the book that the real title came to me. I was standing in line in a supermarket one Saturday here in Brooklyn, and some silly musak was playing, and all of a sudden I thought: *The Music of Chance*. The words just jumped into my head, standing there waiting to pay for my groceries. [Laughs.]

MC: Let's come to the first sentence, or maybe the first paragraph. Is it a question of rhythm or of meaning?

PA: Of everything. And also, more subtly, and maybe even more importantly: tone. Everything should be in that first paragraph. After all, you are asking someone to enter an imaginary world, and I think you want to establish everything right from the start, so there is no turning back.

MC: And when, in the process, comes the idea of the ending? At an early stage?

PA: The ending is always linked to the beginning, as far as I'm concerned. I've changed my ideas about what the ending should be as I've progressed with the book, but I can't begin until I have the sense of what you might call the trajectory of the book, the arc of it. It might be a preliminary plan, but you need some plan or idea in order to start, because everything you say in the beginning of the book is somehow reflected in the end. So if you don't have a sense of the whole shape of it, it makes the beginning lose its meaning also.

MC: Does this mean that you have the last sentence in mind at an early stage?

PA: Sometimes the last sentence, but not always.

MC: But you have the tone.
PA: The tone, yes. And roughly where the story is going to stop.

MC: Which means that you have an early idea of the scope, of the length of the book?
PA: Yes. Or rather no. This is another problem. I've always tended to underestimate how long a book is going to be. With certain books I've written, I originally thought they would be short stories. *The Music of Chance* is a good example. I thought it would be thirty or forty pages. The same with *Mr. Vertigo*. I thought it would be forty pages.

MC: But did you have the idea of the boy getting old and writing the story?
PA: Yes, but I just thought it would be simpler. The ideas turn out to be more complex and richer than you think. That's what I mean when I talk about the adventure of writing a book.

MC: Yes, that's your Scheherazade side.
PA: [Laughs.] Yes, you don't know what's going to happen. When I first started writing *Mr. Vertigo*, for example, Mrs. Witherspoon did not exist, she was not a character. She just came in, she just . . . appeared, and there she was.

MC: She's the counterpart of Slim, the very bad guy.
PA: That's right. [Laughs.] I had no plan for her at all. So, unexpected things are happening all the time.

MC: And is there a central point, too, or do you see the book as an arc, and the acme of it is undecided?
PA: Undecided. There are number of key incidents you have in mind, and the center is there, but not always elaborated as fully as you would like. But once you get your story going, the middle parts begin to take care of themselves. It wouldn't be right to say that you're working with a system, but there is a kind of inner logic to any work of art, and I think that you as the artist are always looking for that inner logic, and if you find it, then you can't really make a big mistake. Every imaginary world, every artificial world—however you want to define what a book is—has its own natural boundaries. And you have to have good instincts to know when you've gone over the

boundary. [He claps his hands.] Sometimes it's very interesting to go right up against them [claps his hands again], sparks can fly. But if you get over them, then you ruin the book.

MC: It's interesting, the gesture you made. Boundaries are like a frame.
PA: It's a page, or a canvas. That's right. That painting [he points to a painting on the wall] does not extend over here; it's in a limited space. And a book is limited to a particular mental space.

MC: You take the metaphor of painting rather than that of melody?
PA: I think in terms of music much more than in terms of painting. But I do sometimes think in terms of maps.

MC: Yes, there is a very interesting sheet of paper for "The Book of Memory." It's like a map, there is an area, a center . . .
PA: I did that at a moment when I was struggling to find the structure of the book. "The Book of Memory" was very complicated. Every event in the book is simultaneous with every other event. But of course a book is a linear work, it unfolds over a time, you can only have one sentence at a time, so the crucial problem with that book was the order of the events, the order of the sections and the paragraphs, and I was very confused, and I just had to make this map, to see how everything fit with everything else. I have never done that since, and I had never done it before.

MC: It was not a narrative, so you had to have this topographical view of the book.
PA: That's right. In the second film that I've been working on, *Blue in the Face*, there's no real narrative—again!—and we've been editing and editing, trying to put all these pieces together in the correct order, and it can drive you crazy. On Thanksgiving last week, last Thursday, we had people over for dinner. This record cabinet had just come, and suddenly Siri and I started rearranging the furniture in the living room, and you move one piece, and then everything else is affected by where you put it, and I was moving everything around and I thought: "This feels very familiar to me. Why am I experiencing the same shudder of doubt and confusion?" Then it occurred to me: "It's like editing the film. This is it. I'm doing this every day with the movie. It's like moving furniture."

MC: The book is made of sequences that get organized in a functional way.
PA: That's right. So you are not banging into a chair if you want to get to the lamp. [Laughs.]

MC: Who is your first reader?
PA: The woman upstairs. [Laughter.]

MC: And before the woman upstairs?
PA: I didn't really have a first reader. Maybe that was my problem.

MC: That is interesting. Because I do think that the first reader is most important.
PA: I trust her completely, her judgment, her sense of things. She understands what I'm trying to do. You can't talk to someone who doesn't share your ideas about the world, or who doesn't at least try to understand what you are trying to do.

MC: What about your editor?
PA: She always has comments. Some of them are minuscule prose questions, and once in a while she asks a bigger question. But I don't think I've ever taken her advice on a big question. Certain bits of prose, mostly, three or four spots in a book, a few words here and there. One thing she did help me with, on *Mr. Vertigo*, was the organization. When I handed her the book, it was in three sections. And she had the feeling that after the Dizzy Dean chapter, something didn't work. It felt strange to her. After our conversation, I realized that there was a problem, and that the solution was to divide the book differently—to add a fourth section that would serve as a kind of epilogue: fifty years in ten pages! And she agreed. And that's how it was done. Her response was a great help to me.

MC: So you never really work on a book with an editor. When you give it, it's final.
PA: It's final except for very small refinements.

MC: Was your first wife a reader too?
PA: She was my reader, but not to the degree that Siri is. She's a writer, too. When I was living with her, I was only writing poems, and she's not a poet, and she doesn't really have much to say about poetry. So I gave her my essays to read.

MC: When the book is published, do you have afterthoughts, maybe alterations you would like to make? Do you consider the possibility of a second edition to amend the first?

PA: There is the stage of the proofs, in between, and I often make changes on proofs.

MC: Like cutting out?

PA: Cutting out a paragraph or part of a paragraph, changing a word, that kind of thing. Again, nothing major. But, to tell you the truth, once the book gets published, I never look at it, I just put it away.

MC: You don't try to read it with the eye of the reader, this kind of hysterical self-reading?

PA: No, I can't. You know the book by heart. And this is a big problem, I've found. You know it too well, and in order to sit back and read it, like a person coming to it for the first time—, well you can't. You can anticipate the next sentence, and therefore you read it too fast, you speed up, there's no sense of discovery, it's just dead. Usually I become very depressed at the proof stage, thinking what a miserable, stupid, unsuccessful work I've written. So I try just to take care of the technical things and forget about the rest.

MC: Do you amend something in the translation?

PA: I have nothing to do with that. For the French editions, for example, Christine Le Boeuf sends me lists of questions. They usually have to do with references to American life that she is not familiar with, or a word that she doesn't know, and I answer those questions, but it would be pointless for me to review the book in French, because I don't know French well enough to make any suggestions. My French is passive, I can understand very well when I'm reading. But to be confronted with choices in the language, I'm not qualified. It requires a deep and intimate syntactical knowledge of the language, and I don't have that.

MC: The general movement of the writing process, as I see it in your manuscripts—very roughly said—is an expansion and then a reduction. You cut a lot, and it seems that you are so filled with ideas and formulas that you write very abundantly, and then you have to go toward sparseness.

PA: In general, that's true. I very rarely add things. It's usually a question of taking things away. I often discover that I've said the same thing three times—without being aware of it. In the effort to articulate the idea, the thought, the sensation, whatever it is you're trying to say, you wind up doing it in a number of different ways, you keep coming at it from different angles. In the first go through you think it's all necessary, but then you realize that it's not. So there's a great deal of reduction that goes on. The big problem in writing anything, whether fiction or nonfiction, is: "What's the next sentence?" Every thought engenders many thoughts, and you can go off in different directions. I have a tendency to fly off and digress. That's the real difficulty for me. Knowing what line to take. That's where all the struggle comes from. That's why it takes me so long to write a paragraph. I know there are people who sit down at their typewriters and bang out ten pages in a day. They just sit, and the ideas are coming, and it's prose, very readable prose, but I can't do that. I wish I could!

MC: Are you sometimes aware of your own censorship? Are there things that you write out of anguish and that you later cross out because you feel you are trespassing on some of your own interdictions?
PA: That's a good question. I think that every once in a while I put in something that I know should not be there, that will later be taken out. But generally, no. Writing fiction is a very strange experience. Part of it is like being an actor, I've found. Every book I've written so far has had one central protagonist—a first-person narrator or a third-person protagonist. And each one of them is quite different from all the others. In order to write the book, I have to inhabit that person. That person is not me. He sometimes resembles me or shares certain of my attributes, but he is not me. Therefore, it's like being an actor. You take on another personality, another role. So the problem of my own personal feelings doesn't often come up, because I'm living the life of the book through this imaginary being that I've become.

MC: Could we focus now on the "Portrait of an Invisible Man?" First I need to ask you a few questions. When did your father die?
PA: My father died on January 15, 1979. Almost sixteen years ago.

MC: And the decision to write was immediate?
PA: As far as I can remember, it was immediate. Within hours I started thinking about sitting down and trying to write something.

MC: But you knew the secret before.
PA: I knew the secret before, yes.

MC: And I have the feeling that this secret is very, very important. It's not the core of the book—I'll tell you later what I think the core of the book is—but it is most important for the narrative. The narrative is organized, in a way, to disclose the secret, to tell this story, which is an amazing story.
PA: Where is the secret revealed? Is it about halfway through, or a little more than halfway through?

MC: No, it's at one third, I guess. Page 34, if I remember, in the British edition. The American edition has a subtitle: it's called "A Memoir."
PA: They put that on. I didn't.

MC: But the first title was "Memoirs of an Invisible Man."
PA: No. Or was it? Is that what it said? And I crossed it out?

MC: You changed it to "Portrait of an Invisible Man."
PA: Because "Memoir" is supposedly only for the one who is writing it.

MC: So you asked for the documentation on the murder in February 1979?
PA: You mean from my cousin?

MC: Yes, you got it only then?
PA: Yes, that's right.

MC: You knew the story.
PA: I knew the story, I had seen it.

MC: You had *seen* the press clips?
PA: I think I had seen the press clips. You know, this is a very good question. I don't even remember anymore. Maybe I was only told about them.

MC: Because your cousins had those clips for years. And my question is . . .
PA: That's right, I also saw the clips as I was writing the book, I mean in that period. But I had been told the whole story.

MC: How long had you known that eventually you were going to write about this secret story [i.e., of your grandmother having murdered your grandfather]?
PA: I never knew that I would write about it until I started writing about it.

There was never any plan at all. The idea of writing anything about myself never occurred to me. I mean, that had never been something I wanted to do.

MC: I just wondered if there had been any attempt at textualizing this story before your father died.
PA: None whatsoever.

MC: Do you think your father had forgotten what had happened?
PA: No. I think he knew it all the time.

MC: And do you think that he confided in your mother? Because you don't say that explicitly.
PA: He didn't. My mother didn't know. From him. But the oldest brother had told his wife, and she had told my mother. But my mother never told me. Nobody told anybody.

MC: So it was a heavy secret.
PA: Yes. And the younger generation, my first cousins and I, only found out about it through that absolutely insane encounter on the airplane—when my cousin accidentally ran into someone who lived in Kenosha, Wisconsin.

MC: And did your sister know before reading the book?
PA: [Long silence]—Yes.

MC: So there was no dangerous betrayal of the family secret when you published that book?
PA: No.

MC: Maybe we will talk about your sister a little later. Because you have taken out a few things from her portrait in the manuscript, and I think I've understood the reasons. Let me start at the beginning, the "incipit." The first drafts contain description of the Invisible Man: "The Invisible Man is wrought in bandages.
PA: That was later. I wrote that much later.

MC: [Surprised]—Really?
PA: I'll tell you why that happened. I was never happy with this. A friend of mine read the manuscript, a good friend, and he suggested a publisher

for the book. The publisher liked it very much. I hadn't published any prose at that point, and he said: "This is good. But somehow you can't begin a book like that, you have to set it up more. I'll publish the book if you have some kind of introduction." And he gave me some suggestions. I thought that maybe he was right, I just wasn't sure, I didn't know what to make of the book yet. And so I sat down and tried to do something, and it was terrible. It didn't belong to the book. I did it, and then I realized that I shouldn't have done it. It was an afterthought, a mistake, and I took it out.

MC: This is very interesting, because you can't know it when you see the manuscripts, at least at first glance.
PA: You're probably right.

MC: There are at least thirteen different versions of that beginning.
PA: Is that so? Well, it probably took so many times because I didn't think it was a good idea, and I was struggling to do it.

MC: Actually the first sentence was: "One day there is life," wasn't it?
PA: Yes.

MC: And then you changed it to: "My father died three weeks ago." There are two versions with this new beginning. And the feeling is that you had the right one from the start, because you come back to it.
PA: I had the right one from the start. The interesting thing about that book is that the first draft is almost identical to the book as published—the first part, at least. But I did a lot of additional work that I eventually scrapped. In 1979, I was invited to go to Yaddo, an artist's colony in Saratoga Springs: a famous American institution where they put up writers and composers and painters. They feed you and give you a nice place to live for a month or two, and all you have to think about is your work. So I took my manuscript, which I had considered a kind of rough draft, and tried to turn it into a more fluid book. I expanded it. That version must be in the Library somewhere. Maybe you saw it.

MC: Yes. What you are telling me now wholly changes my outlook.
PA: I expanded the book, I worked on it very hard for a couple of months, maybe even more. And then, when I looked at it again, I realized that the original approach was better. So I went back to the raw, very immediate

kind of structure that I had organically come up with as I was writing the first draft.

MC: Did you have any models in mind? Had you read anything about the death of a parent?
PA: No. There were two books, but I had read them earlier. One was the little book by Peter Handke about his mother, I think it's the best thing he ever wrote, *A Sorrow Beyond Dreams.* It's only about fifty pages. A very beautiful book. Then there was an American book called *The Duke of Deception*, by Geoffrey Wolff, an excellent book, very interesting, about Geoffrey Wolff's relationship with his father, who was a con-man.

MC: It's become a kind of "genre," the book about one's deceased parent. There are some very good books I can think of: Richard Ford's *My Mother*, Philip Roth's *Patrimony*, Annie Emaux's *Une femme* and *La place*, Simone de Beauvoir's *Une mort très douce*. But yours is very different, because there is this Invisible Man, you really try to invent him, in a way, because he didn't have any real existence for you . . .
PA: It's different. I never thought of this book as an autobiography—not even as a biography. But I was very conscious of what I was trying to do, which was to write a kind of meditation on how you might write a biography. Or, more importantly, how and if anyone can talk about someone else: what you know about other people. This is really what it's about. It's not just about my father. So I don't think this book fits into that "genre."

MC: The "genre" is not very definite: you're not supposed to tell the story of your parents, you're supposed to tell of your sorrow, your grief, your childhood, your relationship with one or both of your parents. And this relationship with your father was obviously so strong that, in a way, we have the feeling that you write to become visible yourself, to become visible to him; but he is dead, he's not there anymore, so you have to invent him, make a person out of him who would be your witness.
PA: Even now, I keep talking to him all the time. And writing the book didn't change anything.

MC: You mean he still exists now?
PA: Well, I mean I talk to him in my mind, I wish he were here so we could continue or begin to talk.

MC: I was wondering if the book had in a way liberated you.

PA: No, I don't think it did at all. Unfortunately. [Laughs somewhat sadly.]

MC: The other very important theme—and I think this is why the ending was worked on so much—the dedication and the ending—is that of the book's being written for Daniel, your son.

PA: That's right. And you have to see the evolution of *The Invention of Solitude*. "Portrait of an Invisible Man" was for Daniel. But that was never published as a book. It wasn't published until the two books came out together, "Portrait of an Invisible Man" and "The Book of Memory." They actually are two books published between the same covers. It's a practical story more than a theoretical story. A friend of mine, a poet, had a very small publishing house in New York called Sun Press, which published poetry. After the fiasco with that other publisher, I gave the book to him as I wanted it to be, as it is now, the little book, "Portrait of an Invisible Man," and he wanted to publish it. But of course he didn't have much money; it was a struggling little enterprise. In the meantime, I worked on "The Book of Memory." By the time he was ready to publish the first book, I had finished the second. And we got together, and I said: "Well, here is this other one." And he said: "I'll publish that one too." But for purely practical reasons, it made more sense to put them together into one book.

MC: And that's when the title was found?

PA: That's where *The Invention of Solitude* came from, that's the title that I gave to the two together.

MC: Did you have that title before?

PA: No.

MC: It's a marvelous invention!

PA: And I don't even know what it means. I still think about the title and I don't know what it means. [We both laugh.]

MC: Well, it's a title that lingers, like the title of a song.

PA: I know.

MC: When were The New York Trilogy and *In the Country of Last Things* written?

PA: It's complicated. *In the Country of Last Things* was started in 1970, and

I finished it in 1985. So that spans a long period. The New York Trilogy I started writing immediately after "The Book of Memory." That's when I started writing *City of Glass.*

MC: So, actually, the "Portrait of an Invisible Man" is your first prose text.
PA: First *published* prose text. Yes.
MC: And it changed your status as a writer?
PA: Well, when *The Invention of Solitude* came out in 1982, it got reviewed, and it was rare for such a small publisher to get reviews. There was a long article in the *New York Times,* I remember, but still it was a very small thing. No big engine of publicity. There was nothing at all. It's a book that sneaked out into the world and some people found it and liked it. Until then, I had only published poetry, which, as you know, fourteen people read, and then occasional book reviews and essays that in the long run didn't mean too much. So that was really the first book of mine that got any attention.

MC: It made you visible.
PA: In a way, yes.

MC: I was thinking of the meaning of that book, before we speak of the way it was written. You crossed out one line about your father, I guess in the third paragraph: *"He didn't have a work to be remembered by."* Something like that. The theme of becoming visible and maybe even immortal in a way through the work you have done underlies the whole book. I have the feeling that you wanted to be a writer very early on . . .
PA: Yes, that's true . . .

MC: And it was against your father, in a way. He didn't want you to be a writer.
PA: I don't know if he actively didn't want me to be a writer. The more I think about this, the more I realize that he was afraid because it was something he didn't understand. And now, being a father myself, I can sympathize much more with his fear about my being able to take care of myself. I think the first thing a parent wants to know about his children is that they will be able to live and feed themselves and have a roof over their heads. And it was as if I were saying to him: "I want to be a bum." He didn't quite understand. But, you see, underneath it all, even during all those years when I was a poet and writing articles, I heard from people, for example an aunt of mine, married to one of my father's brothers, who told me that my father was actually very proud of what I was doing.

MC: You mention his going to a library to read your poems . . .
PA: Isn't that beautiful? I mean, it's so moving that it makes me want to cry when I think about it now. So there was that side of him, too. And sometimes I wish he could see me here, living in this nice house and taking care of everyone, and I think he would be relieved. [Laughs gaily.]

MC: Yes, I think he would be a very proud father.
PA: Happy. He would be. And I constantly think about that.

MC: So, in a way, by writing this book you become a father, you are no longer a son, it's written in the book, maybe you cut it out finally, but there is a passage in the manuscript. Or rather no, I remember, you took it to "The Book of Memory."
PA: I did do some shifting from one book to the other.

MC: In a way, we have the feeling that you were writing this book for your father, in his place, you give birth to him by writing about him and at the same time you give birth to yourself as a writer. A critic wrote that Jean-Paul Sartre's *Les mots* could be wrapped up in the formula "the boy who wanted to become a book." Yours could be "the boy who wanted to make his father a book," so that the book could be transmitted. And that is why the book is addressed to your son, so that he can take his place in the chain of generations. It is a book of immigrants. Emigration cuts the "normal" development of a family in continuation of its own past. The whole story of your grandparents is a story of immigrants, not only a story of insanity. It is the story of people who have been cut from their roots, of people who have lost their culture. Consequently, I see this book as a kind of recapturing of the Jewish tradition of the book, in which you give birth to your father through the book that makes him visible, and at the same time you integrate him into American life, as he becomes a character who is very representative of American materialism. He stands for more than he is. When I read Philip Roth's *Patrimony*—I liked this book very much, I think it is one of his truly great books—I had this feeling that Jewish writers are at this moment giving the real portrait of what America is at its most original. It's not only making money, it's making money to be "worthy of being a Man," to be a "mensch."
PA: Yes, absolutely, to be a "mensch." To be somebody.

MC: And to hand it down to the next generation. This sense of family is very important in the book. This is why I think you have included your sister, in a very discreet way, because in one of the versions you go much farther. I was wondering if you did it out of delicacy . . .

PA: I think so. After all, she is very much alive and still not well. So I didn't want to say too much.

MC: In one of the versions there is a very terrifying portrait of her going out in the streets and making people read your poems, and she appears very disturbed . . . So I was wondering: this part seems to have been reduced out of "respect for the other," but the part about your mother, which was more elaborated, seems to have been reduced because it didn't fit into the main subject.

PA: Well, it was as though I understood at a certain moment what the book was about. It's not the portrait of my family. It was about this very deep emotional and philosophical question as seen through my relationship with my father. But my mother doesn't really enter into the story. I never had problems with my mother it's not a difficulty to be overcome. So those passages were reduced also, I think, for the sake of art.

MC: That's what I meant. To focus on the real subject matter.

PA: This book could only have value if it was concentrated.

MC: And that's why you also cut out most of the unrelated stories of your childhood, like your first friend. There were many pages about him. Suddenly you stop and make a reflexive development on the theme: "This is not an autobiography." Having written this, you can cut it out, and you also cut out everything that was too much of an autobiography.

PA: Right. And it's funny, I don't even remember writing those things.

MC: There is a lot of material that belongs to a "childhood narrative."

PA: I think that this was in the second version, the one that I wrote at Yaddo, when I thought: "Well, I have the kernel of a good book, and now I should develop it."

MC: In one of the versions, you recount that a friend of yours who has not read the book, but knows about it and knows that the book is dedicated to Daniel, that it is written for him, makes a remark about Titus, the dead child of Rembrandt, and in a way he warns you . . .

PA: I put the passage about Titus in "The Book of Memory."

MC: What you say in the manuscript is that you and your friend are drunk, you talk about the book and Daniel, then you look at Rembrandt's picture, and you remember that Titus eventually dies. There is a very tense feeling in the manuscript, because it seems you were realizing that, in a way, you have a death-wish for your own son. You take this out in the next version; for what reasons, I don't know. It seems that you were in a very emotional state to end this book.

PA: Yes. But you see, all that material is in the next book; it revolves around a whole cluster of images about young children: Titus, Mallarmé's Anatole, there is even the story of the missing child in New York at that time. Everywhere you turned, during those months, you saw a poster that said: "Missing child," and that boy looked a lot like Daniel, too.

MC: You were saying that you never had a desire to write an autobiography and that you are probably not going to.

PA: No, certainly not.

MC: Is it that you dislike autobiographical literature?

PA: Not at all. It has nothing to do with that. On some very deep level I think I never found my life very interesting, it wasn't something that seemed worthy of writing about. I went through a long crisis as a writer, which preceded the writing of this book. I hadn't written much for quite a while, and I had more or less stopped: I didn't think I was going to be a writer anymore—and when I started again, it just didn't seem to matter anymore. It wasn't as though I found my life particularly interesting, it was just something that I wanted to write about, it felt appropriate and necessary at the time, and so I did it. Since then I haven't felt the same compulsion, so I haven't done it.

MC: Do you have the feeling that, for example, *Mr. Vertigo* is a metaphor for your own life: the boy loses his power when he gets to be an adult, and what he loses actually is his creative power? He gains sexual power, but loses his "artistic" power to walk in the air. Do you have this anguish for yourself?

PA: No. [Laughs.] No. No, I don't see this novel as a personal story. At least, as I was writing it, I didn't feel that it was my story. It was something else altogether, deeper than just my own life. I really don't understand what I write. I wish I could talk about it more intelligently, with more understanding and knowledge. I don't understand it. I don't know where *Mr. Vertigo* came from. I've even thought that to the degree I don't understand something, that's precisely the degree to which it's interesting and important to do. But that doesn't really solve any problem. I seem to be writing out of some compulsion to write and to tell stories, but even though the act of doing it is satisfying to a certain degree and keeps me going from day to day, the fact that I have to keep writing books means that all the books I have published so far haven't really done anything for me, except to sustain me at the moment I was writing them.

MC: So there would be sort of a fantasy of the vanishing book.
PA: I might have thought that twenty years ago, but I don't think it anymore. I'm not looking for any ultimate solutions. Life is confusing and complicated, and it's so short [laughs] that I guess I'm doing what I have to do for very complicated reasons and I think it's just the ongoingness of the struggle that finally makes it interesting. There is no definitive book, there is no last word on any subject.

MC: I was thinking there are manuscripts in your books. *Mr. Vertigo* leaves a manuscript and it's his whole life.
PA: That's right. It's his summing up.

MC: And you also had a book that had to be written, in *Leviathan*.
PA: That's right. *In the Country of Last Things*, too, has a manuscript and in *City of Glass* there are notebooks. The private act of writing as something necessary: this interests me, and this happens at the level of the manuscript.

MC: It's not the *book* . . .
PA: It's the writing.

MC: But it has to stay as a testimony of the life.
PA: That's right. And I think that's why the books I publish don't interest me so much. I don't spend time looking at them or thinking about them. Let me put it this way: if I didn't publish the books, the manuscripts would be the most precious things to me in the world. I would guard them with my life. But once they become books, the words no longer belong to me.

MC: So you wouldn't say, like Chateaubriand quoted by Sartre: "Je sais bien que je ne suis qu'une machine à faire des livres [I know that I am only a bookmaking machine]"?
PA: No.

MC: You are not making books, you are writing. But what are you writing if it isn't your life?

PA: That's a very hard question. What am I writing? The story of my inner life, I suppose. But metamorphosed through art. Through poetry, through images, through metaphors. Because there is nothing to grab on to. It always eludes you. And I think telling stories is one way to give things concreteness and some kind of shape. It's precisely the imaginary story that resists understanding. I mean, we can talk about it endlessly. But the fact that it's not mathematics, that it's not a science that we can deduce a formula from, is what makes it interesting. We've been talking about Shakespeare for four hundred years. It's inexhaustible. But I don't think anyone is talking about how Isaac Newton came up with his formula for gravity.

MC: Some questions about the making of books are just unanswerable, and they are answered through the work itself.

PA: I don't know why I do it. And these last months, you know, doing this film work, I've gone through a long period without writing.

MC: You can live without it?

PA: Well, I've learned to live without it in a certain way, and I'm very unhappy. I can't wait to get going again. And then I'm afraid. I don't know if I'm going to be able to do it anymore.

MC: Don't you have the feeling that you have your craft in your hand?

PA: No. I think it gets harder and harder. The more you know, the harder it is. At the same time, I don't fall into the kind of despair I used to when I was very young. When I come up against problems and difficulties in a book, I tend to be more patient with myself now. You have the experience of working out problems, so you feel: "Well, you'll be able to do it again." But I don't know, I haven't written anything now in about nine months.

MC: But you started something.

PA: I started something, I have about thirty or forty pages, but I haven't looked at them for a while. I'm sure it won't be finished for several years. I think it will be a fairly long book. It has a very strange title: *Dream Days at the Hotel Existence.*

MC: Oh, it was in the titles enumerated in the margins of many of your notebooks. *Hotel Existence.*

PA: I've had this title for years. This book has been with me for years. It's the first book I'm attempting to write in which there are several key characters. It's not all from the point of view of one person. In fact, I would say the most constant character in it is a dog. And I started writing about this dog before we got Jack [Auster's dog]. And then, not long after, Jack suddenly came into our lives.

MC: Is it a talking dog?
PA: No, it's a thinking dog. [Laughs.] He would like to be able to talk, but he can't. So that's what I want to get back to.

MC: No more movie scripts?
PA: No. That was an interesting detour, but it's not what I really want to do.

MC: Just one question about the father figures. Do you still have one? You say somewhere that you kept looking for fathers everywhere.
PA: I think all my father figures are dead. Everyone has died now. Edmond Jabès is dead. He was more like a grandfather than a father. We had a very warm friendship. I think I looked up to Beckett in a way, even though he was not someone I was close to personally. We met a couple of times, corresponded a little bit, but he was certainly a paternal figure for me.

MC: I have always thought that the last sentence of "The Invisible Man" ["To end with this."] was very Beckettian.
PA: Probably.

MC: Is there another meaning? It's kind of mysterious to me. "To end with this." It can be matter of fact: "let's end with this" . . .
PA: No, "to end with this," meaning on this image, on this thought. This is the place where the story comes to an end. "To end with *this*." Not this [shows something large], but this [shows something tiny]. Very small.

MC: Another phrase you took out was maybe a little pathetic. The narrator cries and feels very depressed and he wonders if he'll ever get out of his chair.
PA: I crossed that out too. Well, self-pity is never good.

MC: You crossed out everything that was too sentimental and too moving. But it's all the more effective. We are moved.

PA: In all art, the power of restraint is important. I don't know if people think about this enough. This is where all the tension in art comes from. And that's where all the real feeling comes from. The sense that there is a whole life behind every statement made, that there is a whole world echoing behind the words that are spoken. If you try to say everything, you don't wind up saying very much at all. You put down the sentence, and it seems like a good thing to say, and then ultimately it's not. So you take it out.

MC: So you have to be your own reader at one time.

PA: Most definitely. And a very hard-hearted, cruel reader. You can't accept any bullshit.

MC: "To end with this."

An Interview with Paul Auster

Ashton Applewhite / 1994

From Penguin Reading Guide for *Mr. Vertigo*. Reproduced with permission of Paul Auster

Applewhite: What drew you to the story of *Mr. Vertigo*?
Auster: That's a great mystery to me. I don't know where it came from. For years I'd been walking around with a tale of a master and a disciple in my head, never very clearly defined, and never much of a story, just a situation. When I sat down to write it, I thought it would be about twenty pages. Obviously, I was wrong.

Applewhite: You once told an interviewer that "very strong emotions, traumas even, generate [my] stories." Was that the case with *Mr. Vertigo*?
Auster: Again, every book I've ever written has been a conundrum to me. I don't know what I'm doing, or why I'm doing it. There is simply the compulsion to do it, the absolute necessity of getting that story down on paper. Sometimes, later, after a book is written, I have little glimmers of understanding about where it came from, little hints. With *Mr. Vertigo*, I think it has something to do with the idea of falling from high places. I say that in the way an anthropologist would say it, strictly based on observation and the evidence of my own eyes. I can think of several books I've written in which people fall. In the most important scene of *In the Country of Last Things*, Anna Blume jumps through a window on the top floor of a building in order to save herself; she's not killed, but it changes the course of her life. In *Moon Palace*, Fogg's obese father falls into an open grave and breaks his back. Everything in *Leviathan* revolves around a man falling off a fire escape. All this, I think (but how can I really know?) might be connected to something that happened to my father when I was a little boy. He was working on a roof in Jersey City and fell off, just like that. He slipped and started tumbling through the air. If not for a clothesline that broke his fall, he probably would have been killed. Though I didn't see it happen, I walked

around with that image in my head all through my childhood: my father flying through space. Maybe that's the source, the thing at the bottom of my strange obsession.

Applewhite: One of my favorite things about the book is the combination of the spiritual and the utterly mundane. Both are certainly present in the character of Master Yehudi: sometimes he sounds like a Zen priest, sometimes like a carnival huckster.

Auster: He's a very complex character. On the one hand he's a con man, a charlatan, an operator trying to make a lot of money—just like everyone else in America. On the other hand, he has a very deep spiritual side. He's interested in spiritual truths. Defying the laws of nature, as he proposes to do with Walt, puts him in a very precarious and interesting position with God, with the universe, with man. And Master Yehudi thinks about these things. He takes them seriously.

Applewhite: Where does he come by his spiritual leanings?

Auster: Hard to say. He was there, fully formed in my head before I started writing. Later on, I realized that his biography was quite similar to Houdini's, who was also a Hungarian Jew who came from a family of rabbis. His real name was Erich Weiss. The contrast between what you might call the mythical and the everyday, how they combine and live side by side in the same world, is part of what this book is about. It's what establishes its tone.

Applewhite: Walt uses a lot of religious language and imagery too. Where does it come from?

Auster: What interests me about American language, the language of the people, is that it's very crude, very lively, very inventive. But at the same time, there's a Biblical component to it, especially the Bible in the King James version, which is undoubtedly the most read book in American history, as well as the book that has been most listened to. For many people, especially people of earlier generations, it was the only literature they knew. So there's an astonishing combination in the American vernacular of what you might call the high and the low. Walt's speech is a perfect example of that.

Applewhite: Isn't Walt searching for some sort of truth?

Auster: No more or less than anyone else. We're all looking for the truth, aren't we? Something to believe in, something solid to stand on. You can read this book in many different ways, and I don't think that one reading is more valid than another. They all coexist. You can look at it as a parable of childhood, but you can also look at it as a piece of American history. You can look at it as a novel about the public and the private, about money, about show biz, about success and failure. I would be the last person to try to impose an interpretation on a reader.

Applewhite: Why did you write the story in the first person?

Auster: Another question I can't answer. That's just how it came to me, the old man looking back. You could say, though—assuming you're a literary critic—that a first-person narration is less reliable than a story told in the third person. A third-person narrator is omniscient; you trust the voice, you accept it on faith. A first-person narration is more complex, because you have to take into account who's saying what, and why. What if the narrator is lying on purpose? You can never ignore that as a possibility.

Applewhite: It's pretty dramatic to make poor Walt choose between his testicles and stardom. How come you shaped the story that way?

Auster: I couldn't think of a more dramatic conflict.

Applewhite: Explaining why Mrs. Witherspoon won't be joining them on tour, Master Yehudi says, "If you just stand there and wait, there's a chance the thing you're hoping for will come right to you." Do you think his fix on romantic love is as off-base as Walt does?

Auster: For many of the things one most ardently wants, patience is a great virtue. Sometimes things do come to you, including love. But Master Yehudi makes one mistake after another where Mrs. Witherspoon is concerned. He doesn't play his cards right.

Applewhite: Mrs. Witherspoon's a lusty lady. Do you think sex is important to men and women in the same way?

Auster: I don't think she has a different approach to her sexuality than either Walt or Master Yehudi. Mrs. Witherspoon is my kind of woman, and I would venture to say that her view of sex is a lot less unusual than people might think. To give you some idea of how my books get written, I have to confess that when I started the novel there was no Mrs. Witherspoon. She just emerged. She started making appearances as I was writing, and became more and more important as the book continued. Actually, and this is occurring to me for the first time, if there's any book that Mr. Vertigo is connected to, it's *Pinocchio*, a book that I've thought about long and hard over the years. In some odd way you could say that Walt is Pinocchio, Master Yehudi is Master Geppeto, and Mrs. Witherspoon is the Blue Fairy.

Applewhite: Walt the Wonder Boy says, "You have to keep testing yourself, pushing your talent as hard as you can. . . . People begin to sense that you're out there taking risks for them." Is this true of writing?
Auster: As a writer, I don't think about the audience in the way an actual performer does. When I wrote that passage, I was thinking about real entertainers, people who stand up in public and do their work in front of a crowd of strangers.

Applewhite: In your opinion, who are the great storytellers?
Auster: The anonymous men and women who invented the fairy tales we still tell each other today, the authors of the *1001 Nights*, the European folk tales, the whole oral tradition that started the moment men learned how to talk. They're an unending source of inspiration to me.

Applewhite: Are those the sorts of books you like to read? What's on your bedside table?
Auster: It's very cluttered right now, which probably means it's a good cross-section of the kinds of things that interest me. My wife and I just bought two books for our daughter, who is almost eight, but I claimed them first: a collection of Yiddish folk tales and another one of French folk tales. I was recently sent the enormous, unabridged first English translation of *The Man without Qualities*, by Robert Musil, and that's there too. Then there's a book about intelligence in dogs, because I'm trying to write about a dog. *Low Life* by Luc Sante, and *A Void* by Georges Perec, a novelist I admire very much. Also . . . let me think . . . a book of poems by Charles Simic . . . and one or two others.

Applewhite: Talking about writing in the *New York Times Magazine*, you say, "You suffer a lot. You feel inadequate. The sense of failure is enormous." Do you still feel that way in the light of your growing reputation?
Auster: Oh yes. The longer you go on writing, the harder writing becomes. You set higher and higher standards for yourself, and the risks you take become bigger, more dangerous, more disturbing. Just because you've written one book doesn't mean you'll be able to write a second, and just because you've written a second doesn't mean you'll be able to write a third. The struggles go on right to the end. When I read nice things about myself or

my work, it's as though they're talking about someone else. People also say a lot of nasty things, and if you've made up your mind not to let that get you down, the only honest way to deal with praise is to ignore it, too.

Applewhite: In the same interview you describe writing as "certainly a stupid way to live your life, isolating yourself every day, making something nobody really needs or wants." Do you really believe that?
Auster: Much of the time, yes. Some of the time, no. But, for better or worse, writing is what I do, it's what I do best. I'm not good for anything else.

The Futurist Radio Hour: An Interview with Paul Auster

Stephen Capen/1996

From *The Futurist Radio Hour*, KUSF San Francisco. Reproduced with permission of Paul Auster.

CAPEN: I'd like to delve into the past as our departure point. You were, at one time, a merchant seaman, and I wonder how this came about.

AUSTER: It's true, I did work for about six months on an Esso oil tanker. I got the job after I left college. I didn't know what I wanted to do in life. I didn't want to be an academic, which is probably what I was best suited for, but I just didn't want to be in school anymore, and the idea of spending my life in a university was too horrible to contemplate. I had no real profession, no trade, I hadn't really studied for anything. All I wanted to do was to write. I guess my ambition was simply to make money however I could to keep myself going in some modest way, and I didn't need much, I was unmarried at the time, no children. It turned out that my stepfather, who was a person I was very close to, the person to whom I dedicated *Moon Palace*, Norman Schiff, earned his living as a labor lawyer and negotiator. One of his clients was the Esso Seamen's Union, a company union. So I knew all about these ships, and when I was about to leave school I asked Norman if he could help me get a job on one of them, and he said, "I'll take care of it for you." It's extremely difficult to get these jobs, because you can't get a job on a ship unless you have seaman's papers, and you can't get seaman's papers unless you have a job on a ship. There had to be a way to break through the circle, and he was the one who arranged it for me. So I shipped out. It's quite amusing. I went through all the exams, I got my papers, and then I had to sit around and wait until a ship from the fleet came into the New York area with an opening, not knowing how long this wait was going to be. In the meantime—this is 1970—I took a job with the U.S. Census Bureau. In *The Locked Room*, the third volume of The New York Trilogy, there's a sequence where the narrator talks about working for the census, and I took this straight from life. As in the book, I wound up inventing people. Kind of curious. Anyway, right around that time I had a problem with a wisdom tooth and I had to go to the dentist to have the thing pulled out, and it was while I was sitting in the chair in the dentist's office—the dentist had just picked up a big pair of pliers and was about to yank out my tooth—when the telephone rang. It was my stepfather. "The ship is here," he said. "You have to report in two hours." So I jumped out of the dentist's chair with the bib on and said, "Sorry, I have to leave," and ran out and made my way to a tanker in Elizabeth, New Jersey. The tooth was taken out a week later in Baytown, Texas. The ship traveled around the Gulf of Mexico, and it was all new to me, I hadn't been in the South, I hadn't been in Texas, and I learned a lot during those months. Luckily, the work was well paid. I managed to save several thousand dollars, and it was with that money that I moved to Paris, where I spent the next three or four years.

CAPEN: This was key for you, this move. What was your experience of Paris? It almost seems like you learned the meaning of being a writer there.
AUSTER: Well, it was certainly a fundamental time. I had been writing before that. It was what I wanted to do with my life. But my student years came at a particularly crazy time in America. We're talking about the late '60s, and Columbia University, where I went to school, was a hotbed of activity. It was impossible not to get caught up in it. As a consequence, I didn't do as much writing as I would have hoped. So after I graduated, leaving America for a while made sense. It wasn't that I wanted to become an expatriate. I just needed some breathing room. I'd already been translating French poetry, I'd been to Paris twice before and had liked it very much, and so that was where I went. By the time I returned to New York, it was certain to me that this is what I was doing with my life, there was no turning back.

CAPEN: You entered into it in what may be the most obscure way, through French poetry, translations of Surrealist works. So the '70s were that sort of period for you. Then in the '80s you came into your own as a novelist, and from there it's skyrocketed into this decade.
AUSTER: The funny thing is, as a young person I was trying to write prose, and I wrote a lot of it, but I was never satisfied with the results. Two of the novels I wound up finishing and publishing later I started very early on, in my early twenties, *In the Country of Last Things* and *Moon Palace*. I worked

on both of those books for a long time but never quite got a grip on either one. I put them aside and at a certain point decided that I couldn't write prose, that I would just stick to writing poetry. I was always interested in French poetry and began translating for the pure pleasure of it. That kind of spilled out into translation as a way to earn money, to pay the rent and put bread on the table, but it was grinding and unpleasant work, I really didn't like it. I wound up translating a lot of mediocre books, badly written books on subjects that had no interest to me, for pay that was disastrously low. At a certain point I realized I could probably earn more flipping hamburgers. I mean, it was that bad. By the late '70s, I ran into a crisis—on every level: personal, artistic, and I was absolutely broke, I'd run out of money and . . . hope, I guess. I stopped writing for about a year. The only thing I actually did during that period was write a detective novel under another name, in about six weeks, just to make money, I was so desperately poor, but it took several years before it was actually published. When I started writing again in late '78, it was prose, and the fact is I haven't written a poem since then. I absolutely stopped, and absolutely started again, and the two parts of my life as a writer are very different.

CAPEN: Not many poets come out of Brooklyn, although Whitman certainly is a notable exception.
AUSTER: Actually, Brooklyn has a long literary history. Whitman most famously, but most of the Objectivists lived in Brooklyn—Louis Zukovsky, George Oppen, Charles Reznikoff, and probably one of the great twentieth-century poems, *The Bridge*, written by Hart Crane, was composed in Brooklyn. In fact, there are few places in America with a greater poetic tradition than Brooklyn.

CAPEN: Kurt Vonnegut feels that once he's finished a book, the work is out of his hands, it's out in the world, and it takes on a life of its own. You share this view?
AUSTER: Yes, I agree with that completely. The book is your book. You have been responsible for every single thing on every page, every comma, every syllable is your work. Then you let go of it, you give it to the world and what the world makes of what you've done is unpredictable, out of your control. One of my novels, *City Of Glass*, was turned into a comic book. The project was initiated by my friend Art Spiegelman (*Maus*). I knew that if Art was involved in this project it would be of high quality, so I let it happen. I think it's terrific, by the way. I'm very impressed by how well the artist-writer team

of [David] Mazzucchelli and [Paul] Karasik managed to render this book in images. Another novel, *The Music of Chance*, was turned into a film, but someone also made it into a ballet a couple of years ago. Most moving to me, and this is the best kind of thing that can happen to a writer, another one of my novels, *In the Country of Last Things*, fell into the hands of a theater director from Sarajevo about three years ago—during the siege. He read it under horrible circumstances, no electricity, no heat, in the dead of winter in the middle of a war, but once he started reading it, he told me, he couldn't stop and pushed on to the end in one night with a candle by his bed. For him, the book was a blow-by-blow account of the situation in Sarajevo. He became so impassioned that he decided to mount a stage adaptation with his theater group—and they performed it, in the worst days of the siege. The book, of course, was written many years before the Bosnian apocalypse, and yet the work of one man's imagination, in this case mine, somehow connected with what another man was living through at that moment, years later, and something new happened with it. Books constantly change, even though the words are the same. The world changes, people change, people find a book at the right moment, and it answers something, some need or desire. Why would I want to block something like that? I think you'd be foolish to assume that you know what the fate of your work is going to be.

CAPEN: Let's get metaphysical for a moment. Do you feel as an author that you open yourself to some sort of channel and the story is out there waiting for you?

AUSTER: Well, yes, I suppose so. You just don't know how complex and mysterious the world can be. It's no accident that he should have felt that way, because I was consciously writing a book about events that had taken place earlier in the twentieth century. And so here in the late twentieth century, yet another horror takes place, and the book strikes a chord. You see, the interesting thing about books, as opposed, say, to films, is that it's always just one person encountering the book. It's not an audience, it's one to one. It's me the writer and you the reader, and we're together on that page, and I think it's probably about the most intimate place where two human beings can meet. That's why books are never going to die. It's impossible. It's the only time we really go into the mind of a stranger, and we find our common humanity doing this. So the book doesn't only belong to the writer, it belongs to the reader as well, and the two of you make the book together.

CAPEN: The titles of your books, *In the Country of Last Things, City of Glass,*

The Music of Chance, Smoke . . . they sound like kernels of ideas as opposed to being derived later from an overview in the long run. Is this the case?

AUSTER: I find it impossible to start a project without the title in mind. I can sometimes spend years thinking of the title to go with the thing that's forming in my head. A title defines the project, and if you keep finding the ramifications of the title in the work, it becomes better, I'm convinced of this. So, yes, I think about titles a lot. Sometimes I walk around making up titles for things that don't exist, that will never exist.

CAPEN: Back to the work, once finished, being out of your control. Philip Haas, the director, took *The Music of Chance* and did, to my way of thinking, a brilliant job with this, but it was completely different than the book.

AUSTER: When *The Music of Chance* was published, several people called about turning it into a film. Philip Haas had no money and he had never made a feature film before, but I felt he understood the book and was going to do an honorable job with it. Some things were altered a bit, but I don't feel the movie betrayed the novel.

CAPEN: John Irving says his favorite novel is Thomas Mann's *The Magic Mountain*, and he's read it perhaps a dozen times. Is there a book like that for you?

AUSTER: There are several of them, but if I had to say just one, one book that I keep going back to and keep thinking about, it's *Don Quixote*. That's the one, for me. It seems to present every problem every novelist has ever had to face, and to do it in the most brilliant and human way imaginable.

CAPEN: Are you about to unveil another novel?

AUSTER: I've finished a book, but it's not a novel, it's a nonfiction work. It's hard to describe. I would call it an autobiographical essay about money. Mostly about not having money. It's called *Hand to Mouth*. And since finishing that, I'm creeping my way back into a novel I had started before.

CAPEN: One last thought. Lou Reed, in *Blue in the Face*, says he's been trying to get out of New York for thirty-five years, but he can't seem to leave. Is this your desire? Or have you become fabulously well-to-do, with houses scattered all over?

AUSTER: No, I don't have houses scattered all over, but I do have one house, and I live in it all the time. Lou says in the film, every New Yorker considers leaving New York at one time or another. I used to think about it every now and then, but at a certain point a few years ago, I realized that I had to stay. It's better for me to be there. So . . . I'm staying. Maybe later, maybe somewhere down the road, I'll change my mind. But for now, and for the foreseeable future, I'm not going anywhere.

Paul Auster: Writer and Director

Rebecca Prime/1998

Interview conducted February 22, 1998. Reproduced from *Lulu on the Bridge. A Film by Paul Auster* (Henry Holt, 1998) by permission of Paul Auster.

Rebecca Prime: Three years ago, when you were working on the postproduction of *Smoke* and *Blue in the Face*, you did an interview with Annette Insdorf and the last question she asked you was, "Now that you've caught the bug, do you have any desire to direct again?" You answered her, "No, I can't say that I do." Obviously, you've had a change of heart. Any particular reason?

Paul Auster: I guess it's dangerous to talk about the future, isn't it? The idea for *Lulu* actually came to me around that time, while I was still working on those films. I saw the story as a movie. And because I was feeling burned out by movies just then—postproduction on *Smoke* and *Blue in the Face* dragged on for almost a year—I did everything I could to resist it. But the story kept coming back to me, kept demanding that I do something about it, and eventually I gave in to the impulse. And when I did, I made a fatal mistake.

RP: How so?

PA: I decided to write it as a novel. If the story was good, I said to myself, then it didn't matter how I told it. Book, film, it didn't matter. The heart of the story would burn through no matter what form it took. So I sat down and started writing—and six or seven months later, when I stood up and examined what I had done so far, I realized it was no good. It didn't work. It was a dramatic story, not a narrative story, and it needed to be seen, not just read.

RP: Why?

PA: Because of the stone, to begin with. Because of the film inside the story. Because of the dreamlike structure of events. A whole host of reasons.

RP: And so you went back and started over again . . .
PA: Not right away. I thought the project was dead, and I turned my attention to other things. A year went by, maybe a year and a half, but the story never really left me. When I finally understood that it was something I needed to do, I took a deep breath and started again. But this time I stuck to my original conception and wrote it as a screenplay. So much for trying to force things. I learned a lot from that blunder.

RP: Still, even though you wrote it as a film, the story feels more like a novel than most films one sees. Like one of *your* novels, actually.
PA: Well, habits die hard, as Izzy says at one point. But the fact was that I felt all along that *Lulu* was a continuation of my work, that it's of a piece with everything else I've done.

RP: Most films seem to set out to tell one thing, and they usually proceed in a linear fashion. With *Lulu on the Bridge*, the story works on several different levels at once.
PA: That's what makes it so difficult to talk about. There are a number of threads running through the story, and by the time you come to the end, they're so tangled up with one another, you can't pull one out without disturbing all the others. The most important thing, though, is that at bottom it's a very emotional story, a story about deep and powerful feelings. It's not a puzzle, not some code to be cracked, and you don't have to "understand" it in a rational way to feel the force of the emotions.

RP: Let's talk about the "dreamlike structure of events" you mentioned earlier.
PA: On one level, it's all very simple. A man gets shot, and in the last hour before his death, he dreams another life for himself. The content of that dream is provided by a number of random elements that appear to him just before and after the shooting. A wall of photographs in a men's room featuring women's faces—mostly the faces of movie stars—and a chunk of plaster that falls from the ceiling. Everything follows from those elements: the magic blue stone, the young woman he falls in love with, the fact that she's an actress and lands a role in a film, the title of that film, the director of that film, and so on. That's one way of reading the story—the framework, so to

speak. But that's hardly the most interesting way of looking at it. It gives the film some plausibility, I suppose, but it doesn't take the magic into account. And if you forget the magic, you don't have much of anything.

RP: Can you elaborate?

PA: Because, on another level, all these things really happen. I firmly believe that Izzy lives through the events in the story, that the dream is not just some empty fantasy. When he dies at the end, he's a different man than he was at the beginning. He's managed to redeem himself, somehow. If not, how else to account for Celia's presence on the street at the end? It's as if she has lived through the story, too. The ambulance passes, and even though she can't possibly know who is inside, she does, it's as if she does. She feels a connection, she's moved, she's touched by grief—understanding that the person in the ambulance has just died. As far as I'm concerned, the whole film comes together in that final shot. The magic isn't just simply a dream. It's real, and it carries all the emotions of reality.

RP: In other words, you believe in the impossible.

PA: We all do. Whether we know it or not, our lives would make no sense if we didn't. . . . Think of something like *A Midsummer Night's Dream*. Elves and fairies prancing through the woods. Sprinkle pixie dust in a man's eyes, and he falls in love. It's impossible, yes, but that doesn't mean it isn't real, that it isn't true to life. Love is magic, after all, isn't it? No one understands what it is, no one can explain it. Pixie dust is as good an explanation as any other, it seems to me. And so is the blue stone—the thing that brings Izzy and Celia together. Just because a story is told "realistically" doesn't make it realistic. And just because a story is told fancifully doesn't make it far-fetched. In the end, metaphor might be the best way of getting at the truth.

RP: *Lulu on the Bridge* operates on a metaphorical level, but it is also grounded in reality.

PA: Well, you can never stray too far from the world of ordinary things. If you do, you slip into allegory, and allegory doesn't interest me at all. Two or three years ago, Peter Brook did an interview in the *New York Times*, and he said something that made an enormous impression on me. "In all my work," he said, "I try to combine the closeness of the everyday with the distance of myth. Because, without the closeness you can't be moved, and without the distance you can't be amazed." A brilliant formulation, no? *Lulu on the Bridge* is that kind of double work, I think. At least I hope it is.

RP: When all is said and done, *Lulu* could probably be described as a love story, couldn't it? That seems to be the heart of the film, at least for me. What happens between Izzy and Celia.

PA: Yes, I think you're right. Izzy is a man who's led a less than noble life. He's selfish, quick-tempered, incapable of loving anyone. He's cut off from his family, and his marriage to Hannah—a beautiful, goodhearted young woman—ended after just a few years. Probably because he couldn't keep his hands off of other women. Then he's shot, and in the delirium of his final moments, he conjures up a great and overpowering love. In doing so, he reinvents who he is, becomes better, discovers what is best inside him. It's a big love, of course. A love so big he's actually willing to die for it.

RP: Izzy is willing to die for Celia, but Celia also sacrifices herself for Izzy.

PA: Precisely. It works both ways. Celia jumps off the bridge and disappears. You think that might be the end of her. Then Izzy dies, and just as he is pronounced dead in the ambulance, we see Celia again, walking down the street. It's as if his death has resurrected her, as if he's died in order to give her another chance at life.

RP: Tell me about the stone. It's probably the strangest element in the story, and yet the odd thing is that everyone seems to accept it. I've attended several screenings of the film, and not once has anyone questioned it or been confused by it.

PA: To tell the truth, I don't really understand what the stone is. I have ideas about it, of course, many feelings, many thoughts, but nothing definitive.

RP: Each person finds his or her own meaning in it . . .

PA: Yes. It becomes more powerful that way, I think. The less fixed, the more pregnant with possibilities. . . . When I first wrote the story, I suppose I thought of the stone as some kind of mysterious, all-encompassing life force—the glue that connects one thing to another, that binds people together, the unknowable something that makes love possible. Later on, when we filmed the scene of Izzy pulling the stone out of the box, I began to have another idea about it. The way Harvey played it, it began to feel to me as if the stone were Izzy's soul, as if we were watching a man discover himself for the first time. He reacts with fear and confusion; he's thrown into a panic. It's only the next day, when he meets Celia, that he understands what's happened. You find your essence only in relation to others. That's the great paradox. You don't take hold of yourself until you're willing to give it away. In other words, you don't become who you are until you're capable of loving someone else.

RP: The stone is one of the elements in the film that clues the viewer to the fact that you can't read the film as a straightforward narrative, that we're clearly in some sort of altered universe. At the same time, it has a very straightforward narrative function. It's the prime mover in what could be called the "thriller" aspect of the story. What compelled you to make use of this genre?

PA: Because it seemed right, it felt right. Thrillers are very much like dreams. When you strip away the surface details, they begin to function as metaphors of our unconscious. People without faces pursuing you through dark, abandoned streets. Men hanging from the edges of buildings. Fear and danger, risk, the contingencies of life and death.

RP: With *Lulu*, how would you describe the thriller aspect of the plot?

PA: It's fairly rudimentary. Dr. Van Horn is associated with the group that developed the magic stone. Various scoundrels representing other groups are trying to gain possession of this priceless object. Stanley Mar would be one. The three thugs who assault Izzy would be another. They lock him up, thinking he knows where the stone is. Then Van Horn's group tracks down this other group and eliminates them. Van Horn then begins to interrogate Izzy.

RP: But he's interested in more than just the stone, isn't he?

PA: Of course he is. He's interested in Izzy's soul. Van Horn isn't at all what he first appears to be. He's an interrogating angel. He's the figure standing between Izzy and the gates of death. His job is to find out who Izzy is.

RP: In their last conversation, when Izzy refuses to reveal that he knows Celia Burns, Van Horn storms out in a fit of anger. Why?

PA: Because he wants the stone, and he understands that Izzy isn't going to help him. At the same time, I see his anger as a test. He wants to know if Izzy will buckle under the pressure or try to protect the person he loves. Izzy stands firm, and even though Van Horn doesn't get what he seems to want, in the end this might be an even more satisfying outcome for him. Remember, he doesn't rush out. He turns at the last moment and says to Izzy, "May God have mercy on your soul." And he means it. There's tremendous ambiguity in that line, of course, but it also represents a spontaneous outburst of compassion.

RP: And then there's Celia—what might be called the "feminine" side of the movie. In some sense, she's everything Izzy is not.

PA: Her most important quality, I think, is vitality. Celia is *alive*. She's generous, she's fetching, she's desirable—the kind of young woman every man can fall in love with. At the same time, she's not a pushover. She's not some simpering cutie-pie. She has opinions, she's capable of anger, she's willing to stand up for herself.

RP: And she's also an actress. I was particularly struck by the line she says to Izzy about playing a prostitute: "I really liked doing that scene." It gives us a glimpse into how she might be capable of playing Lulu.

PA: Yes. It's a jocular, offhanded kind of line, but it does establish an important link. It's a little fulcrum that connects Celia to Lulu.

RP: Celia is a flesh-and-blood character, but at the same time there's a fascination with female archetypes in the film. Just under the surface, the story seems to be making constant references to myth. When Celia looks up at Izzy after she's taken hold of the stone for the first time and says, "Come on, don't be afraid, it's the best thing, it really is," you feel this is just the kind of thing Eve might have said to Adam in the Garden of Eden. When Izzy opens the three boxes and finds the stone in the last one, you can't help but think of Pandora's box.

PA: All the images in the story are connected; everything bounces off of everything else. To a large degree, the film is about how men invent women. It begins with the very first shot—when we see that wall of photographs of women's faces. All those movie stars! I'm intrigued by the fact that for most of this century images of beautiful women have been projected on screens and have fed the fantasies of men all over the world. That's probably why movie stars were invented. To feed dreams. Izzy invents a new life for himself through the medium of a picture. There's Mira Sorvino's face on the wall—and the movie begins. In a way, it duplicates what we all experience when we watch movies. We walk into a dark place and leave the world behind. We enter the realm of make-believe.

RP: Why Lulu and *Pandora's Box*? What exactly were you trying to do by introducing that element into the story?

PA: It pushes the dream farther, throws Celia from one end of her femininity to the other. From good girl to bad girl. It's Izzy's dream, after all, and in some way you can see Lulu as a female version of who Izzy used to be.

RP: I see what you mean when you say that "everything bounces off everything else."

PA: That's why I was so gripped by the Lulu story. Lulu is a completely amoral, infantile creature, a person without compassion. Men lose their minds over her. She doesn't intend to hurt anybody, but one by one all her lovers are driven to suicide, insanity, debasement—every horror you can imagine. Lulu is a blank slate, and men project their desires onto her. They invent her. Just as men invent the women they see in movies. The Lulu plays were written before the invention of movies, but Lulu is a movie star. She's the first movie star in history.

RP: How did you go about adapting the Lulu material?

PA: I went back to Wedekind's two plays, *Earth Spirit* and *Pandora's Box*. I greatly admire Pabst's film, particularly Louise Brooks's performance, but I didn't make much use of it when writing the screenplay, and I certainly didn't want to refer to it in the film. The two plays tell a continuous story, and they add up to nine long acts. Obviously, I couldn't deal with all that. The most I could do was suggest the arc of Lulu's life, and I tried to achieve that by concentrating on what I felt were a few of the most interesting and pertinent scenes. I also decided not to do it as a period piece, to modernize the details, the settings, and so on. The plays are a hundred years old now, and there's so much dreadful writing in them, so much that creaks and grates, there seemed to be no point in trying to restage them as they were written. In the first scene, I changed the painter Schwarz into the photographer Black. The Pierrot costume became a Charlie Chaplin costume. All in the spirit of the original—but different. In the dressing-room scene, I changed the musical revue into a rock and roll performance. That kind of thing. It's never a word-for-word translation, but at the same time I tried not to stray too far from the gist of Wedekind's dialogue.

RP: Once you started writing the screenplay, were you also planning to direct the film yourself?

PA: Not at first. The original idea was for Wim Wenders to direct it. Wim and I have been friends for a long time now; and we've always talked about doing a project together. For a while, it looked as though *Lulu* would be that project. We even went so far as to have a number of conversations about the story, and when I sent him the finished screenplay, he was very happy with it. I assumed that would be the end of my involvement with the film, that the torch had been passed, so to speak. Then, just a few days later, a funny thing happened. Wim was interviewed by a journalist, and at one point she said to him, "Mr. Wenders, do you realize that the past four or five movies you've made have all been about making movies?" The question caught him by surprise. As a matter of fact, he hadn't been aware of it. *Lulu on the Bridge*, of course, is yet another movie with a movie inside the movie, and Wim called me up the next morning to say that he was suddenly feeling worried. Was that his destiny—to be a filmmaker who could only make films about films? He wasn't backing out of the project, but he wanted to think it over for a while before committing himself. Was that okay? Of course it was okay. So I hung up the phone and realized that the film no longer had a director.

RP: How could you be sure?

PA: Making a movie is such a difficult, exhausting process, you can't go into it with anything less than total enthusiasm. The slightest doubt, the smallest flicker of uncertainty, and you're sunk. If Wim was wobbling about it, then my feeling was that he probably shouldn't do it. . . . He was going to call me back with his decision the following week, and in the meantime I started thinking about who else should do it, who else *could* do it. No names jumped out at me. The script is so strange, I suppose, so particular to me and my own private universe, that I couldn't think of anyone whose sensibility would be compatible with the material. That was when it occurred to me that perhaps I should do it myself. It was my story, after all, and why not see the thing through to the end? At least it would be made exactly the way I wanted it to be made—for better or for worse. So I wrote Wim a fax saying that if he decided not to direct the film, I was inclined to do it myself. I sent the letter through the machine, and one minute later the telephone rang. It was Wim. "I just tore up a letter I was going to fax to you," he said, "trying to persuade you to direct the movie yourself." And that was that. Without really intending to work in the movies again, not only had I written another screenplay, but now I was going to direct as well.

RP: And you weren't scared?

PA: No, not really. I had spent two years working on *Smoke* and *Blue in the Face* and had a very clear idea of what I was getting myself into. No one twisted my arm to do it. It was a decision I made on my own, which means that somewhere, deep down, I probably had a real hankering to do it.

RP: You finished writing the script in early February 1997. Now, almost exactly a year later, you're in postproduction. How did it happen so fast?

PA: Two words: Peter Newman. Peter was the producer of both *Smoke* and *Blue in the Face*, and once we started working together, we became great friends. I can't say enough good things about this man. His integrity, his optimism, his sense of humor, his resilience. When I told him about this new project that I wanted to do, he simply went out and raised the money. In record time. It only took about two months.

RP: Peter Newman was also responsible for one of the scenes in the film, wasn't he?
PA: I'm not sure he'd want me to talk about it—but yes, he was. The airplane story that Philip Kleinman tells at the dinner party early in the film came directly from Peter. It's a true story, something that really happened to him. I know it's rather disgusting, and more than a little disturbing, but the fact was that I was very impressed when Peter told it to me—for what it revealed about his moral qualities, his goodness as a human being. That's how it stands in the film: as a moral tale.

RP: How did you go about casting the film? Did you write the script with any specific actors in mind?
PA: Harvey Keitel. He was the only one. It's not that I set out to write a role for Harvey, but once I got into the story a bit, I began seeing him in my mind, and at a certain point it became inconceivable to think of Izzy without also thinking of Harvey.

RP: You'd worked together before, of course.
PA: Yes, and we'd both developed a great deal of respect for each other. It goes without saying that Harvey is a superb actor. But there's something more to it than that. The way he moves, the irresistible qualities of his face, his groundedness. It's as if Harvey embodies something that belongs to all of us, as if he *becomes* us when he's up on the screen. When he agreed to play Izzy, I knew that we were going to have an extraordinary time together. And we did. Working with him on this role was one of the best experiences of my life.

RP: Mira Sorvino plays Celia, but at an earlier stage in the project the part was supposedly offered to Juliette Binoche. Is that true?
PA: Yes. But that was very early, when Wim still thought he would be involved. Juliette was the actress he proposed, and she was interested. But then she won her Academy Award, and in all the uproar that followed, it

became difficult for her to decide what to do next. So I moved on. It's not as though this kind of thing doesn't happen every day when you're trying to put together a movie. Early on, I formulated a little phrase to help me get through the inevitable disappointments and hard knocks ahead. "Every person and every thing is replaceable," I told myself, "except the script." I've repeated those words to myself a thousand times since then, and they've helped; they've more or less allowed me to keep my head screwed on straight.

RP: So you lost one Academy Award actress and got another. Not such a bad trade-off!

PA: The gods were smiling on me, there's no question about it. . . . It's such a difficult, complex role—in effect two roles, many roles—and only a very gifted actress could begin to do it justice. I had worked with Mira for one day on *Blue in the Face* and had been impressed with her intelligence and talent. She has a fierce commitment to getting things right, and you can't learn that kind of attitude—it's who you are. Last spring, we both happened to wind up on the jury at Cannes. We saw each other every day for two weeks and got to know each other better, to become friends. When it finally became clear to me that Juliette wasn't going to be in the film, I didn't hesitate to ask Mira. It turned out to be my luckiest stroke, the smartest move I made. I knew she was going to be good, but I had no idea she had it in her to reach the heights she did, to touch such deep emotional chords. Mira is a very brave person, a girl with guts. And yet she's also immensely fragile. Her pores are open to the world, and she feels everything, registers everything happening in the air around her. Like a tuning fork. It's rare to find this combination of strength and sensitivity in one person. Mix that in with a keen mind and a heavy dose of natural talent, and you really have yourself something. And Mira is really something. I loved the whole adventure of working with her.

RP: What about the other actors? There are at least thirty speaking parts in the film.

PA: In many cases, I approached actors I had worked with before. Giancarlo Esposito, Jared Harris, Victor Argo, Peggy Gormley, and Harold Perrineau had all been involved with *Smoke* and *Blue in the Face*. It was a great advantage to be able to turn to them, because I knew that I could trust them—not just as actors, but as people. Gina Gershon is a close friend of one of my wife's sisters, and we've known each other for years. Mandy Patinkin had played the lead in *The Music of Chance*. Vanessa Redgrave was also a friend. And even Stockard Channing, who couldn't be in the film, did me a little favor a couple of weeks ago when she came in and recorded the phone message that Celia receives from her agent telling her she's been given the part. You might not see Stockard in the film, but you hear her voice!

RP: Do-it-yourself casting.
PA: To a small degree. All the other actors came through Heidi Levitt, who was in charge of casting. Auditions, video reels, telephone calls, nail-biting decisions.

RP: What about Willem Dafoe?
PA: That was a different story, a completely different story. Originally, Dr. Van Horn was called Dr. Singh, and the role was going to be played by Salman Rushdie. Salman is another friend, a very good friend, but also—believe it or not—a wonderfully able actor. I asked him to be in the movie just after I finished the script, and he accepted. We were both very excited about it.

RP: What were your reasons for thinking of him?
PA: First of all, as a recognizable figure, his presence would have reinforced the constant overlapping of dream and reality in the film. A man who has been forced into hiding through terrible, tragic circumstances suddenly appears as a man in charge of interrogating someone who is being held against his will. The captive made captor. It was my little way of trying to turn the tables on the world. I wanted to make a gesture in Salman's defense, to reinvent reality just enough for it to be possible to have Salman Rushdie appear in the film—not as himself, but as an imaginary character. Finally—and most important of all—I knew that he would give an excellent performance.

RP: Why didn't it happen?
PA: Fear, mostly. And bad planning on my part, bad planning all around. I've spent so much time with him, have been in so many public places with him—restaurants, theaters, the streets of New York—that I forget that most people think of him as a walking time bomb, that if they get anywhere near him, they're likely to be blown to bits. Nine years have gone by since the *fatwa* was declared, and he's still, mercifully, very much with us, but his name seems to trigger off an irrational panic in many people, and a certain percentage of the crew wanted extra security guarantees if he was going to appear in the film. The cost of doing such a thing would have been prohibitive, and eventually I had to abandon the idea. I fought tooth and nail to

make it happen, but it didn't. It was a tremendous disappointment to me. I consider it a personal defeat, a moral defeat.

RP: The film was already in production at that point, wasn't it?
PA: We were in our sixth week, and those scenes were scheduled for the eighth week—the last days of shooting in New York.

RP: It didn't leave you much time, did it?
PA: Our backs were right up against the wall. I thought the movie would have to shut down, that we wouldn't be able to finish. It was an awful period, let me tell you.

RP: So Willem stepped in—literally at the last minute.
PA: The very last minute. He received the script on a Sunday, accepted the role on Monday, and when he showed up for a rehearsal with me and Harvey the following Sunday, he had his part down cold. He knew every line perfectly. The next day, Monday, we filmed his first scene. Can you imagine? He's positively brilliant in the role, and he prepared the whole thing in a week. Willem saved the movie. He stepped in and single-handedly rescued us all. It was heroic what he did, and I'm so grateful to him, so deeply in his debt, that I can hardly think about it without getting a little weak in the knees.

RP: You learn to roll with the punches, don't you?
PA: You don't have any choice. Things are going to go wrong. You never know when, and you never know how, but you can be sure it will happen when you're least expecting it. That's why you need to have a good group of people around you, people you can depend on. I was very lucky in that regard. I had a game and cooperative cast, a valiant first assistant director—Bobby Warren—and the people I hired to head the various departments all broke their backs to make the film work. It's not just a matter of knowledge and technical skill. It comes down to character and soul, the way you live your life. Not losing your temper, keeping your sense of humor under trying circumstances, respecting the efforts of others, taking pride in your own work. All the old-fashioned virtues. I can't emphasize how important these things are on a movie set. You have to create a good environment for people to work in, to establish a sense of solidarity. If that doesn't happen, the whole thing can go to hell in about two seconds.

RP: How did you go about choosing the different creative department heads—production designer, costume designer, director of photography, and so on?

PA: I suppose it was similar to the casting. A combination of people I had worked with before, friends, and absolute strangers.

RP: Kalina Ivanov, the production designer, was a *Smoke* and *Blue in the Face* veteran.

PA: Exactly. We had remained friends in the interim, and the truth is that it never occurred to me to ask anyone else to handle the job. Kalina is more than just a designer. She's a real filmmaker, a participant in the whole process. And she also has one of the most energetic, ebullient personalities I've ever encountered—with this great big Bulgarian laugh and a wicked sense of humor. You need people like Kalina with you—people who love challenges, who never take no for an answer, who walk through fire if that's what it takes to get the job done.

RP: And Adelle Lutz, the costume designer?

PA: Known to everyone as Bonny. A friend. But also someone whose work I had admired for a long time. Costumes are an important element in *Lulu*, especially in the *Pandora's Box* sections, and I needed someone with tremendous flair and imagination, a person with original ideas. Just as important, I knew that Bonny was a grown-up and would be able to handle the pressures of the job—which were clearly going to be enormous.

RP: Why enormous?

PA: Because there were so many characters to dress and design costumes for—and so few dollars and days to do it in. A lesser person would have cracked up and jumped out the window.

RP: Surely you exaggerate.

PA: Well, maybe a little—but not as much as you might think. The whole film had to operate on a very restricted budget, but the wardrobe department got the worst of it, I think. One example stands out very vividly in my mind. In the original script, the last segment from *Pandora's Box*—the one that Izzy watches in silence on his VCR—was an elaborate wedding scene that had at least fifty actors and actresses in it. It was supposed to be from an earlier moment in the story, and therefore everyone who had died later on—Peter Shine, Candy, and Lulu—would be seen alive again, in the pink of health, happy, resurrected, with a resplendent Lulu floating among them in her wedding dress. It would have been beautiful, but the hard fact was that we couldn't afford to do it. The extras were one thing, but once Bonny toted up the costs of dressing fifty actors in evening clothes, the expense proved to be too great. At first, I thought about reducing the number of guests at the party, but as I continued to whittle down the list, this compromise began to look rather dismal. What saved the scene was the extraordinary dress that Bonny designed for Mira—the one with the peacock feathers. It was so striking, so sublime, that it allowed me to rethink the scene and do it with no guests at all. Just Lulu alone in her bedroom, right after she's climbed into the dress. It turned out well, I think, and visually it's one of the strongest scenes in the film. But it was motivated by desperation. Without Bonny, I would have been lost.

RP: And what about Alik Sakharov, the director of photography? How did you decide to work with him?

PA: Because I knew the schedule was going to be very intense and grueling, I wanted to hire someone who was rather young—a person with a lot of physical stamina, who still had something to prove to the world. I interviewed quite a few people, some of them very well known. At first, Alik wasn't even on the list. But then Kalina called me up and urged me to meet with him. She talked about his work so enthusiastically, I couldn't resist—even though I was on the verge of hiring someone else. It was a sunny day in late spring, I remember, and Alik came to my house. Not only had he read the script thoroughly, and not only did he understand it and admire it, but he had written out extensive notes about how he would go about filming it. I myself had very definite ideas about how I wanted the film to look and had already thought about how many of the scenes should be shot. For the first thirty or forty minutes, I didn't say much. When you're interviewing someone, it's always more important to hear what the other person has to say. So I asked Alik how he would approach this scene, and then that scene, and then this other scene, and after awhile it was as if I were listening to my own thoughts. Shot for shot, look for look, he had almost the same idea about the film that I did.

RP: What kinds of preparations did you and Alik make before filming began?

PA: We worked for weeks, just the two of us, all through the late summer and early fall, talking through every scene again and again, making up shot lists, analyzing the story in visual terms. That was the foundation of the film. Everything grew from those early conversations. Not only did we develop a plan that we both believed in, but we learned to trust each other, to depend on each other's insights and judgments. By the time filming began, we were comrades, partners in a single enterprise. We worked together in a state of tremendous harmony, and I can't tell you how important that was to me on the set. Alik was a rock of dependability, and I could always count on him, could always get my ideas through to him. He's a man of great dignity and depth of soul, and he has the endurance of a marathon runner. We were on the set for at least twelve hours every day, would go to the Technicolor lab in midtown for dailies every night, and often had to squeeze in time to scout new locations before, between, or after the day's work. And from start to finish, Alik kept going at full tilt. He was my closest collaborator on the film, the one person who was with me every step of the way.

RP: What was it like working with the actors?

PA: That's the fun part, the best part of the job. Four years ago, when Wayne [Wang] and I started rehearsing for *Smoke*, I discovered that I felt naturally connected to actors, that I had an innate sympathy for what they do. A startling discovery to make so late in life, no? But when you stop and think about it, there's a definite affinity between acting and writing novels. In both cases, the object of the work is to bring imaginary beings to life, to take something that doesn't exist and make it real, make it believable. A writer does it with his pen, and an actor does it with his body, but they're both trying to achieve the same thing. In writing my books, I always have the feeling that I'm inside my characters, that I inhabit them, that I actually become them. Actors feel the same way about what they do, and because of that I don't have any trouble understanding what they say to me. Nor do they seem to have any trouble understanding what I say to them.

RP: As a director, you're part of a collaborative process. Did you miss the creative control you have as a writer?

PA: When I was a kid, I was very involved in sports. I played on a lot of teams—baseball teams, basketball teams, football teams—and until I was well into high school, it was probably the biggest thing in my life. Then I grew up, and for the next twenty-five years or so I spent most of my time alone, sitting in a room with a pen in my hand. You have to enjoy being alone to do that, and I do enjoy being alone, but that doesn't mean I don't enjoy working with other people, too. When I began collaborating with Wayne on our two movies, it brought back memories of playing on those sports teams as a kid, and I realized that I had missed it, that I was glad to be participating in a group effort again. Yes, as a writer you have total control over what you're doing, and as a filmmaker you don't. But that's like saying oranges taste like oranges, and apples taste like apples. The two experiences are entirely different. When you write a book, you have all the time in the world. If you make a mistake, nobody sees you make it. You can just cross out the sentence and start over again. You can throw out a week's work, a month's work, and nobody cares. On a film set, you don't have that luxury. It's do or die every day. You have to accomplish your work on time, and you don't get a second chance. At least not with a tightly budgeted film like ours. So, needless to say, things can get pretty nerve-racking at times. But that doesn't mean they aren't enjoyable. When things go well, when everyone is doing his or her job the way it's supposed to be done and you pull off the thing you've set out to do, it becomes a beautiful experience, a deeply satisfying thing. I think that's why people get addicted to working in movies—the grips, the gaffers, the camera team, the prop men, the sound people, everyone. They work terribly hard, the hours are long, and no one gets rich, but every day is different from the day before. That's what keeps them at it: the adventure of it, the uncertainty, the fact that no one knows what's going to happen next.

RP: Did you find that the imaginative process involved in directing differs significantly from the one involved in writing?
PA: Not as much as you might think. The outward circumstances are utterly different, of course—one person sitting alone in a room as opposed to dozens of people on a noisy set—but at bottom you're trying to accomplish the same thing: to tell a story. *Lulu* was my script; it wasn't as if I was directing someone else's work. And I tried to use all the tools at my disposal to tell that story as well as I could: the actors, the camera, the lights, the locations, the sets, the costumes, and so on. Those elements create the syntax of the story. There were times when I thought the camera is the ink, the lighting setups are punctuation marks, the props are adjectives, the actors' gestures are verbs. Very strange. But standing there on the set every day with the crew, I somehow felt that they were creating the story with me—with me and for me. It was as if they were all inside my head with me.

RP: Earlier, you talked about things going wrong on the set. Can you give me an example of what you meant?
PA: I could give you dozens of examples. Some big, some small. A lighting

setup that short-circuited at the worst possible moment. A prop gun that kept misfiring. A dress that tore. All the usual mishaps. Once, I even ruined a take myself by laughing too hard. Jared Harris was doing something so funny, I just couldn't control myself any more. . . . The incident I learned the most from, though, would have to be something that happened in the second or third week of shooting. During preproduction, I had had several meetings with Jeff Mazzola, the prop master, and we had made a thorough list of all the things that would have to be on hand for every scene in the film. Jeff was an integral part of what we did every day, and beyond being a pleasant person to be around, he brought a lot of intelligence and enthusiasm to his work. He was the one who helped me design the stone that Izzy finds in the briefcase. He was the one who worked out the pie-in-the-face scene with me—and actually threw the pie at Mira. He was the one who drove the ambulance in the last scene. I mention these things so you'll have an idea of how closely we worked together. Anyway, for the scene in which Celia says good-bye to Izzy and drives off to the airport, we needed a black town car. I had specifically told Jeff that I wanted a car that had a back window that went all the way down—so that Celia would be able to lean out and blow Izzy a kiss as the car drove away. Most cars these days have windows that go only halfway down, and Jeff had given precise instructions to the car rental place that we needed an older-model car. So, the day arrives when we're supposed to shoot the scene, and the car shows up on the set. There was an establishing shot we had to do—the car parked in front of Celia's building—and since Harvey and Mira were still in the hair-and-makeup trailer getting ready for their first scene together, I figured we could knock off the establishing shot first, which would help us save time for more important things later in the day. Just to make sure, though, I told Jeff that we should check to see if the window went all the way down. No point in doing the shot if we had the wrong car, was there? And lo and behold, the window went only halfway down. I was furious. We were working on a very tight schedule, and I knew this little blunder was going to cost us precious time and money. What could I do? I couldn't very well turn on Jeff and start blaming him. It wasn't his fault. He had ordered the right car, and I wasn't about to criticize him for not doing his job. He *had* done his job. But still, you feel this anger surging up inside you, this horrible sense of frustration. Fortunately, Jeff was just as angry as I was. Even angrier, probably. He's so conscientious about his work, and he treated this screw-up as an insult to his professional pride. That's when I learned an important lesson about being a director. You can actually live your anger through other people. Jeff called up the car rental place, and as I stood there next to him, listening to him scream and curse at the man responsible for the mistake, I began to feel much better. Jeff's anger was my anger, and because he could express it for me, I was able to stay calm. At least on the outside.

RP: Of all the hundreds of things that happened on the set, what moment are you proudest of?

PA: That's hard to say. In general, I'm proud of everything we did, of everyone's work. Even when we made mistakes, we always managed to fix them—so there's really nothing I look back on with any deep regret. But the proudest moment, I don't know. There's one *happy* moment that jumps out at me, however. I don't know why I think of this one now, but there it is. The pie-in-the-face scene. Maybe because I just mentioned it a few minutes ago. It's such a small part of the film, but it took a lot of careful preparation to get it right, and Mira was a great sport about it. We all had fun doing those four little video scenes. The horror movie, the pie-in-the-face, the nun praying over the dying child, and the hooker bit with Lou Reed in the bar. I gave Mira a different name for each of these parts, just to keep things amusing. The nun, I remember, was Sister Mira of the Perpetual Performance. We probably had such a good time with these things because all the other work we did was so intense, so demanding, and these little clips gave us all a chance to relax a little, to play in a different key. Not just Mira and the other actors, but the crew as well. Anyway, I was very keen to do a pie-in-the-face gag. It's a lost art, an ancient turn that's vanished from films, and no one knows how to do it anymore. I asked a couple of older directors for advice, but they couldn't help me. "Just make it funny," one of them said. Yes, but how? So I had to sit down and figure it out for myself. The problem was that I didn't have any room for flubs. It had to be done perfectly on the first take. Otherwise, we would have needed three or four hours to set up the shot again, and we didn't have that kind of time to spend on such a small thing. If we got it wrong, the whole set would have to be redone, Mira's hair and makeup would have to be redone, and we couldn't afford to do that. The only solution was to devise a fail-proof technique.

RP: What did you use for the cream?

PA: Reddi Wip. We experimented with shaving cream, but it wasn't as good. Once everything was prepared and we'd gone through a couple of dry runs, I turned on some crazy Raymond Scott music to get everyone in the mood, and then I started giving instructions to Mira and David Byrne, who played the escort. The whole crew was watching anxiously, hoping it would work, and when it did, the whole place erupted in wild cheers and laughter. It was a wonderful moment. Not just for me, but for all of us. I remember saying to myself, "Good grief, I think I'm actually getting the hang of this job."

RP: Is it a job you'd like to do again?
PA: This is where we came in, isn't it?

RP: Not really. It's three years later, and you've just finished directing a film. Would you like to do it again?
PA: All things being equal, yes. But things are rarely equal, so I'm not going to speculate about the future anymore. The only thing I can say with any certainty is that I've poured myself into making *this* film, and I'm glad I had the chance to do it. It's been a big experience for me, and I'm never going to forget it.

Off the Page: Paul Auster

Carole Burns/2003

Reproduced by permission of washintonpost.com.

Carole Burns: Hello, booklovers. Welcome to "Off the Page" and welcome to Paul Auster, whose latest novel, *Oracle Night*, was just released (and is slated to be reviewed by Michael Dirda in *Book World* this Sunday). We have a geographically diverse group of questioners today, and let's get to them.

Harrisburg, Pa.: It is great to see writing with skillful comedic touches. That is a difficult type of writing to do well. How do you approach adding humor to your work? Do you have a conscious plan in developing humor in your writing, or do you, say, simply write what you yourself find funny?
Paul Auster: Life is both funny and not funny. It has its tragic moments and its hilarious moments. I try in my work to embrace all aspects of what it means to be alive, and humor is an important part of that. So even in some of my grimmest works, there have been comic touches. There have to be, because that's the way we're built as human beings, and often when we're in dark circumstances we survive them by cracking jokes.

Kassel, Germany: First I'd like to thank you for making me more aware of life by writing unforgettable novels like *City of Glass* and *Oracle Night*. Strange things keep happening to me while reading your novels. Last summer, for example, I was standing under the Eiffel Tower in Paris when a huge screw fell down just some feet away from me. It could have killed me, just like the gargoyle almost did to Nick in *Oracle Night*. Well, I didn't start a new life after that, but it kind of changed my life. So, do you think it could be that books have an equally mysterious influence on people like the blue notebook?
Paul Auster: I think it can happen. I tend not to be a mystic. I tend not to believe in magic. But it's undeniable that weird things happen in the world

all the time, and one has the feeling that books can sometimes provoke these events. The story that is told by Trause to Sidney toward the end of the novel, *Oracle Night*, is a true story. I didn't put in the name of the writer, but the facts as I know them are very, very close to what's in the novel. A man wrote a narrative poem about a drowning child, and not long after the book was published, his own child drowned. Sidney responds by saying that it's just a coincidence, a terrible, terrible coincidence. At the same time, in a state of grief and wretchedness, it's perfectly understandable that the writer would make a connection between the book and the death of his child.

Carole Burns: It struck me when reading *Oracle Night* that it might not be the notebook that disrupts Sidney Orr's life, but the act of writing in it. Is writing a dangerous activity?

Paul Auster: It can be. It can be very bad for one's mental health. It looks innocent enough from the outside, but when a man or a woman is living every day in an imaginary world, it's often difficult to separate your own reality from the imaginary reality you're writing about. But no, I don't really believe that the book has any magic property. It's simply that Sidney at times believes that it does. But of course, everything that's happening in the book is very subjective. Sidney is telling the story of his life and also his inner life. And that life is in turmoil during the days that he's writing about in 1982.

Helsingborg, Sweden: Dear Mr. Auster,

I'm an American living in Sweden and I work as a teacher, writer, and translator. Do you have any suggestions for how to maintain the writer's voice when translating, especially if the writer has a significantly different writing style than you do? Also, do you think a translator of literary works must also be a creative writer himself?

Thank you very much for your time and consideration. And thank you, also, for your wonderful contributions to literature.

Paul Auster: Thank you for saying such nice things. Having translated myself for many years, I feel that your primary job is to give yourself up to the writer you're translating. You have to try to become that person, in a way. To think like that person. To write like that person. It's a creative act, almost like embodying a role in a play. So your particular style as a writer has nothing to do with what your style will be as a translator, because you're serving the text written by the other person.

You don't have to be a creative writer to be a translator, because translation itself is a creative act. The very fact that you're doing it makes you a creative writer—you are by definition a creative writer, even though the work is not originally yours. Bringing it into another language requires all the skill, all the poetic gifts, that any novelist or poet needs to write his work. In fact, some of the very best translators only translate.

Sacramento, CA: In a recent chat Martin Amis said that the humor novel would be dead in twenty years because there is a butt to every joke and the culture just won't stand for that much longer. On the other hand, Aristophanes has been packing them in for several years. Do you foresee today's comedy becoming as dated as, say, Tex Avery cartoons are now?
Paul Auster: Humor is eternal. Comedy is eternal. And no matter what the circumstances of a particular moment, there are always going to be people making jokes about what is happening. Styles of humor change over the years, but to say that humor in general would die would be like saying the human race is going to die.

Tel-Aviv, Israel: Fate and coincidence play a large role in your books. Is it something that derives from your personal life?
Paul Auster: In my nonfiction I've recorded some of the wilder, more unsettling coincidences that have occurred in my own life. At times in my fiction, similar kinds of events take place. But I don't believe in the idea of fate. I don't believe that our destinies are mapped out in advance. We create our lives every day, and they're constantly shifting, and each one of us, I think, has the potential to live many different lives. And circumstances, coincidence, accidents and choice and desire and will all play their part in the paths we take. But I don't believe that these paths are preordained. Life would be terrible if we thought that were true.

Fresno, Calif.: I noticed a reference to Wittgenstein in *The Book of Illusions*, where Zimmer remarks that Wittgenstein is his sort of thinker, or words to that effect. While one should not assume that Zimmer=Auster, do you draw anything from Wittgenstein's work? If so, the earlier or the later? Many thanks.
Paul Auster: As the young student at Columbia in the '60s, I read Wittgenstein's work very carefully and very avidly. I didn't always fully understand it. But I was always intrigued and inspired by it. Definitely the later work interests me more than the early work, particularly the *Philosophical Investigations*.

NYC: I was wondering if you'd read fellow Brooklynite Jonathan Lethem's new novel *Fortress of Solitude.* It basically lives off of the author's experiences growing up in the borough, and I was curious as to how being a Brooklynite affects your writing.

Paul Auster: I wrote before I ever moved to Brooklyn, and I've continued to write ever since I've been here, which is now almost twenty-four years. It's my place. It's the little spot on earth that I inhabit. And because I'm surrounded by it every day, it's only natural that I'd want to write about it at times, which I've done. But it's not the only subject that interests me.

Lenexa, Kan.: Mr. Auster: I've read four of your novels but so far only reviews of your latest. I especially enjoyed *The Music of Chance*—a bad poker night and its aftermath. I really enjoyed Durning and Walsh in the movie version. I'm also a big fan of the film *Smoke.*

Two questions: Are there any plans to film *Vertigo*? Are you a fan of Millhauser's writing? Thanks.

Paul Auster: There are no plans to make a film out of *Mr. Vertigo.* And Millhauser is a writer I admire—I've read several of his books and I've liked them all.

Washington, D.C.: Love your work. Just actually finished reading The New York Trilogy. I was wondering, who are some of the authors that you feel have most influenced your writing? Also, who are some of your favorite authors writing fiction these days? Thanks.

Paul Auster: The list is too long to enumerate today, but I'll give a few names. Montaigne, Shakespeare, Cervantes, Dickens, Dostoyevsky, Tolstoy, Hawthorne, Melville, Thoreau, Kafka, Beckett, Joyce, Céline, Fitzgerald, Faulkner, etc.

These days, in the United States, I'm very fond of Don DeLillo's work. Robert Coover, García Márquez, Kundera.

Toronto, Ontario: Thank you for *Oracle Night*—I just read it and enjoyed it very much.

Do you have any plans to visit Toronto in the near future? We would very much like to see you here, but I haven't heard about any planned appearances . . .

Paul Auster: I'm not going to Toronto any time soon, but I will be in Montreal on March 31. I'm getting some kind of prize up there, at a festival called

Blue Metropolis. Every year they give a literary Grand Prix and this year they're giving it to me.

Other travels: In May I'm going to a few places in Europe—London and Berlin and Amsterdam. And then in the summer, Brazil, for the first time.

I'm reading in Washington on January 13 (I think at Politics and Prose) and later in January I'm reading in Boston. I've done the New York reading—I read the entire contents of *Oracle Night* over two nights at the Paula Cooper Gallery in Chelsea, in the middle of the blizzard. It was an exhausting but invigorating experience for everyone, myself included.

Tel-Aviv, Israel: Mr. Auster, I have read almost all your books in translation to Hebrew although I am capable of reading them in English. Is it, in your opinion as a both writer and translator, possible for a translation to be superior to the original?

Paul Auster: Yes, it's possible, but only when the original work is badly written. If you can read in English, I think you'll have a more enjoyable experience tackling the book in the original.

San Francisco, CA: Mr. Auster—

First off, let me say that *The Book of Illusions* and *Oracle Night* are two of the most amazing books I have ever read. Thank you for them! As a young reader, I became aware of you and your writing when Don DeLillo dedicated *Cosmopolis* to you . . . I figured if my all-time favorite author liked you, I should check you out! Boy, am I glad I did.

So, how does it feel to have a book by DeLillo dedicated to you? Cheers!

Paul Auster: I was extremely touched. Don is a very close friend of mine, but I didn't know that he was dedicating the book to me until I received a copy of the bound galleys. When I get a new book in my hands, I usually flip through it at random. So I didn't see the dedication page until I'd been looking at the book for a few minutes, which somehow made it a double shock. And all the more moving because in 1992, I dedicated one of my novels, *Leviathan*, to Don.

Carole Burns: Your work is so strong on story, and yet they are also novels of ideas. Which aspect of your novels comes to you first? How do the ideas and the stories evolve?

Paul Auster: It's always the story. The story first and last. And the stories come to me out of my unconscious. I never look for them. They find me. And I'm not consciously writing about so-called ideas, but the thoughts and ideas of the characters become crucial to the telling of the story. Sometimes you start with something, and then the more you explore it, the more ramifications you discover in a particular image or event. But I rarely know exactly what I'm doing. I don't work from a prearranged outline. I have a general sense of the shape of the story, who the characters are, and a sense of the beginning, the middle, and the end, and yet once I start to write, things begin to change, and I've never written a book that ended up the way I thought it would be when I started. For me, I find the book in the process of writing it. Which makes it a great adventure. If it's all mapped out in advance, there's nothing to discover. It's happened to me that I've thought of stories so much and for such a long time that by the time I sit down to try to write them, they're already dead, and I no longer want to write them, because I know them too well. It's the not knowing that makes it exciting.

Williamsburg, Va.: I selected *The Book of Illusions* for a local book group, and got a wide variety of responses to it—I loved it, but was in the distinct minority. If you had the chance to talk to a new Auster reader and tell them why they should read you, what would you say?

Paul Auster: I would never tell anyone to read my books. It's not my job to do that. But all my life as a writer, I've had very disparate responses, contradictory responses, to the work I do. Some people love it, and other people simply despise it. I get the best reviews and the worst reviews of any writer I know, and there's nothing, nothing in the world I can do about it. I would of course prefer that everyone love what I do, but I've been doing this work long enough to know that that's never going to happen. But I'm very happy that you enjoyed it.

Alex, VA: Thanks for doing this chat. Is this sort of "publicity" fun or torture? Would you rather just be able to write and stay locked away somewhere? I am so intrigued by the descriptions of your work. I would not have heard about your books without this. Thanks for your time.

Paul Auster: I would prefer not to say a word to anybody. But I do feel an obligation to my publisher to cooperate on a small scale in helping to present the book to the public. But I try to keep it to the absolute minimum.

Kassel, Germany: Dear Mr. Auster, I guess you read a lot while not writing. What is the last novel you read? Any recommendations?

Would you consider yourself as a postmodernist writer? What's your opinion about comparisons between you and authors like Thomas Pynchon and John Barth?

Paul Auster: The last novel I read is the new translation into English of *Don Quixote*, by Edith Grossman, which I enjoyed very much. *Don Quixote* is probably my favorite novel of all time, and I've read it at least five times.

As for the postmodern question, it's a term that doesn't mean anything to me. People keep using it, but I truly don't understand what it means. And I don't put labels on what I do. If other people want to do that, that's their privilege, but I'm not interested in looking at myself from the outside.

I admire both Pynchon and Barth, but I don't feel my work has much to do with theirs.

Carole Burns: Thanks so much, Paul, for coming online today, and to everyone from around the world who submitted questions. Look for *Book World's* review of *Oracle Night* this weekend.

Paul Auster: The Art of Fiction

Michael Wood/2003

Reproduced from *The Paris Review Interviews IV* (Macmillan, 2009), pp. 308–34.

INTERVIEWER: Let's start by talking about the way you work. About how you write.

PAUL AUSTER: I've always written by hand. Mostly with a fountain pen, but sometimes with a pencil—especially for corrections. If I could write directly on a typewriter or a computer, I would do it. But keyboards have always intimidated me. I've never been able to think clearly with my fingers in that position. A pen is a much more primitive instrument. You feel that the words are coming out of your body and then you dig the words into the page. Writing has always had that tactile quality for me. It's a physical experience.

INTERVIEWER: And you write in notebooks. Not legal pads or loose sheets of paper.

AUSTER": Yes, always in notebooks. And I have a particular fetish for notebooks with quadrille lines—the little squares. I think of the notebook as a house for words, as a secret place for thought and self-examination. I'm not just interested in the results of writing, but in the process, the act of putting words on a page. Don't ask me why. It might have something to do with an early confusion on my part, an ignorance about the nature of fiction. As a young person, I would always ask myself, Where are the words coming from? Who's saying this? The third-person narrative voice in the traditional novel is a strange device. We're used to it now, we accept it, we don't question it anymore. But when you stop and think about it, there's an eerie, disembodied quality to that voice. It seems to come from nowhere, and I found that disturbing. I was always drawn to books that doubled back on themselves, that brought you into the world of the book, even as the book was taking you into the world. The manuscript as hero, so to speak.

Wuthering Heights is that kind of novel. *The Scarlet Letter* is another. The frames are fictitious, of course, but they give a groundedness and credibility to the stories that other novels didn't have for me. They posit the work as an illusion—which more traditional forms of narrative don't—and once you accept the "unreality" of the enterprise, it paradoxically enhances the truth of the story. The words aren't written in stone by an invisible author-god. They represent the efforts of a flesh-and-blood human being and this is very compelling. The reader becomes a participant in the unfolding of the story—not just a detached observer.

INTERVIEWER: But what about the famous Olympia typewriter? We know quite a bit about that machine—last year you published a wonderful book with the painter Sam Messer, *The Story of My Typewriter*.
AUSTER: I've owned that typewriter since 1974—more than half my life now. I bought it secondhand from a college friend, and at this point it must be about forty years old. It's a relic from another age, but it's still in good condition. It's never broken down. All I have to do is change ribbons every once in a while. But I'm living in fear that a day will come when there won't be any ribbons left to buy, and I'll have to go digital and join the twenty-first century.

INTERVIEWER: A great Paul Auster story. The day when you go out to buy that last ribbon.
AUSTER: I've made some preparations. I've stocked up. I think I have about sixty or seventy ribbons in my room. I'll probably stick with that typewriter till the end, although I've been sorely tempted to give it up at times. It's cumbersome and inconvenient, but it also protects me against laziness.

INTERVIEWER: How so?
AUSTER: Because the typewriter forces me to start all over again once I'm finished. With a computer, you make your changes on the screen and then you print out a clean copy. With a typewriter, you can't get a clean manuscript unless you start again from scratch. It's an incredibly tedious process. You've finished your book, and now you have to spend several weeks engaged in the purely mechanical job of transcribing what you've already written. It's bad for your neck, bad for your back, and even if you can type twenty or thirty pages a day, the finished pages pile up with excruciating slowness. That's the moment when I always wish I'd switched to a computer, and yet every time I push myself through this final stage of a book, I wind

up discovering how essential it is. Typing allows me to experience the book in a new way, to plunge into the flow of the narrative and feel how it functions as a whole. I call it "reading with my fingers," and it's amazing how many errors your fingers will find that your eyes never noticed. Repetitions, awkward constructions, choppy rhythms. It never fails. I think I'm finished with the book, and then I begin to type it up and I realize there's more work to be done.

INTERVIEWER: When did you first realize you wanted to be a writer?
AUSTER: About a year after I understood that I wasn't going to be a major league baseball player. Until I was about sixteen, baseball was probably the most important thing in my life.

INTERVIEWER: How good were you?
AUSTER: It's hard to say. If I'd stuck with it, I might have made it to the low minor leagues. I could hit well, with occasional bursts of power, but I wasn't a very fast runner. At third base, which was the position I usually played, I had quick reflexes and a strong arm—but my throws were often wild.

In some mysterious way, baseball provided me with an opening onto the world, a chance to find out who I was. As a small child, I wasn't very well. I had all kinds of physical ailments, and I spent more time sitting in doctors' offices with my mother than running around outdoors with my friends. It wasn't until I was four or five that I was strong enough to participate in sports. And when I was, I threw myself into it with a passion—as if making up for lost time. Playing baseball taught me how to live with other people, to understand that I might actually be able to accomplish something if I put my mind to it. But beyond my own little personal experiences, there's the beauty of the game itself. It's an unending source of pleasure.

INTERVIEWER: Baseball to writing is an unusual transition—in part because writing is such a solitary enterprise.
AUSTER: I played baseball in the spring and summer, but I read books all year long. It was an early obsession, and it only intensified as I got older. I can't imagine anyone becoming a writer who wasn't a voracious reader as an adolescent. A true reader understands that books are a world unto themselves—and that that world is richer and more interesting than any one we've traveled in before. I think that's what turns young men and women into writers—the happiness you discover living in books. You haven't been

around long enough to have much to write about yet, but a moment comes when you realize that's what you were born to do.

INTERVIEWER: What about early influences? Who were the writers you were reading in high school?

AUSTER: Americans, mostly . . . the usual suspects. Fitzgerald, Hemingway, Faulkner, Dos Passos, Salinger. By my junior year, though, I began discovering the Europeans—mostly the Russians and the French. Tolstoy, Dostoyevsky, Turgenev, Camus, and Gide. But also Joyce and Mann. Especially Joyce. When I was eighteen, he towered over everyone else for me.

INTERVIEWER: Did he have the biggest impact on you?

AUSTER: For a while, yes. But at one time or another, I tried to write like each one of the novelists I was reading. Everything influences you when you're young, and you keep changing your ideas every few months. It's a bit like trying on new hats. You don't have a style of your own yet, so you unconsciously imitate the writers you admire.

Dozens of writers are inside me, but I don't think my work sounds or feels like anyone else's. I'm not writing their books. I'm writing my own.

INTERVIEWER: You also have a longstanding interest in Hawthorne, don't you?

AUSTER: Of all writers from the past, he's the one I feel closest to, the one who talks most deeply to me. There's something about his imagination that seems to resonate with mine, and I'm continually going back to him, continually learning from him. He's a writer who isn't afraid of ideas, and yet he's also a master psychologist, a profound reader of the human soul. His fiction was utterly revolutionary, and nothing like it had been seen in America before. I know that Hemingway said that all American literature came out of *Huck Finn*, but I don't agree. It began with *The Scarlet Letter*.

But there's more to Hawthorne than just his stories and novels. I'm equally attached to his notebooks, which contain some of his strongest, most brilliant prose. The diary he kept about taking care of his five-year-old son for three weeks in 1851 is a self-contained work. It can stand on its own, and it's so charming, so funny in its deadpan way, that it gives us an entirely new picture of Hawthorne. He wasn't the gloomy, tormented figure most people think he was. Or not only that. He was a loving father and husband, a man who liked a good cigar and a glass or two of whiskey, and he was playful, generous, and warmhearted. Exceedingly shy, yes, but someone who enjoyed the simple pleasures of the world.

INTERVIEWER: You've worked in a number of different genres. Not only poetry and fiction, but also screenplays, autobiography, criticism, and translation. Do they feel like very different activities to you, or are they all somehow connected?

AUSTER: More connected than not, but with important differences as well. And also—this needs to be taken into account, too, I think—there's the question of time, my so-called inner evolution. I haven't done any translating or critical writing in many years. Those were preoccupations that absorbed me when I was young, roughly from my late teens to my late twenties. Both were about discovering other writers, about learning how to become a writer myself. My literary apprenticeship, if you will. I've taken a few stabs at translation and criticism since then, but nothing much to speak of. And the last poem I wrote was in 1979.

INTERVIEWER: What happened? Why did you give it up?

AUSTER: I ran into a wall. For ten years, I concentrated the bulk of my energies on poetry, and then I realized that I'd written myself out, that I was stuck. It was a dark moment for me. I thought I was finished as a writer.

INTERVIEWER: You died as a poet, but eventually you were reborn as a novelist. How do you think this transformation came about?

AUSTER: I think it happened at the moment when I understood that I didn't care anymore, when I stopped caring about making "Literature." I know it sounds strange, but from that point on writing became a different kind of experience for me, and when I finally got going again after wallowing in the doldrums for about a year, the words came out as prose. The only thing that mattered was saying the thing that needed to be said. Without regard to preestablished conventions, without worrying about what it sounded like. That was the late seventies, and I've continued working in that spirit ever since.

INTERVIEWER: Your first prose book was a work of nonfiction, *The Invention of Solitude*. After that, you wrote the three novels of The New York Trilogy. Can you pinpoint the difference between writing in the two forms?

AUSTER: The effort is the same. The need to get the sentences right is the same. But a work of the imagination allows you a lot more freedom and maneuverability than a work of nonfiction does. On the other hand, that freedom can often be quite scary. What comes next? How do I know the next sentence I write isn't going to lead me off the edge of a cliff? With an autobiographical work, you know the story in advance, and your primary obligation is to tell the truth. But that doesn't make the job any easier. For the epigraph of the first part of *The Invention of Solitude*, I used a sentence from Heraclitus—in Guy Davenport's unorthodox but elegant translation: "In searching out the truth be ready for the unexpected, for it is difficult to find and puzzling when you find it." In the end, writing is writing. *The Invention of Solitude* might not be a novel, but I think it explores many of the same questions I've tackled in my fiction. In some sense, it's the foundation of all my work.

INTERVIEWER: And what about your screenplays—*Smoke*, *Blue in the Face*, and *Lulu on the Bridge*? How does screenwriting differ from writing novels?

AUSTER: In every way—except for one crucial similarity: You're trying to tell a story. But the means at your disposal are utterly dissimilar. Novels are pure narration; screenplays resemble theater, and as with all dramatic writing, the only words that count are in the dialogue. As it happens, my novels generally don't have much dialogue, and so in order to work in film, I had to learn a completely new way of writing, to teach myself how to think in images and how to put words in the mouths of living human beings.

Screenwriting is a more restricted form than novel-writing. It has its strengths and weaknesses, the things it can do and the things it can't do. The question of time, for example, works differently in books and films. In a novel, you can collapse a long stretch of time into a single sentence: "Every morning for twenty years, I walked down to the corner newsstand and bought a copy of the *Daily Bugle.*" It's impossible to do that in a film. You can show a man walking down the street to buy a newspaper on one particular day, but not every day for twenty years. Films take place in the present. Even when you use flashbacks, the past is always rendered as another incarnation of the present.

INTERVIEWER: There's a phrase in *The Invention of Solitude* I've always liked: "The anecdote as a form of knowledge." That strikes me as the guiding spirit behind the pieces in *The Red Notebook*.

AUSTER: I would agree. I look at those stories as a kind of *ars poetica*—but without theory, without any philosophical baggage. So many strange things have happened to me in my life, so many unexpected and improbable events, I'm no longer certain that I know what reality is anymore. All I can do is talk about the mechanics of reality, to gather evidence about what goes on in the world and try to record it as faithfully as I can. I've used that approach in my novels. It's not a method so much as an act of faith: to present things as they really happen, not as they're supposed to happen or as we'd like them to happen. Novels are fictions, of course, and therefore they tell lies (in the strictest sense of the term), but through those lies every novelist attempts to tell the truth about the world. Taken together, the little stories in *The Red Notebook* present a kind of position paper on how I see the world. The bare-bones truth about the unpredictability of experience. There's not a shred of the imaginary in them. There can't be. You make a pact with yourself to tell the truth, and you'd rather cut off your right arm than break that promise. Interestingly enough, the literary model I had in mind when I wrote those pieces was the joke. The joke is the purest, most essential form of storytelling. Every word has to count.

INTERVIEWER: There's a story in *The Red Notebook* about something that happened when you were fourteen years old. You and a group of boys went out on a hike in the woods, and you were caught in a terrible electric storm. The boy next to you was struck by lightning and killed.
AUSTER: That incident changed my life, there's no question about it. One moment the boy was alive and the next moment he was dead. I was only inches away from him. It was my first experience with random death, with the bewildering instability of things. You think you're standing on solid ground, and an instant later the ground opens under your feet and you vanish.

INTERVIEWER: Tell me about the National Story Project you did with NPR. As I understand it, they liked your voice and wanted to find a way to have you on the air.
AUSTER: It must have something to do with all the cigars I've smoked over the years. That rasping rumble in the throat, the clogged-up bronchia, the diminished lung power. I've heard the results on tape. I sound like a piece of sandpaper scraping over a dry roof shingle.

INTERVIEWER: Your wife, Siri Hustvedt, suggested that the listeners send in their own stories, which you would select and read on the air.
AUSTER: I thought it was a brilliant idea. NPR has millions of listeners around the country. If enough contributions came in, I felt we would be able to form a little museum of American reality. People were free to write about anything they wanted. Big things and little things, comic things and tragic

things. The only rules were that the pieces had to be short—no more than two or three pages—and they had to be true.

INTERVIEWER: But why would you want to take on such an enormous job? In the space of one year, you wound up reading over four thousand stories.
AUSTER: I think I had several motives. The most important one was curiosity. I wanted to find out if other people had lived through the same sorts of experiences that I had. Was I some kind of freak or was reality truly as strange and incomprehensible as I thought it was? With such a large reservoir of possibilities to draw from, the project could take on the dimensions of a genuine philosophical experiment.

INTERVIEWER: And what were the results?
AUSTER: I'm happy to report that I'm not alone. It's a madhouse out there.

INTERVIEWER: Did anything else draw you to this project in particular?
AUSTER: I've spent most of my adult life sitting alone in a room, writing books. I'm perfectly happy there, but when I got involved in film work in the mid-nineties, I rediscovered the pleasures of working with other people. It probably goes back to having played on so many sports teams as a kid. I liked being part of a small group, a group with a purpose, in which each person contributes to a common goal. Winning a basketball game or making a film—there's really very little difference. That was probably the best part of working in the movies for me. The sense of solidarity, the jokes we told each other, the friendships I made. By 1999, however, my movie adventures had pretty much come to an end. I was back in my hole again writing novels, not seeing anyone for weeks at a stretch. I think that's why Siri made her suggestion. Not just because it was a good idea, but because she thought I'd enjoy working on something that involved other people. She was right. I did enjoy it.

INTERVIEWER: Didn't it take up a lot of time?
AUSTER: Not enough to interfere with my other work. The stories came in slowly and steadily, and as long as I kept up with the submissions, it wasn't so bad. Preparing the broadcasts usually took a day or two, but that was only once a month.

INTERVIEWER: Did you feel you were performing a public service?

AUSTER: To some degree, I suppose I did, it was an opportunity to engage in guerilla warfare against the monster.

INTERVIEWER: The monster?

AUSTER: The "entertainment-industrial complex," as the art critic Robert Hughes once put it. The media presents us with little else but celebrities, gossip, and scandal, and the way we depict ourselves on television and in the movies has become so distorted, so debased, that real life has been forgotten. What we're given are violent shocks and dimwitted escapist fantasies, and the driving force behind it all is money. People are treated like morons. They're not human beings anymore, they're consumers, suckers to be manipulated into wanting things they don't need. Call it capitalism triumphant. Call it the free-market economy. Whatever it is, there's very little room in it for representations of actual American life.

INTERVIEWER: And you thought the National Story Project could change all that?

AUSTER: No, of course not. But at least I tried to make a little dent in the system. By giving so-called ordinary people a chance to share their stories with an audience, I wanted to prove that there's no such thing as an ordinary person. We all have intense inner lives, we all burn with ferocious passions, we've all lived through memorable experiences of one kind or another.

INTERVIEWER: In *City of Glass*, you use yourself as a character in the story. Do you often draw on autobiographical material for your novels?

AUSTER: To some extent, but far less than you might think. After *City of Glass*, there was *Ghosts*. Other than announcing that the story begins on February 3, 1947—the day I was born—there are no personal references in it. In *The Locked Room*, however, several incidents come directly from my own life. Ivan Wyschnegradsky, the old Russian composer who befriends Fanshawe in Paris, was a real person. I met him when he was eighty and saw quite a lot of him when I lived in Paris in the early seventies. The business about giving Ivan the refrigerator actually happened to me—in the same way it happens to Fanshawe. The same holds for the slapstick scene in which he delivers the captain breakfast on the oil tanker—inching along the bridge in a seventy-mile-an-hour gale and struggling to hold onto the tray. It was the one time in my life I truly felt I was in a Buster Keaton movie. And then there's the crazy story the narrator tells about working for the U.S. Census

Bureau in Harlem in 1970. Word for word, that episode is an exact account of my own experience.

INTERVIEWER: You really invented fictitious people and filed their names with the federal government?
AUSTER: I confess. I hope the statute of limitations has run out by now or I might wind up in jail for doing this interview. In my own defense, I have to add that the supervisor encouraged this practice—for the same reason he gives in the novel. "Just because a door doesn't open when you knock on it doesn't mean that nobody's there. You've got to use your imagination, my friend. After all, we don't want the government to be unhappy, do we?"

INTERVIEWER: What about the novels after the Trilogy? Are there any other autobiographical secrets you're willing to share with us?
AUSTER: I'm thinking . . . There's nothing that jumps to mind from *The Music of Chance* . . . or *In the Country of Last Things* . . . or *Mr. Vertigo.* A couple of small elements in *Leviathan,* however, and one amusing bit in *Timbuktu*—the story about the typing dog. I projected myself into the book as Willy's former college roommate—Anster or Omster (Mr. Bones can't quite remember the name)——and the fact is that I did go to Italy when I was seventeen to visit my aunt, my mother's sister. She had been living there for more than a decade, and one of her friends happened to be Thomas Mann's daughter, Elisabeth Mann Borgese, who was a scientist involved in the study of animals. One day we were invited to her house for lunch and I was introduced to her dog Ollie, a large English setter who had been taught how to type out his name with his snout on a specially designed typewriter. I saw it with my own eyes. It was one of the most preposterous and extraordinary things I've ever witnessed.

INTERVIEWER: In *Leviathan,* the narrator has your initials—Peter Aaron. And he's married to a woman named Iris, which is your wife's name spelled backwards.
AUSTER: Yes, but Peter isn't married to Siri. He's married to the heroine of her first novel, *The Blindfold.*

INTERVIEWER: A transfictional romance.
AUSTER: Exactly.

INTERVIEWER: You haven't mentioned *Moon Palace,* which reads more like an autobiography than any of your other novels. Fogg is exactly your age, and he goes to Columbia exactly when you did.

AUSTER: Yes, I know the book sounds very personal, but almost nothing in it comes from my own life. I can think of only two significant details. The first has to do with my father, and I look on it as a kind of posthumous revenge, a way of settling an old score on his behalf. Tesla is a minor character in the novel, and I devote a couple of pages to the AC-DC controversy that flared up between Edison and Tesla in the 1890s. Effing, the old man who tells Fogg the story, heaps quite a lot of abuse on Edison. Well, it turns out that when my father graduated from high school in 1929, he was hired by Edison to work as an assistant in the lab at Menlo Park. My father was very gifted in electronics. Two weeks into the job, Edison found out that he was Jewish and fired him. Not only did the man invent the electric chair, but he was a notorious anti-Semite. I wanted to get back at him for my father's sake, to square the account.

INTERVIEWER: And what's the other detail?

AUSTER: The night when Effing hands out money to strangers in the street. That scene comes straight out of something that happened to me in 1969— my meeting with H. L. Humes, better known as Doc Humes, who was one of the founders of the *Paris Review*. It was such a wild business, I don't think I could have invented it myself.

INTERVIEWER: You wrote some memorable pages about Doc Humes in *Hand to Mouth*, which is about your struggles as a young man to keep yourself afloat. What prompted you to take on that subject?

AUSTER: I'd always wanted to write something about money. Not finance or business, but the experience of not having enough money, of being poor. I'd been thinking about the project for many years, and my working title had always been "Essay on Want." Very Lockean, very eighteenth century, very dry. I was planning to write a serious, philosophical work, but when I finally sat down to begin, everything changed. The book turned into the story of my own problematic dealings with money, and in spite of the rather dismal subject matter, the spirit of the writing was largely comic.

Still, the book wasn't only about myself. I saw it as an opportunity to write about some of the colorful characters I'd met when I was young, to give these people their due. I'd never had any interest in working in an office or holding down a steady, white-collar job. I found the idea extremely distasteful. I gravitated toward more humble kinds of work, and that gave me a chance to spend time with people who weren't like me. People who hadn't gone to college; people who hadn't read a lot of books. In this country, we tend to underestimate the intelligence of working-class people. Based on my own experience, I found most of them to be just as smart as the people who run the world. They simply aren't as ambitious—that's all. But their talk is a lot funnier. Everywhere I went, I had to struggle to keep up with them. I'd spent too much time with my nose buried in books, and most of my coworkers could talk circles around me.

INTERVIEWER: Who is the source for Hector Mann, the silent comedian in *The Book of Illusions*?

AUSTER: He appeared in my head one day about ten or twelve years ago, and I walked around with him for a long time before starting the book. But Hector himself was fully formed right from the beginning. Not only his name, and not only the fact that he was born in Argentina, but the white suit and the black mustache and the handsome face—they were all there, too.

Physically, Hector Mann bears a strong resemblance to Marcello Mastroianni in *Divorce, Italian Style*, a film from the early sixties. The mustache and the white suit could have come from that movie, although I'm not certain. Hector also shares certain characteristics with Max Linder, the earliest of the great silent comedians. And perhaps there's a touch of Raymond Griffith in him as well. Most of Griffith's films have been lost, so he's become a rather obscure figure. But he played a dapper man of the world—just as Hector does—and he also had a mustache. But Hector's movements are crisper and more artfully choreographed than Griffith's.

INTERVIEWER: The descriptions of the films are extraordinary acts of visualization in words. How did you go about writing those passages?

AUSTER: It was a question of striking the right balance. All the visual information had to be there—the physical details of the action—so the reader could "see" what was happening, but at the same time, the prose had to move along at a quick pace, in order to mimic the experience of watching a film, which is rushing past you at twenty-four frames per second. Too many details, and you would get bogged down. Not enough, and you wouldn't see anything. I had to go over those pages many times before I felt I had them right.

INTERVIEWER: *The Book of Illusions* tells a very complex story, but at its heart, I would say it's an exploration of grief. Do you think you could have written that book when you were younger?

AUSTER: I doubt it. I'm well into my fifties now and things change for you as you get older. Time begins slipping away, and simple arithmetic tells you there are more years behind you than ahead of you—many more. Your body starts breaking down, you have aches and pains that weren't there before, and little by little the people you love begin to die. By the age of fifty, most of us are haunted by ghosts. They live inside us, and we spend as much time talking to the dead as to the living. It's hard for a young person to understand this. It's not that a twenty-year-old doesn't know he's going to die, but it's the loss of others that so profoundly affects an older person—and you can't know what that accumulation of losses is going to do to you until you experience it yourself. Life is so short, so fragile, so mystifying. After all, how many people do we actually love in the course of a lifetime? Just a few, a tiny few. When most of them are gone, the map of your inner world changes. As my friend George Oppen once said to me about getting old: what a strange thing to happen to a little boy.

INTERVIEWER: You quote that line in *The Invention of Solitude*.
AUSTER: It's the best comment about old age I've ever heard.

INTERVIEWER: In *Leviathan*, your narrator Peter Aaron writes: "No one can say where a book comes from, least of all the person who writes it. Books are born out of ignorance, and if they go on living after they are written, it's only to the degree that they cannot be understood." How close is that to your own belief?
AUSTER: I rarely speak directly through my characters. They might resemble me at times, or borrow aspects of my life, but I tend to think of them as autonomous beings with their own opinions and their own ways of expressing themselves. But in this case Aaron's opinion matches my own.

INTERVIEWER: Do you work from a plan when you start writing a novel? Have you figured out the plot in advance?
AUSTER: Each book I've written has started off with what I'd call a buzz in the head. A certain kind of music or rhythm, a tone. Most of the effort involved in writing a novel for me is trying to remain faithful to that buzz, that rhythm. It's a highly intuitive business. You can't justify it or defend it

rationally, but you know when you've struck a wrong note, and you're usually pretty certain when you've hit the right one.

INTERVIEWER: Do you jump around in the story as you write?
AUSTER: No. Every book begins with the first sentence, and then I push on until I've reached the last. Always in sequence, a paragraph at a time. I have a sense of the trajectory of the story—and often have the last sentence as well as the first before I begin—but everything keeps changing as I go along. No book I've published has ever turned out as I thought it would. Characters and episodes disappear; other characters and episodes develop as I go along. You find the book in the process of doing it. That's the adventure of the job. If it were all mapped out in advance, it wouldn't be very interesting.

INTERVIEWER: And yet your books always seem to be so tightly constructed. It's one of the things you're most admired for.
AUSTER: *The Book of Illusions* went through a number of radical shifts along the way, and I was rethinking my ideas about the story right up to the last pages. *Timbuktu* was originally conceived as a much longer book. Willy and Mr. Bones were supposed to have no more than minor, fleeting roles in it, but once I started writing the first chapter, I fell in love with them and decided to scrap my plan. The project turned into a short lyrical book about the two of them with scarcely any plot. With *Mr. Vertigo*, I thought I was writing a short story of thirty or forty pages, but the thing took off and seemed to acquire a life of its own. Writing has always been like that for me. Slowly blundering my way toward consciousness.

INTERVIEWER: Can we go back to the phase "a paragraph at a time"?
AUSTER: The paragraph seems to be my natural unit of composition. The line is the unit of a poem, the paragraph serves the same function in prose— at least for me. I keep working on a paragraph until I feel reasonably satisfied with it, writing and rewriting until it has the right shape, the right balance, the right music—until it seems transparent and effortless, no longer "written." That paragraph can take a day to complete or half a day, or an hour, or three days. Once it seems finished, I type it up to have a better look. So each book has a running manuscript and a typescript beside it. Later on, of course, I'll attack the typed page and make more revisions.

INTERVIEWER: And little by little, the pages mount up.

AUSTER: Yes, very slowly.

INTERVIEWER: Do you show your work to anyone before it's finished?
AUSTER: Siri. She's my first reader, and I have total faith in her judgments. Each time I write a novel, I read to her from it every month or so—whenever I have a new stack of twenty or thirty pages. Reading aloud helps to objectify the book for me, to hear where I've gone wrong or failed to express what I was trying to say. Then Siri makes her comments. She's been doing this for twenty-two years now, and what she says is always remarkably astute. I can't think of a single instance when I haven't followed her advice.

INTERVIEWER: And do you read her work?
AUSTER: Yes. What she does for me, I try to do for her. Every writer needs a trusted reader—someone who has sympathy for what you're doing and wants the work to be as good as it can possibly be. But you have to be honest. That's the fundamental requirement. No lies, no false pats on the back, no praise for something you don't believe deserves it.

INTERVIEWER: What contemporary novelists do you read?
AUSTER: Quite a few—probably more than I'm able to count. Don DeLillo, Peter Carey, Russell Banks, Philip Roth, E. L. Doctorow, Charles Baxter, J. M. Coetzee, David Grossman, Orhan Pamuk, Salman Rushdie, Michael Ondaatje, Siri Hustvedt. . . Those are the names that jump out at me right now, but if you asked me the same question tomorrow, I'm sure I would give you a different list. Contrary to what many people want to believe, the novel is in good shape these days, as healthy and vigorous as it's ever been. It's an inexhaustible form, and no matter what the pessimists say, it's never going to die.

INTERVIEWER: How can you be so sure?
AUSTER: Because a novel is the only place in the world where two strangers can meet on terms of absolute intimacy. The reader and the writer make the book together. No other art can do that. No other art can capture the essential inwardness of human life.

INTERVIEWER: Your new novel, *Oracle Night*, will be out at the end of the year. That's just fifteen months after the publication of *The Book of Illusions*. You've always been prolific, but this seems to be some kind of record.
AUSTER: Actually, I started writing *Oracle Night* before *The Book of Illu-*

sions. I had the first twenty pages or so, but then I stopped. I realized that I didn't quite understand what I was doing. *The Book of Illusions* took me roughly three years to write, and all during that time I continued thinking about *Oracle Night.* When I finally returned to it, it came out with remarkable speed. I felt as if I was writing in a trance.

INTERVIEWER: Was it smooth sailing all the way through—or did you run into difficulties along the way?

AUSTER: Not until the end, the last twenty pages or so. I had a different conclusion in mind when I started the book, but when I wrote it out as originally planned, I wasn't happy with it. It was too brutal, too sensational, and undermined the tone of the book. I was stuck for several weeks after that and for a while I thought I would have to leave the book unfinished. Just like Sidney's story in the novel. It was as if I had fallen under the spell of my own project and was living through the same struggles as my hero. Mercifully, something finally came to me, and I was able to write the last twenty pages.

INTERVIEWER: It's an intensely intimate novel.

AUSTER: I think of it as a kind of chamber piece. There are very few characters, and all the action takes place in just two weeks. It's very compact, tightly coiled in on itself—a strange little organism of interlocking parts.

INTERVIEWER: There are a number of elements you've never used before. Footnotes, for example.

AUSTER: Hardly an original idea, of course, but for this particular story, I felt they were necessary. The main body of the text confines itself to the present, to the events that take place during those two weeks, and I didn't want to interrupt the flow of the narrative. The footnotes are used to talk about things that happened in the past.

INTERVIEWER: In *Oracle Night* there are two photographs—of a 1937–1938 Warsaw telephone book. How did you come to have that telephone book, and what made you decide to include those pictures?

AUSTER: I went to Warsaw for the first time in 1998, and my Polish publisher gave it to me as a gift. There's an Auster in that book, no doubt some one murdered by the Nazis just a few years later. In the same way, Sidney, the narrator of *Oracle Night*, finds the name of someone who could possibly have been a relative of his. I needed the photos to prove that the book really exists—that I wasn't just making it up. The entire novel is saturated with references to twentieth-century history. World War II and the Holocaust. World War I, the Chinese Cultural Revolution, the Kennedy assassination. It's a book about time, after all, and fleeting as those references might be, they're an essential part of the story.

INTERVIEWER: *Oracle Night* is your eleventh novel. Has writing fiction become easier for you over the years?

AUSTER: No, I don't think so. Each book is a new book. I've never written it before, and I have to teach myself how to write it as I go along. The fact that I've written books in the past seems to play no part in it. I always feel like a beginner, and I'm continually running into the same difficulties, the same blocks, the same despairs. You make so many mistakes as a writer, cross out so many bad sentences and ideas, discard so many worthless pages, that finally what you learn is how stupid you are. It's a humbling occupation.

INTERVIEWER: Do you think you've had a strange career: all that hard work and patience, but finally also all that success?

AUSTER: I try not to think about it. It's difficult for me to look at myself from the outside. I simply don't have the mental equipment to do it, at least where my work is concerned. It's for other people to make judgments about what I've done, and I wouldn't want to presume to have an answer to that question. I wish I could, but I still haven't mastered the trick of being in two places at the same time.

Jonathan Lethem
Talks with Paul Auster

Jonathan Lethem/2005

Reproduced from *The Believer*, February 2005, with permission of Jonathan Lethem.

I. MUSIC

JONATHAN LETHEM: What were you doing today before I appeared in your house?
PAUL AUSTER: The usual. I got up in the morning. I read the paper. I drank a pot of tea. And then I went over to the little apartment I have in the neighborhood and worked for about six hours. After that, I had to do some business. My mother died two years ago, and there was one last thing to take care of concerning her estate—a kind of insurance bond I had to sign off on. So, I went to a notary public to have the papers stamped, then mailed them to the lawyer. I came back home. I read my daughter's final report card. And then I went upstairs and paid a lot of bills. A typical day, I suppose. A mix of working on the book and dealing with a lot of boring, practical stuff.

JL: For me, five or six hours of writing is plenty. That's a lot. So, if I get that many hours the other stuff feels satisfying. The other stuff feels like a kind of grace. But if I have to do that stuff when I haven't written—
PA: Oh, that's terrible.

JL: That's a terrible thing.
PA: I've found that writing novels is an all-absorbing experience—both physical and mental—and I have to do it every day in order to keep the rhythm, to keep myself focused on what I'm doing. Even Sunday, if possible. If there's no family thing happening that day, I'll at least work in the morning. Whenever I travel, I get thrown off completely. If I'm gone for two

149

weeks, it takes me a good week to get back into the rhythm of what I was doing before.

JL: I like the word "physical." I have the same fetish for continuity. I don't really ask of myself a given word or page count or number of hours. To work every day, that's my only fetish. And there is a physical quality to it when a novel is thriving. It has an athletic component. You're keeping a streak going.

PA: Writing is physical for me. I always have the sense that the words are coming out of my body, not just my mind. I write in longhand, and the pen is scratching the words onto the page. I can even hear the words being written. So much of the effort that goes into writing prose for me is about making sentences that capture the music that I'm hearing in my head. It takes a lot of work, writing, writing, and rewriting to get the music exactly the way you want it to be. That music is a physical force. Not only do you write books physically, but you read books physically as well. There's something about the rhythms of language that correspond to the rhythms of our own bodies. An attentive reader is finding meanings in the book that can't be articulated, finding them in his or her body. I think this is what so many people don't understand about fiction. Poetry is supposed to be musical. But people don't understand prose. They're so used to reading journalism— clunky, functional sentences that convey factual information. Facts . . . just the surfaces of things.

JL: This relates to the acute discomfort of publicity, so much of which consists of requests to paraphrase the work. Which inevitably results in something unmusical. It's as if you've taken the body away, then drawn its outline and described its contents.

PA: I don't know why the world has changed so much that writers are now expected to appear in public and talk about their work. It's something I find very difficult. And yet, one does have some sense of responsibility towards one's publishers, to the people trying to sell the book.

I've tried to pick my spots. I don't do it that often. But every once in a while I'll come out and do it as an act of good faith. Then I hope I'll be left alone again for a while. For example, with the last novel I published, *Oracle Night*, I refused to go on book tours. I just didn't have the stamina for it.

JL: Kazuo Ishiguro has a funny way of talking about it as if it's a giant, consensual mistake all authors made together, by agreeing to this. And then suggesting we need to end it together. It's like a version of Prisoner's Dilemma. If one of us tours, we all have to tour. If everyone refuses . . .

PA: He's speaking from deep experience. He did something that no one else I know ever did. He was on book tour for about two years. He went everywhere, to every country in the world where his book was published. In the end, it probably nearly killed him.

JL: Did you read *The Unconsoled*?
PA: I've wanted to.

JL: It's one of my favorite novels by a living writer. An epic Kafkaesque account of a pianist's arrival in a city to give a recital which never seems to happen. One possible description of it is as the longest and bitterest complaint of a book-touring author ever written.

PA: There's a great entry in Kafka's diaries in which he describes an imaginary writer in the process of giving a public reading. So-and-so is up there on stage and people are getting restless and bored. "Just one more story," he says, "just one more. . . ." People start getting up and leaving. The doors keep slamming shut, and he goes on begging "just one more, one more," until everyone is gone and he's left alone at the podium, reading to an empty room.

II. FILM

JL: It does seem that lately you've managed to reinstate your primary relationship with novel-writing. I mean, judging from the degree of concentration evident in the two recent novels and from your testimony that you're already deep in another one, which is nice news.
PA: Yeah, deep, deep in it.

JL: When you talk about the exclusivity that the novel demands I'm very much in agreement with you. So I wonder about the years when you were apparently happy in the world of film. Did you feel that you had to retrench?
PA: I stumbled into filmmaking by accident. I've always been passionately in love with movies, to such a degree that as a young person of about nineteen or twenty I thought maybe I would try to become a film director. The reason I didn't do it was because I felt I didn't have the right personality. At that time in my life, I was mortally shy. I couldn't speak in front of other people, and I thought: if I'm going to be this silent, morose, brooding person, I'm not going to be able to communicate effectively with the actors and the crew

and so on. So I gave up that idea. And then, ironically enough, it was only after I started publishing novels that I got involved with film—because people
started calling me about potential film rights, writing original screenplays,
and eventually I got lured into it.

JL: In your recent novels I imagined I'd spotted a subtle turn from film,
toward fiction. That is to say, the last two books both portray artists. In
The Book of Illusions, your main character is a filmmaker, and the reader
encounters extensive—and beautiful—descriptions of his films. In *Oracle
Night* the main character is a novelist, and we read a portion of his novel-in-
progress. Does this match a turn in your own attentions?

PA: I want to disentangle this a little bit. During the years I was making
films, I never believed I was abandoning the novel. The two films with
Wayne Wang took two years of my life. It was a wonderful experience. One
of the great pleasures was getting out of my room for a while, working with
other people, opening up my mind to new ways of thinking.

Lulu on the Bridge was an accident. I wrote the screenplay for Wim
Wenders, and then he had a conflict; he wasn't able to direct the film. At his
urging, I decided to take on the job myself. And so, boom, there went another two and a half years of my life. But, then again, it was an irreplaceable
experience, and I'm glad I did it. Then came the promotional tour, which
was far more exhausting than making the film itself. You think books are
hard. Films are deadly. I can remember doing forty interviews in two days
in Japan. Long interviews, one after the other, one after the other. I was so
worn out, I got sick and wound up in the hospital. That was when I came
to a decision. As much as I enjoyed making films, and as much as I thought
I was beginning to get the hang of it, I understood that it's a full-time job.
You can't do it as a hobby. In order to go on making films, I would have
been forced to give up writing, and that was out of the question. There was
no doubt in my mind that what I'm supposed to do is write novels. So, very
happily, without any regret at all, I retired. I'm not in the movie business
anymore.

But to get back to *The Book of Illusions*, to Hector Mann and his film
career: the fact is that Hector was born inside me long before I got involved
with the movies myself. He came to me one day in the late eighties or very
early nineties, full-blown in his white suit with his black mustache, and I
didn't know what to do with him. I thought perhaps I would sit down at
some point and write a book of stories that would describe his silent films—
each story a different film. I walked around with him for years before the

book finally coalesced into the novel it is now. People have said, "Oh, this is a result of Auster's foray into filmmaking," but it really predated all that.

The last thing to say about this little adventure into moviemaking is that it's rare that a person gets a chance at a somewhat advanced age—I'm talking about my mid-forties—to learn something new. To get involved in something you've never tried before. In that way it was good for me. It was good for me not to write a novel for five years. The only piece of prose I wrote during that period was *Hand to Mouth*, my little autobiographical essay about money.

JL: This is something I wrestle with. I am actually in the middle of the longest break from novel writing of my adult life. I began trying to write novels when I was eighteen.
PA: Me too.

JL: They weren't any good, of course, but I've never been away from the activity since then. But in the past two years I've done a tremendous amount of promotion, and then worked on assembling two collections—a book of stories and a book of essays.
PA: Nothing to be ashamed about.

JL: Thank you. But it means that this body that's been accustomed for twenty years to this practice, as an athlete's body is accustomed to showing up at the clubhouse and putting on the cleats and running, my writer's body is—
PA: Atrophied a little bit.

JL: Yes, atrophy. It's a bit dismaying. I have a friend, a novelist with a delightfully unembarrassed sense of ambition. He's got a bit of that Norman-Mailer-getting-into-the-boxing-ring-with-Tolstoy thing. He says a thing that haunts me: "If you look at the record, with very few exceptions novelists are at their best between the ages of thirty-five and fifty. The crossroads of youthful energy and experience." And here I am kissing off a couple of years at the start of my forties.
PA: Just to reassure you, I'm a firm believer that there are no rules in art. Every trajectory is different. My French publisher once told me that a novelist has twenty years, that all his best work will be done in that span of time. I don't necessarily buy that. But the interesting thing is how easy it is not to work. Yes, writing is a necessity and often a pleasure, but at the same time, it can be a great burden and a terrible struggle.

JL: I'm glad to hear you say that.

PA: In my own case, I certainly don't walk into my room and sit down at my desk feeling like a boxer ready to go ten rounds with Joe Louis. I tiptoe in. I procrastinate. I delay. I take care of little business that I don't have to do at that moment. I come in sideways, kind of sliding through the door. I don't burst into the saloon with my six-shooter ready. If I did, I'd probably shoot myself in the foot.

III. PLACE

JL: You've reminded me of another thought I had when you mentioned going to your little apartment. I hope you don't mind me saying you have an extraordinary house. The sort of house which, in my fantasies, I would never leave. There'd be a beautiful office in it and I would write in that office. In fact, you've arranged to slip out of this house. That slippery, crabwise kind of movement is one the writer thrives on. Or, anyway, another thing I identify with.

PA: It's complicated. When we lived in a crowded apartment with children, there was nowhere for me to work, so I found a little studio apartment for myself. I worked there for six or seven years, and then we bought this house. In the beginning, there were tenants downstairs, but eventually they left and I decided to move my operation here. For quite a number of years, I contentedly worked downstairs. But last year we started doing work on the house. We were invaded by contractors, carpenters, plumbers, electricians, painters. There was so much noise. The doorbell was ringing all the time. The phone was ringing all the time. I realized I wasn't able to concentrate. And I thought, maybe I should go back to the old way. I rented a little apartment in the neighborhood about nine months ago, and I find it good, very good. This is a magnificent house. It's the product of Siri's [Siri Hustvedt, Auster's wife] tremendous aesthetic sense, her brilliant eye for harmony and order. But I think working in a rougher, meaner environment is good for me. I've always been a kind of Caliban. I feel happier in a bare space.

JL: My equivalent, perhaps, is that I enjoy an indirect relationship to place. People understandably think I moved back to Brooklyn in order to write about it, but the odd truth is that I've written the majority of these Brooklyn books in Toronto or Saratoga Springs or German hotel lobbies. I seem to write most happily about Brooklyn from a little distance, glancing back, yearning for it.

PA: Like Joyce and Dublin. As it happens, I'm writing about Brooklyn now as well. The last book, *Oracle Night*, was Brooklyn twenty-two years ago. Now, I'm writing about the Brooklyn of today. I can tell you the title of the new novel because I'm not going to change it: *The Brooklyn Follies*. It's an attempt to write a kind of comedy. I've never been in this territory before, and I'm having a lot of fun with it, doubting every word I write, and yet finally, I think, producing something that's interesting. I hope so, anyway.

JL: I can't wait.

PA: You try to surprise yourself. You want to go against what you've done before. You want to burn up and destroy all your previous work; you want to reinvent yourself with every project. Once you fall into habits, I think, you're dead as an artist. You have to challenge yourself and never rest on your laurels, never think about what you've done in the past. Just say, that's done, now I'm tackling something else. It's certain that the world's large enough and interesting enough to take a different approach each time you sit down to write about it.

JL: Anyway, your voice is going to be helplessly your own. And so the books will be united despite your attempts to ignore your own earlier work.

PA: Exactly, because all your attempts to flee from yourself are useless. All you discover is yourself and your old obsessions. All the maniacal repetitions of how you think. But you try. And I think there's some dignity in that attempt.

JL: I'm laughing, because now, as I'm about to begin a new novel at last, the only thing I'm certain of are the exclusions, the things I'll refuse to do again. I'm avoiding Brooklyn. I'm going to avoid writing about parents and children. And I'd noticed that each book, as different as I thought they were, had mortal stakes attached. Someone was capable of pulling a gun on someone else. So I decided to restrict myself to emotional stakes.

PA: Well, that's good. When you become aware of what your limits have been so far, then you're able to expand them. And every artist has limits. No one can do everything. It's impossible. What's beautiful about art is that it circumscribes a space, a physical and mental space. If you try to put the entire world into every page, you turn out chaos. Art is about eliminating almost everything in order to focus on the thing you need to talk about.

IV. TECHNOLOGIES

JL: Do you find it difficult to include certain technologies, now deeply imbedded, such as email and cell phones, in your fiction? I find that technologies invented beyond a certain date—for me it might be 1978, or 1984—don't seem to belong in the realm of fiction.

PA: That's a very interesting question. In *The Book of Illusions*, which is set in the late eighties, there's a fax machine. Something very important happens through a fax machine. So, I'm not, per se, against talking about technology. In the book I'm working on now, there's a reference to email. Also to cell phones.

I'm one of the few people left without a computer. I don't write on a word processor, and I don't have email and I'm not really tempted to get it. I'm very happy with my pen and my old portable typewriter, but I'm not against talking about anything, actually. I think the glory of the novel is that you're open to everything and anything that exists or has existed in the world. I don't have any proscriptions. I don't say, "This is not allowed because . . ."

JL: Not an ideological boycott, of course, but more a tendency to flinch from including those things. I email frequently. But if I include it in fiction I begin disbelieving the fiction instantly. It seems to disqualify the reality of the page.

PA: But this leads to a much larger and more interesting question that I've debated with various people over the years. You know, there are the enthusiasts for technology and they always say—and this has been happening now for probably 150 years—they say that new technology is going to change the way people think and live. It's going to revolutionize our lives. Not just our physical lives, but our inner lives as well. I am not at all a believer in this view for the simple reason that we have bodies. We get sick. We die. We love. We suffer. We grieve. We get angry. These are the constants of human life whether you live in ancient Rome or contemporary America. I really don't think that people have changed because of the telegraph or the radio or the cell phone or the airplane or, now, computer technology.

Seven or eight years ago, I was invited to Israel by the Jerusalem Foundation and stayed at an artists' center called Mishchanot. A wonderful place. I was fifty years old, and I'd never been to Israel, a Jew who had resisted the idea my entire life. I was waiting for the right moment, and when the letter from Teddy Kollek came and he said they wanted to invite me for three or four weeks to stay there and live in that building and write and do whatever I wanted, I thought it was the appropriate moment to go. Siri and Sophie [Auster's daughter] went with me. At one point, we took a tour around the country. We visited the town of Qumran, where the Dead Sea Scrolls were discovered. There's an extraordinary museum there with the scrolls and other artifacts that were found in the cave and around the site. These artifacts are so fascinating because there are plates that look like plates you could buy in a store today, with the same patterns, the same design, or baskets that any French or Italian person would use to take to the market today. And I had a sudden revelation about the extraordinary sameness of human life through the ages. That's why we can read Homer and Sophocles and Shakespeare and feel that we're reading about ourselves.

JL: I spent my early twenties in the Bay Area during the late eighties. I was witness to this extraordinary boom in the ideology of computing, the birth of *Wired* magazine and all that gave it context. There was a tremendous excitement at the idea that human life would never be the same once virtual reality existed. But if you read Dziga Vertov, the great Russian theorist of cinema, a hundred years earlier he was making the same claim for film. And then, if you search just a decade or so earlier, the advent of radio was surrounded by the same rhetoric.

PA: It must have seemed revolutionary then. The world—people from distant places, were suddenly in contact. This isn't to say that there aren't dangers in technology. We're all too aware of teenagers today spending their lives in front of their computer screens, dulling their senses, not living fully anymore. But, I think as they grow up and life begins to impinge on them, they're going to join the rest of us.

JL: The sweet irony is that so much of the online world takes a written form. What was meant to be a post-literate or visually literate culture is now obsessed with epistolary exchange. Letters. Or diaries.

PA: Exactly. That gets us back to the question of fiction. Over the generations, countless people have predicted the death of the novel. Yet I believe that written stories will continue to survive because they answer an essential human need. I think movies might disappear before the novel disappears, because the novel is really one of the only places in the world where two strangers can meet on terms of absolute intimacy. The reader and the writer make the book together. You as a reader enter the consciousness of another person, and in doing so I think you discover something about your own humanity, and it makes you feel more alive.

JL: I like your emphasis on the privacy of the experience. No matter how enormous a novel may become, the physical act of reading determines that there's no way it can become a communal experience. To read is intimate. It's almost masturbatory.

PA: There's only one reader of a novel. That's the crucial fact about all this. Only one person. Every time, only one person.

V. EXPHRASIS

JL: I'm also fascinated by this notion of the novel's capacity for extensive descriptions of other art forms. It seems to me one of the novel's defining strengths: that it can swallow a song, a poem, or a film—

PA: Or a painting.

JL: Or a painting. It has a scope that other art forms are denied, because a novel can't be recapitulated in some other art form.

PA: I think the word is exphrasis, which is a rhetorical term meaning the description of imaginary works of art. It's so interesting to me that one of the things that novels have tended not to concentrate on over the centuries is the fact that people read books. I show books and the experience of reading as part of the reality of the world. And the same goes for film. Why not describe movies? After I published *The Book of Illusions*, I sent a copy to my friend Hal Hartley, the filmmaker. And he said to me, "You know, I think maybe written films are better than real films. You can see them in your head, and yet everything is exactly as you want it to be."

JL: Novelists get to direct the perfect films. We get to cast every part. We dress the set exactly as we wish.

PA: With a book you can read the same paragraph four times. You can go back to page 21 when you're on page 300. You can't do that with film. It just charges ahead. It's often difficult to keep up, especially if you're watching a film you admire very much. Good films demand to be looked at several times in order to be observed completely.

I think one of the mistakes I made with *Lulu on the Bridge* was that I wrote the script too much as if it were a novel. I think the film has to be seen several times before you can really penetrate what's going on. There's a moment early in the film when Harvey Keitel is walking down the street and there's a little graffito on the wall that says "Beware of God." I had seen this on a T-shirt and liked it very much. It's the dyslexic "Beware of Dog." Later on, I very consciously put a barking dog in the distance. That dog, to me, was a deity. And that's when Harvey's character discovers the dead man in the alley. Nobody, nobody could possibly understand what I was trying to do.

JL: A reader, encountering a sentence about a barking dog, would have to dwell on why that choice was made at that moment. Everything in a novel is explicitly chosen, whereas some of what a film captures feels incidental, according to the vagaries of photography and sound recording.
PA: Exactly.

JL: Meanwhile, I just can't help noticing that while you described that, a dog was barking in the distance, here in Brooklyn.
PA: Yes.

JL: So what's your fondest example of exphrasis—the work of art depicted in another work of art?
PA: There's a great moment in *War and Peace* when Natasha is taken to the opera and Tolstoy deconstructs the whole experience. Rather than write about it from an emotional point of view or an artistic point of view, he depicts it simply from a raw, physical point of view. You know, "Then some fat woman came on stage and started gesturing, and then a gong sounded in the background, and then lightning struck, and then a skinny man sang an aria that no one understood." And I think that's probably the funniest description of a work of art I've ever read. But, probably the best and most beautiful, and I'm doing this right off the top of my head—

JL: That's ideal.
PA: I hate to bring this so close to home, but I think it's Siri's last novel, *What I Loved.* The painter's artworks are of a sublime profundity, and the artworks are part of the novel. It was so beautifully articulated. I don't know that I've read another novel in which art has played such an integral role in the story.

JL: I'm remembering the description of a painting in which the artist's presence is shown, just barely, at the edge of the frame.
PA: A little shadow.

JL: Yes.

PA: Over the years, I've been intensely interested in the artificiality of books as well. I mean, who's kidding whom, after all. We know when we open up a book of fiction that we're reading something that is imaginary, and I've always been interested in exploiting that fact, using it, making it part of the work itself. Not in some dry, academic, metafictional way, but simply as an organic part of the written word. When I was a kid, I'd pick up a novel written in the third person, and I'd say to myself, "Who's talking? Who am I listening to here? Who's telling this story?" I can see a name on the cover, it says Ernest Hemingway or Tolstoy, but is it Tolstoy or Hemingway who is actually talking?

I always loved the books in which there was some kind of excuse for the fact that the book existed. For example, *The Scarlet Letter*, where Hawthorne discovers the manuscript in the custom house and then proceeds to print it in the subsequent pages. It's all a ruse. Art upon art upon art. And yet it was very compelling to me. I think that's why most of my books have been written in the first person rather than the third.

JL: When you first started out, did you think that would be the case? I, too, gravitate towards the first person, but when I was a young reader, I thought of third person as the more pure. It seemed to me in some way the higher form of fiction.

PA: Perhaps, but I like the low. I'm very interested in the low, the close to the ground, something that's almost indistinguishable from life.

JL: At what point in a project are you certain of which you'll choose?

PA: I think in every case I've known from the beginning. The only time I was confused was when I was writing a book of nonfiction, *The Invention of Solitude*. The first part of that book is written in the first person, and then I started the second part in the first person as well. But there was something that I didn't like about it. I couldn't understand why I was dissatisfied. I wrote, I wrote, I wrote and then I had to stop. I put it away, meditated for several weeks, and understood that the problem was the first person. I had to switch to the third. Because in the first part I was writing about somebody else—my father. I was seeing him from my point of view. But, in the second part, I was mostly writing about myself. By using the first person, I couldn't see myself anymore. By shifting to the third person, I managed to get a certain distance from myself, and that made it possible for me to see myself, which in turn made it possible for me to write the book. It was very strange.

JL: You use the word distance. And it seems to me one aspect of your work—omnipresent, but very elusive, and difficult to speak of—is a quality of reserve.

PA: This might come as a surprise to you, but I tend to think of myself as a highly emotional writer. It's all coming out of the deepest feelings, out of dreams, out of the unconscious. And yet, what I'm constantly striving for in my prose is clarity. So that, ideally, the writing will become so transparent that the reader will forget that the medium of communication is language. So that the reader is simply inside the voice, inside the story, inside what is happening. So, yes, there is a certain—I wouldn't call it reserve, but precision maybe, I don't know. At the same time, I'm trying to explore the deepest emotional questions I know about: love and death. Human suffering. Human joy. All the important things that make life worth living.

JL: Yes, I certainly didn't mean to suggest I experience the books as dispassionate. I found *Oracle Night* a wrenchingly emotional book. I'm not surprised by that. I do think you're right, that what I'm trying to characterize proceeds from the precision of the prose, its exacting quality. The effect is one of timelessness.

PA: I want to write books that can be read a hundred years from now, and readers wouldn't be bogged down by irrelevant details. You see, I'm not a sociologist, and the novel has often concerned itself with sociology. It's one of the generating forces that's made fiction interesting to people. But that's not my concern. I'm interested in psychology. And also certain philosophical questions about the world. By removing the stories from the morass of things that surround us, I'm hoping to achieve some kind of purer approach to emotional life.

JL: What's lovely is that you grant that same imperative to the characters themselves. They are often looking to purify their relationship to their own lives.

PA: I suppose in a way most of my characters are non-consumers, not terribly interested in all the little baubles and artifacts of contemporary life. Not to say that there aren't many specific things mentioned in my books, it's just that I don't dwell on them excessively.

JL: Yes, even the most contemporary references in your work seem to float off into a timeless place.

PA: I'm very concerned that every word, every sentence in my book is pertinent. I don't want to indulge myself in the luxury of writing beautiful paragraphs just for the sake of making beautiful writing. That doesn't interest me. I want everything to be essential. In a sense, the center is everywhere. Every sentence of the book is the center of the book.

A Conversation with Paul Auster

Mary Morris/2005

Reproduced from "Paul Auster: Purgatory," a special issue of *Storie* (2005) with permission of Paul Auster.

Interviewer: Midway through *The Brooklyn Follies*, Nathan's nephew Tom asks him about his work in progress, "The Book of Human Folly," and Nathan responds that he is "charging ahead with no end in sight," that each story he writes seems "to give birth to another story and then another story and then another story." Would you say that this in some way describes your own process in writing this book, one story giving way to another, and perhaps your process as a writer in general? Is that somehow a description of your own self?

Auster: Possibly, although in this particular case I conceived of this book as a whole. It's not a linear novel in which one episode or narrative thread generates another. *The Brooklyn Follies* had been brewing inside of me for a long time before I started to write it, well over ten years.

Interviewer: But not the ending, of course, which is based on more recent events.

Auster: Not the ending, no. Things always change after you begin. But, I would say, taking the long view, it's quite possible that one book seems to have generated another book. I tend to think of each book as a response to the proceeding one. In some sense I try to annihilate what I've done before, go against it, start all over again.

Interviewer: Are you in some way posing a question in a previous novel that you are answering in the next?

Auster: No, it's more of a dialectic, I think. If one book is a kind of chamber piece, like *Oracle Night* was, then the next book has to be more symphonic in scope. If one book is linear in the sense that, say, *The Music of Chance* is linear—it's a story that goes from A to B to C all the way to the end—then the next book, *Leviathan*, is going to be a labyrinth. More structurally complex. You don't want to keep playing the same piece over and over again.

Interviewer: Is that an intentional decision, to annihilate the ones that come before? Or is that just the way your mind works when you come to the next story?

Auster: I think it's just an instinct. It's a matter of self- preservation more than anything else.

Interviewer: But, in a way what you're talking about here is the form of the work, less than the substance. Because, I think, thematically the links in your work—the role of chance and coincidence, the mysteries of the self—are quite strong.

Auster: True. Although, again, there's really quite a wide range. If you take the extremes of my work, say a book like *In the Country of Last Things*, as compared to *Timbuktu*, they seem to have nothing to do with each other. But, in the middle, of course, there are many overlaps. I'm perfectly willing to agree with that.

Interviewer: There seems to be a very strong fable-like tradition in some of your writing such as *Timbuktu*, *In the Country of Last Things*, even *Moon Palace*, *Mr. Vertigo*, of course. By the same token, there's kind of a noir feeling that some of the books have. *The Book of Illusions*, I think, had a little bit of that as well as The New York Trilogy. How do these two extremes of the lighter, more childlike, and the darker, less innocent, play out in your work?

Auster: I tend to think of it as a narrative spectrum, different ways of telling a story. Some of the books are quote unquote more realistic than others. For example, this new book is very much grounded in the everyday. There's nothing fantastical about it. But, then, of course, I've written other books that are more fabular, more metaphorical. I like working in different modes. I don't want to feel stuck, to delude myself into thinking there's only one way to approach the world.

Interviewer: So, in other words, you'll make a decision to try comedy—because in many ways, *The Brooklyn Follies* is strongly comedic. Whereas *The Book of Illusions* is very serious.

Auster: It's a dark book. *Oracle Night* is also a dark book. But, as Billy Wilder said—and I had this in my mind while I was writing this story—when you're feeling really happy, that's the moment to write a tragedy. And when you're feeling low, do a comedy. And I've been feeling so bad about America, and Bush, and the war, and all the terrible things we've gotten ourselves into, that I've tried to keep my spirits up by writing a comedy.

Interviewer: Yet your comedy ends with a very dark vision, doesn't it, of 9/11.

Auster: In essence, I think of *The Brooklyn Follies* as a hymn to the ordinary, a hymn to the beauty of everyday life. The mystery and joy of being alive.

Interviewer: And all of life's exuberant possibilities?

Auster: That's one way of putting it, and then, yes, our lives are overshadowed by tragedy, cataclysms, historical upheavals, murders, deaths, wars. That's the context. We live and suffer and make countless mistakes. We grumble about our problems, and then something monstrous happens, and we understand how lucky we were to have those problems.

Interviewer: We're talking about the writer's perception of the world beyond himself, and, perhaps, a sense of social responsibility: Bush, Iraq, 9/11, all the things that we've been embroiled in in the last few years. By the same token, in the novel, Harry has his Hotel Existence, and there's the whole philosophical discussion of imaginary Edens and a sense of the need for an inner refuge. In the novel when you talk about Poe there is this need to create a safe haven for oneself as a writer. How do you balance those two parts of yourself—the part that is deeply engaged in the world and the part that needs extreme solitude to work?

Auster: I'm a writer, but I'm also a citizen. I'm both, and I also happen to have strong political opinions. When circumstances require it, when I'm asked to do something or say something or write something, I do it—as a citizen. I don't think my work is overtly political. I'm interested in politics, yes, but more deeply about simply what it means to be alive. That's what my books are about.

Interviewer: But, look at a book like *In the Country of Last Things*. It's a book about what it means to be alive, but it also gets to the heart of how we live in society.

Auster: It's a book about a collapsing society.

Interviewer: And *Leviathan* too.

Auster: Of course. Yes. I've even thought of *The Music of Chance* as a kind of political parable about power, with the building of the wall and the imprisonment of these two luckless people. But there are different ways of approaching it. It's not overt, even in *In the Country of Last Things*. There's scarcely a word about politics in that novel. It's about how one lives in a kind of chaos.

Interviewer: It's a parable in the way *Waiting for the Barbarians* by J. M. Coetzee is a parable. But what about the whole question of the writer being engaged in the world in some way? Do your views and your feelings move into action? Or is it all in the texts, in the writing?
Auster: I've written a few political pieces over the years. I've spoken out at various times over the years. I've marched in demonstrations—is that action?

Interviewer: Yes, that's action.
Auster: Okay, so that's action. But, by and large, I spend my days alone in my room trying to write stories.

Interviewer: Is that your imaginary Eden? Your Hotel Existence?
Auster: Perhaps. I've certainly been there a long time now. And I don't have any great urge to leave it, so it must be a pretty good place for me.

Interviewer: You're a writer who's very visible in the world. You have a lot of demands on you. How do you keep that safe haven for yourself? Is that hard to do, keep the world away?
Auster: It's a juggling act.

Interviewer: To be true to your imagination?
Auster: Siri calls me Dr. No, because I turn down nearly every request. And then, occasionally, I'll accept and go off and do something. And then, you know, one has a commitment to one's publishers. You can't just ignore them. They're making big efforts to try to get your books out there. And to be a snob about it and say I don't want to dirty my hands with any of this journalistic nonsense, I think it's a bit unfair. On the other hand, you have to draw the line. So I try to pick my spots, do enough to keep everybody happy, but not so much that I feel exhausted and overwhelmed by it.

Interviewer: The room you work in—there's a reference in here to Poe's philosophy of furniture, and that whole question of creating that whole dream of perfection. Can the world call you? Are you completely isolated when you're working?

Auster: Over the years, I've worked in different places, under different circumstances. I used to work at home, in whatever little apartment I happened to be living in. Then, a number of years ago, when our daughter was born, and we were living in a fairly small place, there was simply no room for me anymore. She needed a room, and so I didn't have one. That's when I got that little studio, which used to be across the street from where you lived. I worked in there for quite a few years, probably eight to ten years. I liked it there. Then we moved to this house, and suddenly there was room for me to work here. I did that for a number of years. And then, we started doing work on the house. There was so much commotion here—the doorbell was ringing every five minutes, the phone was ringing, the interruptions never stopped. I was so distracted that I decided to go back to my old system and work outside of the house. So, last winter I rented an apartment in the neighborhood. I've been going there ever since, and I've enjoyed it a lot. It's very quiet. There's no fax. I don't have email, as you know. . . . I have a phone, but only a few people have the number. When it rings, I know it's something important.

Interviewer: In her book on boxing, Joyce Carol Oates compares the writer to the boxer. She says, "the writer, like the boxer, is always redefining the parameters of self." Do you find yourself doing that, like when you leave this world and go to that room where you work? I think about your characters because you have a lot of characters who are alone in rooms, observing the world, especially in The New York Trilogy.

Auster: I don't know. Do I redefine myself? I don't know.

Interviewer: Not redefine, but just carve out that space.

Auster: I just think of it as an adventure. I never know what's going to happen next. You keep discovering things. And as you discover things about the story you're working on, you discover things about yourself, too. I don't start books blindly, I have some sense of what I want it to be; and then, when I start, things begin to change. No book I've written has ever turned out the way I thought it would when I began.

Interviewer: We've talked before about your process and heard you say that you write one sentence and then the next.

Auster: I always write in sequence. If I'm stuck, I just stop. Sometimes I have to stop for two weeks. I don't know what to do. I know the story, and yet things that I thought were good before I started writing turn out to be bad, and things that had never even occurred to me pop up while I'm writing and then I begin to adjust and shift and change everything. When I started writing *Mr. Vertigo*, for example, there was no Mrs. Witherspoon. She came up when I was a few weeks into the project, and I realized I needed this character. She became quite a significant force in the novel. But she wasn't born until after I started writing.

Interviewer: Were there any surprises in *The Brooklyn Follies* as you were writing it? You said it was a book you'd thought about for many years. For example, the ending must have surprised you at some point.
Auster: I had different endings in mind earlier. Then, that changed. I'm trying to think . . . this book, no, things didn't change that much.

Interviewer: Harry is quite a character in the book. Did you know him before?
Auster: Harry was a character I had been walking around with for a long time. You see, originally, this book was going to have Willy and Mr. Bones in it, who, of course, became the characters in *Timbuktu*. It had an entirely different configuration. It was a third-person novel. There was no Nathan at the time. But there was Harry and Tom. And then, there was going to be Mr. Bones. Willy was going to die. In the original story, Tom's sister has committed suicide in Baltimore. Tom goes down to Baltimore to fetch his niece, and while he's walking along on the street with her he comes upon Willy and Mr. Bones. Willy gives his long speech and dies, and they take the dog with them. Mr. Bones was going to be with Lucy and Tom throughout the story.

Interviewer: So, in a way, you took this one story and pulled it apart into two novels.
Auster: Yes. The first chapter was going to be identical to the first chapter of *Timbuktu*. Then it was going to move on to Tom, and suddenly the book would take a sharp turn. After I started writing it, I realized that I loved these two characters. I felt they deserved a book of their own. So I scrapped the big book and wrote a little poetic novel instead. Then it took me years to figure out how to bring back Harry and Tom and the rest of that story—Lucy and Aurora, and all of those characters that I'd had in my head. It just took a while.

Interviewer: Is it difficult for you to jettison something or put it aside? Is there a place where the novels and stories that might see the light of day in another time go?

Auster: The funny thing is that very few things get lost forever. For example, in *Oracle Night* there's the story that Sidney is writing about Nick Bowen. That story originated as an idea for a film I was going to do with Wim Wenders way back in 1990. Wim wrote to me and said he was reading my books. He wanted to do a project together, and we met and became friends. It was his idea—Wim's. He said, Let's take the Flitcraft story from *The Maltese Falcon* and use that as our premise. I sat down and wrote out an outline of the story which is pretty much what you get in *Oracle Night*. It's very similar, up to a certain point. There was a denouement that is not in the novel. But the backer who was going to put up the money for the film disappeared, and we never made the film. So I had these pages, these handwritten pages, in my drawer for how many years? Eleven years, twelve years. And I kept thinking about them, kept hoping that one day I would be able to do something with them.

Interviewer: The part where Nick Bowen winds up locked in the underground telephone book museum—which is, I think, one of my favorite moments in that novel—is when Sidney realizes that there's absolutely nowhere to go with that character, that that's the end of the story. He can't do anything to take care of it.

Auster: Yes, he's blocked, he's stuck.

Interviewer: Was that in the film? Or was that a writerly decision?

Auster: In the film there was a resolution at the end. I used material from that story, but I recast it for the novel.

Interviewer: On those days in your studio—you said that sometimes when something is not going the right way, you said that you can be stuck for two weeks. How do you get unstuck, and what do you do during those two weeks? Do you walk? Do you—

Auster: No, I usually keep trying. I go in and I write.

Interviewer: You'll stay.

Auster: I'll say, is this the next sentence? And then I'll work on a passage, and I'll realize, no, it's not. I'll throw it away and start again, and then just keep hacking away at it until the wall crumbles. When I was younger, these were the moments when I'd panic and feel that everything was disintegrating around me. That the whole project was a failure and I'd never write another word for the rest of my life. The one good thing about getting older, and I can't think of too many good things about getting old, is that I don't panic anymore. I realize that eventually, if the book is worth writing, I'm going to find the way to write that next sentence.

Interviewer: Michael Cunningham once said to me that half the time he feels like a poseur, or just a complete fraud in his writing life, and the other half he has delusions of grandeur. And then there are days in between where he actually gets things done. Do you have those kinds of swings of your own? Or do you try to keep—
Auster: No, I don't think of myself as either a poseur or someone with an inflated sense of himself.

Interviewer: More like a bricklayer?
Auster: Not even a bricklayer. I'm just so damn interested in what I'm doing that I don't think about myself. The day flies by, six, seven hours pass in the blink of an eye.

Interviewer: And all the time you're scribbling?
Auster: I'm scribbling, or walking around the apartment, thinking about the next sentence, the next word.

Interviewer: Reading? Would you do any reading during that period, or no?
Auster: Almost never. Sometimes, when I eat my little meager sandwich for lunch, I might read something.

Interviewer: You have a little lunch?
Auster: There's a kitchenette in the apartment, so I prepare some food for myself.

Interviewer: It sounds almost monastic.
Auster: It is. It's very simple, but it's bright, and this has been a great change. The old studio was dark; it was on the ground floor of the apartment building. My place here was on the garden floor, dark. I think it had something to do with Siri changing her study. Last year she took over a bigger room

upstairs, and it's so bright and peaceful there, I think there was a sense of envy, to work in such a beautiful—
Interviewer: You don't seem to be someone who experiences envy.
Auster: Well, not envy, just admiration. I decided that I wanted that, too. The apartment I rented is on the top floor of a four-story brownstone. There are two skylights, and lots of sun pouring through.

Interviewer: I've often thought of you as a dark writer and this is probably one of the first—well, *Moon Palace* has a lot in it too that I thought was funny. Well, look, this is a truly comic novel. Does the light affect you in any way? Do you think that the change in environment had any . . .
Auster: No, because this was always going to be a comic novel, even when I was working in my dingy basement.

Interviewer: So, the inner space and the outer space are not necessarily having a conversation.
Auster: No. Not really, no. Because, when you're working, the environment is not the room you're in, it's the page that's sitting in front of you. That's the universe you're living in.

Interviewer: You write a lot about notebooks. There's *The Red Notebook*, of course, and there's the notebook in *Oracle Night*. Is the notebook important to you? Do you go and buy a special notebook for each book?
Auster: No, I tend to be very particular about them. I like a brand of French notebook called Clairefontaine, which has very nice paper, and I always work with a fountain pen or a pencil. With the pen, the ink doesn't blot.

Interviewer: Pencil?
Auster: I often write with pencils. Mechanical pencils. I like them. I generally use a pencil when I'm not sure of what I'm doing, so I can erase. Clairefontaine is very good, but I have other brands, too. Whenever I go to a foreign country, I buy notebooks. I have Norwegian ones, German ones, French, Italian. But I only use quadrille lines. You know, squares, graph paper.

Interviewer: Oh really? Graph paper?
Auster: I can't write on a traditional—

Interviewer: A straight line, like a cahier?

Auster: No, always with the rectangles.

Interviewer: That's somewhat of a fetish.
Auster: I suppose.

Interviewer: The character in *Oracle Night* is obsessed with his notebook—the one he buys in the store that then is gone. There's no more of this notebook. And that notebook has magical powers.
Auster: He feels it does, but that doesn't mean he's right.

Interviewer: He feels he cannot write. I'm always interested in the autobiographical in your work and how it comes into play. For example, in The New York Trilogy there's the character Paul Auster. But he virtually has nothing to do with you.
Auster: No, nothing. I was trying to make fun of myself. Everything he says is stupid. Someone said just the other day that you should take your work seriously, but you shouldn't take yourself seriously. I think that's a very good rule.

Interviewer: Let's talk a little bit about your relationship to Brooklyn, since this is *The Brooklyn Follies*. Kafka had Prague, Dostoyevsky had St. Petersburg. Many writers draw strongly from a sense of place, and a place can even become a character. I have two questions about sense of place. One is, you moved in The New York Trilogy to this book, which is really, I think, not about Brooklyn—you don't even describe Brooklyn—but it's based here, perhaps more than any other novel, I think.
Auster: It's about the spirit of Brooklyn.

Interviewer: That's right. The complete serendipity, these wacky characters, the people you might meet on the street. The coincidences that can happen in this neighborhood. There's that great line, the first line in the book. I love that line.
Auster: I'm glad you like it. "I was looking for a quiet place to die. Someone recommended Brooklyn."

Interviewer: It reminds me of that famous line from the film *Casablanca*. "I came to Casablanca for the waters . . . I was misinformed." Anyway, if you live in Brooklyn, you appreciate Brooklyn, and your opening line is somehow perfect for this place. Do you feel as if this book might enter some kind of oeuvre of novels set in Brooklyn?

Auster: I have no idea. I don't think about those things. But I have to say that the BPM in the book, the Beautiful Perfect Mother, was based on a real character. I used to walk my daughter, Sophie, to school, on Carroll Street. And every morning across the street there was this beautiful woman with her two kids. She fascinated me. I never spoke to her, I don't know who she is. But in my mind I started calling her the Beautiful Perfect Mother. And so she becomes the BPM, Nancy Mazzucchelli. After Sophie went to middle school, I lost track of this woman and didn't see her for years. Oddly enough—and these things happen to me all the time—just as I was writing the chapter in *The Brooklyn Follies* where the BPM is introduced, I saw her again. Walking down Seventh Avenue toward the F train. The BPM, in the flesh, looking as beautiful as ever. She was all dressed up in a very attractive way, going off to do whatever it was she was going to do. I thought, dammit, here she is and I'm writing about her and she doesn't even know it.

Interviewer: Were you tempted to go up and say, you're a character in my next book?

Auster: No, not at all. But anyway, Brooklyn. We made *Blue in the Face*, which is all about Brooklyn. *Smoke* is set in Brooklyn as well. *Oracle Night* is set in Brooklyn. This book is set in Brooklyn. *Ghosts* is set in Brooklyn.

Interviewer: And there's a Brooklyn moment in *Moon Palace*. Doesn't he go to the Brooklyn Museum?

Auster: Absolutely. With his eyes closed.

Interviewer: Your work is deeply rooted in American literature. Of course there's fellow Brooklynite Walt Whitman. In this book your influences seem to be particularly the American transcendentalists. Are those among your strongest antecedents?

Auster: I think so. I keep going back to them. As you know, a couple of years ago, I did a preface for a Hawthorne text. It was an excerpt from his notebooks, a very fascinating fifty- or sixty-page passage that I think is one of the most remarkable things in American literature. Nobody knows about it. It's buried in the *American Notebooks*, which I recommend to everybody. It's one of Hawthorne's great works. It's equal in power to Kafka's diaries. Fantastically interesting, beautifully written, both personal and also philosophical, and so many ideas for stories that he jotted down and never wrote.

People tend to think of Hawthorne as an ornate, complex stylist. But the prose in the *Notebooks* flows like water. It's extraordinarily alive.

Interviewer: Why do you think that was?
Auster: He was writing for himself. It was more notational. But he wrote so well that he couldn't help but write good, musical sentences. Anyway, in 1851 Hawthorne and his family were living in the Berkshires. He's already published *The Scarlet Letter*. *The House of Seven Gables* is about to come out, and Sophia, his wife, gives birth to their third child, Rose. In July, she went to West Newton to visit her parents with their older daughter, Una, and the baby, leaving Hawthorne alone with his five-year old son, Julian. So he writes this piece in his notebook called *Twenty Days with Julian and Little Bunny* by Papa. I think it's the first account in Western literature of a man taking care of a child alone. It's very funny, and also moving. This was the moment when Hawthorne and Melville were becoming friends, so Melville is a character in this story as well. I thought it deserved to be published separately, as a little book. The *New York Review* did it a couple of years ago. I wrote a preface, which I think is more than half the length of the text. I loved going back into Hawthorne—his mind, his life, his work. I feel very close to him. Our sensibilities, our personalities, our whole way of being, are very similar.

Interviewer: Can you elaborate on that similarity?
Auster: There's a fabular aspect to his writing that I'm very drawn to. And I think his combination of shyness and affability is similar to mine.

Interviewer: Did you name your daughter after his wife?
Auster: In *The Locked Room*, Sophie is married to Fanshawe. Fanshawe, of course, is a character from Hawthorne's first novel. He wrote *Fanshawe* when he was about twenty-three. After it was published, he felt so mortified that he bought up every copy he could find and burned them. But enough copies survived so that we still have the book. For me, *Fanshawe* became the name or the image of a writer who turns against himself. And that's why I gave that name to the character in the book. His wife, Sophie, is based on Sophia, Hawthorne's Sophia. And we named our daughter Sophie, after the character in the novel. So indirectly, she's named after Sophia Hawthorne.

Interviewer: When did you discover Hawthorne, and when did the connection begin?

Auster: I started reading Hawthorne seriously after college. I never took an American fiction course in school. I mostly studied Renaissance and six-teenth- and seventeenth-century literature in English, French, and Italian, though I was technically an English major. I wasn't doing modern stuff at all. I was reading it, but not studying it. So, when I moved to Paris in my early twenties, I started reading Hawthorne. I read *The Scarlet Letter* when I was about twenty-four. It absolutely knocked me over. I think it's the first great American novel. Hemingway says all American literature comes out of one book: *Huckleberry Finn*. I disagree vociferously. *The Scarlet Letter* was really our first important novel. It deals with all the questions that have plagued American life since the beginning.

Interviewer: More than *Moby-Dick*?
Auster: *Moby-Dick* is different. *Moby-Dick* is a genetic sport. It doesn't fit into any category, and it doesn't resemble any novel written before or since. It's a towering work of genius, but I don't think it has engendered anything. It just stands alone as a perfect crazy book that continues to obsess us. But *The Scarlet Letter* bore children. I can't imagine *The Great Gatsby* without it, for example.

Interviewer: Okay, do the math for me.
Auster: The small, jewel-like novel about a society, and the hypocrisy of that society, and the delusions of that society.

Interviewer: And the human foibles that shape it.
Auster: There's also Thoreau. If we're talking about American writers, we mustn't forget him. I can't think of an American writer who has written better discursive prose. You watch how, in *Walden*, which he worked on, and worked on, and worked on, how the sentences move one into the other, through these leaps that are absolutely brilliant, that take your breath away.

Interviewer: It's actually a very modernist book, in a way, isn't it? It's sort of like Hemingway before Hemingway. The theme is sentences and the prose.
Auster: There are so many phrases from that book that have become part of our everyday discourse. "Most men live lives of quiet desperation." Among others.

Interviewer: I think Hawthorne and Poe have a similar surreal edge to them. And in a way, Melville and Thoreau both are kind of writing about

America. They're more rooted in the culture. It's interesting to me that these four writers have had this kind of deep impact on you. I feel that those two threads come together in your own work.

Auster: It's possible. I've never thought about it in those terms, but it's possible. But there are so many other writers I've read who have had a big impact on me. It's hard to disentangle them.

Interviewer: What about foreign writers? What about Kafka?

Auster: To me, Kafka is the giant of the twentieth century. I go back to him again and again. The stories, the novels, the diaries, the letters. Everything. I just read a very interesting biography of Dora, his last mistress. That's where I got the story of the doll, which is in the new novel.

Interviewer: Oh, I love that story. I was going to ask you about the story of the doll because it figures in *The Brooklyn Follies*.

Auster: It's a remarkable story. Dora was the one who told it.

Interviewer: Do those letters exist today?

Auster: No, but in the biography it was mentioned that at some point announcements were published in the newspapers attempting to track down the little girl Kafka wrote those letters to. But they never found her. The letters are lost.

Interviewer: Tell the story.

Auster: It's so moving to me.

Interviewer: Also, contextualize it in terms of *The Brooklyn Follies*.

Auster: It's a story Tom tells his uncle Nathan while they're driving to Vermont. They've been talking about all kinds of things, mostly about writers and literature. Tom gets onto the subject of Kafka, who died of tuberculosis when he was not yet forty-one. In the last months of his life, he finally found the courage to break away from his family in Prague. He moved to Berlin and began living with Dora Diamant, a young woman he'd fallen in love with. It was 1923, 1924, a bad time politically and economically. Hyperinflation, riots, food shortages. Kafka and Dora lived in a quiet place, a little outside of town. Every afternoon, they would take a walk in the park. One day, they're in the park and they see a little girl in tears. She's about four years old. Kafka walks up to her and asks her what's wrong. She explains that she's lost her doll and doesn't know what to do. And Kafka, without missing a beat, says to her, Don't worry. Your doll went away on a vacation. And she says, How do you know that? And he answers, She just wrote me a letter. The girl asks to see the letter, but Kafka says he left it at home. But, if you come back tomorrow, he tells her, I'll give it to you. So Kafka goes home and actually writes the letter from the doll. Dora said that he worked really hard on it, trying to get the prose just right. That's extraordinary enough, I think, but Kafka went on doing it for *two or three weeks*, every day another letter from the doll, which he would read to the girl in the park. It cured her of her misery. And here you have this dying man, this genius of a writer, with just a few months to live, devoting his precious time to helping a little girl he barely even knows. What a person he must have been. It breaks my heart to think about it.

Interviewer: You know, I think about this story, which is an incredibly moving story, but also, thinking about it in connection with your work. I think of the Willie Mays piece in *Why Write?* where you are going to a baseball game to see Willie Mays when you're, what, eight years old, and at the end you're in a situation where you're face to face with Willie Mays, so there's nothing you want more than his autograph. And no one has a pen or pencil. In a way, it's kind of an anti-story to the doll story, right? So I'm wondering if it doesn't touch you in a deep way because—and of course the important part of the Willie Mays story is that from then on you carried a pencil.
Auster: I did, I really did.

Interviewer: And you still write with a pencil.
Auster: Yes, a pen or pencil. But I started that when I was eight. I didn't want to be unprepared, after all.

Interviewer: But there is a reason why this doll story touches us all as writers.
Auster: It's because it's for one person. It's not for publication. It's not for anything but to help. Even if it's a little four-year-old girl.

Interviewer: Nathan, your hero in this new novel, is aging, mortal. He has ailments. Does he represent a character from a new phase of your life?
Auster: Undoubtedly. In fact, I was talking to my British editor at Faber & Faber, Walter Donahue, not long ago and he said, you know, these last novels are all part of a group. I call them the books about wounded men. Starting with Willy, and then onto David Zimmer in *The Book of Illusions*,

who dies of a heart attack, or one assumes he does—he's had heart attacks in the past, and he's dead when the book is published. And then we have Sidney, who's a young man, but very badly hurt and ill, and Nathan, who's recovering from cancer.

Interviewer: Despite its comic nature, there are also deeply moral issues in this novel, aren't there?

Auster: There are many dark passages in this book. It's not slapstick. It's tough. People suffer. Crazy things happen. And yet, finally, most of the characters in the book are a little better off at the end than they were in the beginning. And that's how I would define comedy as opposed to tragedy.

Interviewer: I have a final question along those lines about people being a little better off at the end than they were in the beginning. Given the world as we know it right now, are you hopeful for the future? How do you feel about what's ahead for America, or the environment, for the world?

Auster: Right now, all these things look like disasters. And any one of them can do us in. We truly have the worst government I've experienced in my lifetime. The fact that this, this person was reelected is so appalling to me, I can barely talk about it. At the same time, I don't believe that Bush represents the majority of the American people. And in the end, unless America really destroys itself—which is a possibility—there's going to be some kind of counter-balance in the next years, after he leaves office. We'll correct a lot of the mistakes we made. America always tends to go toward the middle, and now we have extremists running the government.

Interviewer: So you have some hope.

Auster: Well, if you don't have hope, how can you get up in the morning?

The Making of *The Inner Life of Martin Frost*

Céline Curiol/2006

Reproduced from Paul Auster, *The Inner Life of Martin Frost*, pp. 1–19, with permission of Paul Auster.

Céline Curiol: You already wrote part of Martin Frost's story in *The Book of Illusions*. Why go back to it, expand it, and turn it into a screenplay?

Paul Auster: *The Inner Life of Martin Frost* has had a rather complicated history. In 1999, I was approached by a German producer to make a thirty-minute film for a series she was putting together of twelve short films by twelve different directors on the subject of men and women, so-called Erotic Tales. I was intrigued by the proposal and decided to take the plunge. It was early in the year, I remember, February or March, and I sat down and wrote my little script, which came to about thirty pages. Since the budget was going to be low, I confined myself to just two actors and one location—an isolated house in the country. The story of Martin Frost, a writer, and a mysterious woman who turns out to be his muse. A fantastical story, really, more or less in the spirit of Nathaniel Hawthorne. But Claire isn't a traditional muse. She's an embodiment of the story Martin is writing, and the more he writes, the weaker she becomes—until, when he comes to the last word of the text, she dies. He finally figures out what has been happening and burns the manuscript in order to bring her back to life. That's where the short version ended—with Martin bringing Claire back to life.

CC: What was the response from the German producer?

PA: Very positive. Everyone liked the script, and I went ahead and began making preparations to shoot the film. Willem Dafoe and Kate Valk—the great actress from the Wooster Group—were going to be my cast. Peter Newman, the producer of all the previous films I'd worked on, was again

179

going to produce. We made an itemized budget and were starting to look for a house to film in when negotiations with the German company broke down. They wanted to release the money to us in three stages. One-third on signing the contract, one third when we started shooting, and one-third when we were finished—and they approved the film. This last point worried me. What if they didn't like what I did and rejected the results? One-third of the budget would be lacking, and suddenly Peter would be in the position of having to pay off tens of thousands of dollars from his own pocket. I didn't want to put him at risk like that, so I backed out of the project. The thing that clinched it for me was a conversation I had with Hal Hartley. He had just finished shooting one of the twelve films for the series, and lo and behold, the German producer was insisting that he make changes, putting Hal in exactly the same mess I was afraid of getting us into. His advice to me was to pull out, and that's what I did. In the end, it was probably all for the best. For the fact was that not long after I finished writing the short version of Martin Frost, I began thinking I should extend it into a full-length feature film. Martin brings Claire back to life—and then what? That's where the story would start to get even more interesting, I felt. So I sketched out a plan for the rest of the film—nothing definite yet, but a stack of notes to mull over for the future. Then I put it all away and started writing *The Book of Illusions*, which had been brewing inside me for a long time, close to ten years. That was the summer of 1999, and I finished the manuscript two years later, exactly one month before the attack on the World Trade Center. Toward the end of the book, David Zimmer, the narrator, gets to see one of Hector Mann's late films shot in the New Mexico desert. For numerous reasons, *The Inner Life of Martin Frost* seemed to be the perfect story to use at this point in the novel, so I adapted the short version of the script and put it in.

CC: Did you make many changes?
PA: Nothing essential, really. The action had to be shifted to 1946, for example. The location had to move to Hector's house in New Mexico. The film had to be shot in black and white, and I had to abandon the scenario form and describe the film in prose. Quite a challenge, I might add. Those changes aside, however, the film in the book is very close to the original screenplay.

CC: Why didn't you incorporate the longer version into the novel?
PA: I was tempted, but I decided it would take too many pages to do it right, and in the process I would throw off the balance of the narrative.

CC: Why did it take you three years to go back to *Martin Frost* after you finished the novel?

PA: There were other books I wanted to write, books I had been thinking about for many years, and I was reluctant to leave my room. . . . Now that I think about it, September 11 probably had something to do with it as well. It hit me very hard, watching it happen from the window of my house in Brooklyn, and the idea of making another film lost its attraction for a while. I wanted to be alone, to think my own thoughts. Directing a film means giving up a good two years of your life, and except for the writing of the screenplay, you're working with other people all the time. I just wasn't in the mood for that.

CC: What changed your mind?

PA: *The Brooklyn Follies* was the fourth novel I'd written in six years, and I think I was feeling a little burned out, not ready to start writing another work of fiction. And *Martin Frost* was still on my mind. I hadn't been able to get rid of the story, so one fine day I decided to take a crack at finishing it.

CC: The entire movie takes place out in the countryside, in a very isolated house. What was the appeal of that isolation, and what importance does it have in the film?

PA: To be very blunt, it was largely a question of money. If I was going to get a chance to make another film, I knew it would have to be done on a small scale, with an extremely limited budget. That's why I wrote it for just four actors and used just three locations: the house and the grounds of the house; the empty road; and for three days at the end of production, a sound-stage, where we filmed the dream sequences and the shots of the spinning typewriter. I was trying to be realistic. I'm proud of *Lulu on the Bridge*, but it turned out to be a commercial failure, and I understood how difficult it would be for me to raise money for a new project. So, to quote a line from Fortunato in the film, I forced myself to "think small." But when it comes to the isolation of the setting—to answer your question at last—I wanted to create an otherworldly ambience, a place that could be anywhere, a place that felt as if it existed outside time. The action unfolds in Martin's head, after all, and by choosing the house I did, a little domain cut off from the rest of the world, I felt I would be enhancing the interiority of the story.

CC: Why did you shoot in Portugal?

PA: Because the producer of the film, Paulo Branco, is Portuguese. I met Paulo fourteen or fifteen years ago in Berlin—through Wim Wenders, a mutual friend—and we've stayed in touch ever since. After *Lulu on the Bridge*, he told me that if I ever wanted to make another film, all I had to do was call him, and he would produce it. When the script for *Martin Frost* was finished, I called. We explored the possibility of shooting here in America, but we simply couldn't find enough money to do it. Paulo has made close to two hundred movies all over Europe, but Portugal is his home base, and he has all the means at his disposal to work inexpensively there—access to equipment, labs, crew, the whole works—and so we decided to go there. You watch the finished film, and you don't really know where you are. To me, it looks like Northern California. And all the props in the movie are American: the brown grocery bag, the house keys, the yellow legal pad, the eight-and-a-half by-eleven typing paper, the license plates, the books on the shelves, everything.

CC: You put together quite an ensemble of actors. How did you go about casting the film?

PA: In November 2004, just when I was about to start writing the screenplay, I went to France to give a reading tour in five or six cities. In each theater, I would read a couple of paragraphs in English, and then a French actor would read the same passage in translation—and back and forth we'd go until the reading was finished. When my French publisher asked me which French actor I'd like to work with, I suggested Irène Jacob. I had met Irène in 1998 when I went to the Cannes Film Festival with *Lulu on the Bridge*. One afternoon, we wound up sitting next to each other at lunch, and we had a very good talk. When you see her act in a film like *Red* or *The Double Life of Véronique*, her talent and presence on screen are remarkable, but I found her just as remarkable in life. There's a special quality to Irène, something I've never seen in anyone else. A kindness, a goodness, a tenderness—I don't know what to call it—along with a terrific sense of humor and a startling lack of egoism, which is almost unheard of in an actor. In short, she's an exceptional person, and I wanted her to read with me. She happened to be eight months pregnant with her second child at the time, which meant she couldn't go on the tour, but we did the reading in Paris together. A couple of nights later, she invited me to a play she was performing in (yes, acting while eight months pregnant!), and after the play we went out for a drink with some friends. It was raining that night, and she offered to drive me back to my hotel in her car. That was when lightning struck. I looked over at her as she sat behind the wheel, and I realized that I was looking at Claire, the one and only Claire. I said to her: "I'm about to start writing a screenplay, and I think I have a part for you. Would you be interested in reading it when I'm finished?" She said she would, and when I finished in February, I mailed her the script. A few days later, she called me in New York and said she was in.

CC: What about the others?
PA: Michael Imperioli had auditioned for *Smoke* in 1994, and even though we didn't hire him, I was very impressed by his work. I gave him a small part in *Lulu on the Bridge*, but then something bigger came along for him, and I had to let him go. But I always hoped that one day we would wind up working together. He's made a great success in *The Sopranos*, of course, but he told me that the movie scripts he's sent are uniformly dismal. Cops and robbers, always a cop or a robber, and he turns them all down. He's so much better than that, with so much more range and intelligence. When I sent him *Martin Frost*, he accepted right away. One reading, and he was in. As for Sophie, I didn't meet with any resistance either. I know that some people will say I cast her because she's my daughter, but that's not true. There's no one who could have played the part better than she does—an eighteen-year-old who can both act and sing at that level. I feel lucky to have gotten her at the beginning of what promises to be a fine career. You never know in this business, of course, but there's a good chance that it won't be long before people stop thinking of her as my daughter and refer to me as her father.

CC: And your leading man?
PA: Every movie has its problems, and casting Martin proved to be the biggest problem of all. My first choice was Willem Dafoe, who was going to play Martin for the short version in 1999, but he was unavailable. A couple of good actors then turned me down. After that, someone very good accepted with a lot of enthusiasm, but then we ran into scheduling difficulties, and he had to back out. Finally, I found someone else and thought we were home free. The film was set to begin shooting on May 8. In February, I went to Portugal for the first time and found the house with my first assistant director, Zé Maria Vaz da Silva, and the production designer, Zé Branco. Then I returned to New York and worked for the next month with the costume designer, Adelle Lutz, on wardrobe choices for the four actors. The plan was for me to go back to Portugal on April 1 to begin preproduction. On March 15, just two weeks before I was supposed to leave, Adelle and I did a wardrobe fitting with the actor who was going to play Martin. Something wasn't

right. He was very agitated, not at all himself, and then Adelle and I learned that he was in a bad spot financially. We were making the movie for next to nothing, and all the actors had agreed to work for minimum salaries. Now, suddenly, my distraught Martin let it be known that he couldn't do the part for so little and needed more money. What could I do? I understood his dilemma, but there was no way we could satisfy his demands. Fortunately, we parted on amicable terms.

CC: How did David Thewlis enter the picture?

PA: That evening, I asked myself the question: if I could get any English-speaking actor in the world to play the part, who would I want? The answer was: David Thewlis. I had met David only once, all the way back in 1997, when I was a member of the jury at Cannes. Mike Leigh was also on the jury that year, and one morning as we were walking along somewhere, David happened to pass by, and Mike introduced us. After that, David and I talked for a little while, and I remember being very touched when he told me that the last three novels he had read had all been written by me. All well and good. At least David Thewlis knew who I was. But how to get in touch with him without going through an agent? And how could I hope that an actor of his ability would be available? I contacted Heidi Levitt in Los Angeles, the casting director who had worked on *Smoke*, *Blue in the Face*, and *Lulu on the Bridge*, and asked her if she knew someone who could give her David's number. Yes, she said, she thought there was someone, and half an hour later she called back with the number. A promising start. The next morning, I called David in London and left a message on his cell phone. He called back several hours later, and the first thing he told me was that when he heard my message he thought that one of his friends was playing a prank on him. It turned out that for the past several weeks David had been asking around for my telephone number in order to contact *me*. There was a complicated and funny story he wanted to tell me about one of my books, and he couldn't believe that I had contacted *him*.

CC: And then?

PA: The script was e-mailed to David, and the next day he accepted the part. It felt like a miracle, a stroke of astonishing luck. Two and a half weeks later, we met for the first time in Lisbon. He and Irène had both come to rehearse with me for several days, and we hit it off immediately. Not only is he a superb actor, he's an irresistible person: intelligent, funny, a great raconteur, and kind to everyone around him. And—here's where it really starts to get interesting—he's a writer. For five or six years prior to playing a novelist in my movie, David had been writing a novel of his own. Incredibly, he finished the manuscript while we were all in Portugal, just before the first day of shooting.

CC: What were some of the problems you ran into while making the film?
PA: I lost my American DP in early April, just one week before he was supposed to join me in Portugal. Paulo sprang right into action and saved the day by finding me Christophe Beaucarne. As soon as Christophe accepted the job, I flew to Paris to meet him. We talked for six or seven straight hours, going over the thirty-page shot list I had put together in New York with the other DP. This is not to denigrate the man who backed out, but at this point I can't imagine having made the film with anyone other than Christophe. He's smart, fast, sensitive, and experienced. And physically one of the strongest people I've ever known. He was born in Belgium, and after a while David started calling him "Muscles from Brussels." David also told me (and this is someone who's appeared in close to forty films) that Christophe was the best DP he ever worked with. So, another problem solved at the last minute. And then, more recently, after the film had been shot and I returned to New York to begin working with my editor, Tim Squyres, I lost the composer who had agreed to write the score. Music is an essential part of the film. There's more than forty minutes of it in *Martin Frost*, and just when he was supposed to start working, the composer bailed out on me because he was backed up on another project—which, rest assured, was paying him a lot more money than our poor little movie ever could. And so there I was, stuck again, trying to think of a replacement. Two or three days later, Sophie turned nineteen, and Wim Wenders called to wish her happy birthday. He's known her since she was a little tot, and they're very fond of each other. As it happened, I picked up the phone, and before I passed the receiver to Sophie, I told Wim about losing my composer and asked if he had any suggestions. He did. A man named Laurent Petitgand, who had written the circus music for *Wings of Desire* and the scores for several of Wim's movies, including *Far Away, So Close!* Dear Wim. He was the one who introduced me to Paulo Branco, and now he had just given me my composer. I called Laurent right away, and when he said he was interested in the job (low pay or not), Tim and I express-mailed him a DVD of a rough cut of the film. Laurent watched it, and the next thing I knew, he was in. Like everyone else who wound up working on this project, he accepted immediately, was undeterred by the

minuscule salary, and did an outstanding job. I think his score is exceptionally beautiful.

CC: You wore two hats on this movie: writer and director. What are the advantages of doing both? What are the disadvantages?

PA: To tell the truth, I can't think of a single disadvantage. I'm not a full-time filmmaker, after all, and I tend to think of my occasional forays into the world of movies as an extension of my work as a novelist, as a storyteller. Not all stories should be novels. Some should be plays. Some should be films. Some should be narrative poems. In the case of *Martin Frost*, it was conceived as a film from the start—just as *Smoke* and *Lulu on the Bridge* were. By directing my own screenplay, I profit from the fact that I know the text better than anyone else. I know the rhythm of the words, the rhythm of the images, and I can communicate these things directly to the actors and the crew.

CC: You worked with a British actor and an American actor, a French actress and an American actress. Your crew was Portuguese. Your DP was French. Let's call it an international team. Was communication difficult at times? Was it a help or a hindrance to be collaborating with people who had different working methods?

PA: Actually, communication was never a problem. Three languages were spoken on the set, but English was the principal language. Both Irène and Christophe speak English well, and most of the Portuguese crew had fairly good English. The ones who didn't know English knew French, but since I speak French, there wasn't any difficulty. I made a point of speaking in English with Irène from the first moment she accepted the part—to keep her immersed in the language of the film—but naturally, when she and Christophe had a one-on-one conversation, they spoke French. The same with the crew. They spoke in Portuguese with one another, but either in English or in French with me and the actors. There were some funny moments, of course. Zé Maria, the first AD, calling out before each scene: "Let's rehearsal!" Or Diana Coelho, the line producer, trying to explain to me that she and another woman were the same age, uttering this immortal sentence: "She has my old." But I understood exactly what she meant. We were such a small group—the working crew was only about eighteen people—we all became quite close, and while everyone worked very hard—*very hard*—there was a lot of laughter and goodwill on the set. As for different working methods—all very interesting to me, but since film is an international medium, a universal language, really, the differences are rather nuanced. An alternate method for numbering setups in a scene, for example, or the slightly different way the script supervisor wrote up her continuity reports. But there were also many advantages. In America, union rules forbid a DP from operating the camera. Not so in Europe—so Christophe operated himself. And while there's no union in Portugal, there are nevertheless certain unwritten rules. Eleven-hour days, with one hour for lunch. In America, crews work twelve hours. But only five days a week, whereas in Portugal we worked six.

CC: What was your biggest surprise on the set?
PA: The passion and intensity of the crew. The crews I've worked with in America have all been good, but much larger, and so inevitably a lot of people wind up standing around and doing nothing for long stretches of time. Because we were so small, everyone was busy from the beginning of the day to the end. People didn't walk, they ran. I was impressed by how knowledgeable they were and how much they accomplished. In some cases, one person would do the work normally done by three or four people on an American set. I myself like to work intensely, to keep pushing things along. I'm very decisive (I know what I want!), and I'm a stickler for details. The crew seemed to enjoy working at that rhythm, and we actually managed to shoot the film in twenty-five days, not twenty-nine days as originally planned. That allowed me to give the crew two Saturdays off—which was good for morale.

CC: Making a movie on a small budget isn't easy. Did it force you to restrict yourself a lot? Did it feel like a big constraint? Did it help in any way?
PA: One would always like to have more money, but I must say that I enjoyed the challenge of having to make something with very little. It keeps you sharp, on your toes. The film was designed to be small from the start. The previous scripts I'd written for *Smoke* and *Lulu on the Bridge* were quite long—so long that large chunks of filmed material were cut out in the editing room. With *Martin Frost*, I didn't have that luxury. The film was literally edited in the script, so that every scene and every word of dialogue wound up in the finished version of the movie. Not one moment deleted. Tim Squyres, my brilliant, irreplaceable editor (who also cut *Lulu on the Bridge*), edited a big film that came out last year, *Syriana*. He told me they shot over a million feet of film. With *Martin Frost*, we shot about eighty thousand feet—including the slow motion sequences, which eat up film stock at four times the normal rate. The key to pulling off a little film without any resources, I think, is to be prepared. What helped enormously in this case was the rehearsal time I had with the actors before we started shooting. Late last summer, when we were still hopeful that we would begin filming in the fall of '05 in

America, Irène came to New York, and the entire cast (with the old Martin) rehearsed for a solid week in Michael Imperioli's sixty-seat theater in Manhattan, Studio Dante. All-day sessions, from early in the morning until late in the afternoon. On two different trips to Paris, I worked alone with Irène at her house for several days at a stretch. Then there were the four days with Irène and David in Lisbon at the beginning of April. And finally, at the end of the month, a full week of rehearsal with the whole cast (except Sophie, who was finishing her freshman year of college) in the house where we shot the film. All this made a big difference. I cut many lines from the script, and by the time we started filming, the actors were truly prepared, comfortable in their roles. For the last day of that rehearsal period, I devised a nutty experiment: we shot the entire film on video—in order, scene by scene. It took about eight hours, and we were all exhausted at the end, but I think it gave us a sense of the film as a whole, and we came up with some new ideas for blocking and camera setups. That was fundamental, but also having a plan when you show up at the set in the morning, a coherent shot list, and an idea of what you want to accomplish during the hours ahead. Paradoxically, the plan gives you the freedom to be spontaneous, the confidence to change things at the last minute.

CC: How do you see the role of director? Is the focus more on transmitting and putting into images your own vision, or is it about coordinating and using the work of an artistic team?

PA: It's both. It has to be both, because in order to get your vision onto the screen, you need the best work possible from the actors, the DP, and the crew. Because the scope of *Martin Frost* was so small, I was personally involved in every aspect of the production. I actually went out shopping for clothes with Adelle, and every picture on the walls of the house, every book on the shelves, every tablecloth and wine glass, I chose with Zé Branco, the production designer. One crazy Sunday during preproduction, when we were still getting the house ready for the film, I walked into the kitchen and decided that I hated the knobs on the cupboard doors and drawers. They were white porcelain spheres that resembled Ping-Pong balls, and I knew they would look terrible on film—even if you saw them only in the background of a shot. So I unscrewed every damn one of them myself—about fifty or sixty of those hideous Ping-Pong balls—and stashed them away in a drawer.

CC: How do you reconcile what you want with what is being given to you by the actors and the DP?

PA: The director is responsible for everything, and therefore his job is to make every aspect of the film as perfect as possible. If I think something isn't working, we do it again. And again. And again. We keep on doing it until we get it right. Fortunately for me, the actors and the DP on this film were all great artists, and they were as demanding on themselves as I was on myself. There weren't any conflicts. We all kept working until we were happy with the results.

CC: What do you look for in an actor? What is the most important quality?

PA: A good question—and a difficult one to answer. I suppose it begins with a kind of fascination, a desire to watch the person perform. Why do we find some people compelling, while others leave us cold? Why can some actors break our hearts or make us want to laugh our heads off? It's a great mystery to me. How do we know when something is funny or not? If people laugh, it's funny. If they don't laugh, it's not funny. But no comedian has ever known in advance what is going to work or not work. That's why they have to keep trying out their material in front of live audiences. The same with acting. Some people have the gift, others don't. But when you see someone who's really good, you recognize it at once. You're transported, and you can't take your eyes off them.

CC: You collaborated on two films with Wayne Wang, then wrote and directed a film on your own, *Lulu on the Bridge*. Was this experience different—and if so, how?

PA: Some aspects were quite similar, others vastly different. Working with Tim Squyres and Adelle Lutz, for example, a close rapport with the actors, the DP, the crew, the immense pleasure of making a film, the hard work—all that was the same. But *Lulu* was finished eight years ago, and there have been enormous technological changes in filmmaking since then. Not so much with the equipment on the set—we shot *Martin Frost* on thirty-five-millimeter film, the dolly and the dolly tracks were the same, the lights were the same, the boom was the same, and so on—but the way film is processed and edited is very different now. In the old days, you would do a take of a scene, and if you thought it was good, you would say to the script supervisor, "Let's print that one." You don't print anything anymore. The whole day's shooting is digitally scanned from the negative and turned into a DVD. The old ritual of going to a little screening room at the lab every night to watch the rushes is dead. In Portugal, Christophe and I watched the rushes on a TV monitor in my hotel room. And then there are the advances in editing. Tim and I cut *Lulu* on an Avid, which was a fairly big machine in 1998. Now he was able to download the entire Avid program into a laptop, and we've edited the film in my house! That's proved to be a great advantage, since I can smoke my little cigars here while we're working, which keeps me in good spirits. And then, most amazingly, there's the question of the music. Laurent has been composing on a computer in Paris (we'll be recording the music with real musicians in a couple of weeks) and e-mailing the cues to Tim's computer—which we then cut into our digitized version of the film. Luddite that I am, I can only gape. It feels as if we're playing with magic toys.

CC: There are some funny moments in the film. The broken chair, Martin chasing the tire down the road, Fortunato's stories, the outrageous cowboy suit. Yet other scenes are intensely dramatic, or mysterious, at times even mystical. How do you account for these shifts in tone, the oscillation between humor and drama? What role does comedy play in your work—and in *Martin Frost* in particular?

PA: Life is both tragic and funny, both absurd and profoundly meaningful. More or less unconsciously, I've tried to embrace this double aspect of experience in the stories I've written—both novels and screenplays. I feel it's the most honest, most truthful way of looking at the world, and when I think of some of the writers I like best—Shakespeare, Cervantes, Dickens, Kafka, Beckett—they all turn out to be masters of combining the light with the dark, the strange with the familiar. *The Inner Life of Martin Frost* is a very curious story. A story about a man who writes a story about a man who writes a story—and the story inside the story, the film we watch from the moment Martin wakes up to find Claire sleeping beside him to the moment Martin stops typing and looks out the window, is so wild and implausible, so crazy and unpredictable, that without some doses of humor, it would have been unbearably heavy. At the same time, I think the funny bits underscore the pathos of Martin's situation. The tire scene, for example. The viewer knows that Claire has just left the car and run off into the woods, and here comes Martin pushing a tire down the road, unaware that the woman he loves has just disappeared—and suddenly the tire gets away from him. It's classic silent comedy: man versus object. He runs after the tire—only to have it bounce off a stone and knock him to the ground. Funny, but also pathetic. The same goes for Fortunato, with all his weird comments, bad jokes, and ridiculous short stories. He shows up when Martin is at his most abject, suffering over the loss of Claire, and amusing as I find this character to be, his presence underscores the powerful loneliness that has enveloped Martin. The saddest scene in the film is also one of the funniest: when Martin practices Screwdriver Darts on his own. The poor man is so lost, he doesn't know what to do with himself anymore.

CC: Screwdriver Darts. Where did you come up with that idea?

PA: The inspiration came from something that happened in my childhood. I was ten or eleven years old, and one day after school I went back to the house of my best friend. For some reason, he had decided to set up his bedroom in the basement, and there we were, sitting in that room, which had soft, knotty pine walls, throwing a screwdriver and trying to get it to stick in the wood. Don't ask me why we were doing it. That's all I remember. Throwing the screwdriver and trying to get it to stick in the wood. Neither one of us could do it. We threw the screwdriver ten times, twenty times, thirty times, with no success at all. Then my friend's older brother came downstairs and poked his head in the door. He must have been about fourteen and was much bigger and stronger than we were. "What are you two idiots up to?" he asked. We explained that we were trying to get the screwdriver to stick in the wall, but it couldn't be done, it was physically impossible. "Of course it's possible," my friend's brother said. "Do you want to bet?" Naturally we wanted to bet, since we were convinced we would win. The stakes were set at five dollars, a tremendous amount of money for kids back then, the equivalent of ten or twenty weeks' allowance. We gave the screwdriver to the brother, who was still standing by the door, and without even pausing to think, he raised the thing behind his head and let off a fiendishly powerful throw. The screwdriver sailed clear across the room, and then bang, it stuck in the wall. It left an indelible impression on me. And that was how Screwdriver Darts was born. I'm hoping it will catch on after the movie comes out and that Screwdriver Dart leagues will be set up all around the world.

CC: The pivotal scene in the film is when Claire dies and Martin brings her back to life by burning the pages of his story. Do you think writing is a dangerous weapon? Can it kill?

PA: Writing can certainly be dangerous. Dangerous for the reader—if something is powerful enough to change his view of the world—and dangerous for the writer. Think of how many writers were murdered by Stalin: Osip Mandelstam, Isaac Babel, untold others. Think of the fatwa against Salman

Rushdie. Think of all the imprisoned writers in the world today. But can writing kill? No, not literally. A book isn't a machine gun or an electric chair. And yet, strange things sometimes happen that make you stop and wonder. The case of the French writer Louis-René des Forêts, for instance. I first heard about it when I was living in Paris in the early seventies, and it haunted me so much that I wound up incorporating it into one of my novels years later, *Oracle Night*. Des Forêts was a promising young writer in the fifties who had published one novel and one collection of stories. Then he wrote a narrative poem in which a child drowns in the sea. Not long after the book was published, his own child drowned. There might not have been any rational link between the imaginary death and the real death, but des Forêts was so shattered by the experience that he stopped writing for decades. A terrible story. It's not hard to understand how he felt.

CC: *The Inner Life of Martin Frost* begins with a slow tracking shot of a series of family photographs. If one looks closely, one recognizes that these are pictures of you and your wife, Siri Hustvedt. Supposedly, these two people are the owners of the house, Jack and Diane Restau, Martin's friends. If you rearrange the letters of the name *Restau*, it becomes *Auster*. Immediately after we see the photographs, the camera stops in front of the door, and an unseen narrator begins to speak. The name of the narrator is not credited in the film, but the voice happens to belong to you. Would you care to explain?
PA: When I thought about what we would need to make the house look like a real house lived in by real people, family photos were among the first things that sprang to mind. Every family has photos scattered around the house. Rather than go to the expense of taking pictures of actors, I pulled forty or fifty photos from our own albums and took them to Portugal with me. Why not? They were authentic family pictures, and if someone recognized Siri and me, fine. If they didn't, that was fine, too. As for the name *Restau* and the fact that I did the narration myself, I think they add a subtle but interesting element to the film—for those who figure out the scrambled name or recognize my voice. Everyone who sees the film will know from the credits that I'm the writer and the director. I'm the man who wrote the story about the man who wrote the story about the man who wrote the story. Why pretend otherwise?

Interview: Paul Auster

Greg LaGambina/2008

Interview originally published by The A.V. Club/The Onion (www.avclub.com). Reprinted with permission of Greg LaGambina

The A.V. Club: The story of *Man in the Dark* begins literally with a man in the dark, telling himself a story to cope with his insomnia. How did this story come to you? Do different stories come to you in different ways?

Paul Auster: It's always a mystery to me, I have to confess. I've never been able to witness the birth of an idea. It's as if one second, there's nothing going on, and the next second, something is there. Stories come up out of my unconscious, up from places that are inaccessible to me. If it's compelling, if it knocks me down or throws me against a wall, I get interested and start to explore it.

AVC: This book is already being branded as a "post-9/11" novel. Did this story take shape because of September 11?

PA: No. The spark was the 2000 elections, which were a source of tremendous frustration and outrage. Al Gore was elected president, and then, through political and legal manipulations, the Republicans stole it from him. I've had this eerie sense for the last eight years that we've been living in a parallel world, a shadow world. And the reality is that Al Gore is finishing his second term as president, there's no war in Iraq, and there might never have been 9/11. When one considers how thoroughly the Clinton administration was tracking these people, it's possible the towers never would have fallen. I think that sense of unreality is what inspired me to write the story that [August] Brill tells himself.

AVC: We tell ourselves stories to fend off reality, like Brill does when he says, "Give me my story . . . to keep the ghosts away." On the other hand, some argue that Bush told us a story so he could involve us in the actuality of the war in Iraq.

PA: Yes, that's a good example. You're right: a fiction creating reality.

AVC: Is that something that's going on in this novel?

PA: No, because that fiction is propaganda. That fiction is just lies. The kind of fiction I'm trying to write is about telling the truth.

AVC: Is *Man in the Dark* a story you constructed to help you deal with the catastrophe of 9/11, or with other violence around the world?

PA: It's possible. There was another very important factor, too. I don't know if you noticed, but the book is dedicated to David Grossman and his family. He's an Israeli novelist and essayist. A great writer, in fact. And a very close friend of mine, someone I admire as much as anyone I have ever met. Two years ago, when David's son Uri was twenty years old, he was killed in the war between Israel and Lebanon. I knew the boy, and his death was a shattering experience. Not just for David and his family, of course, who are still suffering horribly, but for me too. I haven't been able to stop thinking about it.

AVC: Does making art out of these events help us heal? Do you admire any particular so-called post-9/11 novels?

PA: I don't know if it helps. I doubt it. As for the novels you refer to, Don DeLillo's *Falling Man* is the one I like the best. I thought there were some beautiful things in it, particularly the relationship between the man who finds the briefcase and the woman whose husband owned the briefcase. It's quite a beautiful passage.

AVC: In the novel, Brill spends a lot of time with his granddaughter Katya, watching and discussing films. At one point, Brill says, "Escaping into a film is not like escaping into a book." You've written and directed films yourself. Can you elaborate on this idea?

PA: Books demand more. You have to be a more active participant. Brill says, "You can actually watch a film in a state of passivity and even enjoy the film." Films often go right through us. You see the film, you might even find it entertaining, and later it's gone. Books stay with us a lot longer.

AVC: When Brill is talking about the film *Tokyo Story* with Katya, he mentions that "some films are as good as books," but compares the film to a Tolstoy novella. Can the best films be only as good as the best novellas, falling short of the scope of a full novel?

PA: Having made films, I feel that the scope of the average 90- to 120-minute movie has about the same narrative heft as a long short story or novella. Movies are not novels, and that's why when filmmakers try to adapt novels, particularly long or complex novels, the result is almost always a failure. It can't be done. You need six hours, twenty hours, to do it justice. The best filmmakers, I think, have always had very narrow frameworks for their stories, and then they can go deeply, rather than skimming the surface. When I think of *Tokyo Story*, yes, it's like a novella. That doesn't mean it's not great. Some of my favorite Tolstoy works are his novellas.

AVC: In the act of discussing books and films with others who have read or seen the same things, do we ever really arrive at a certain truth about the work, or can we only come as close as a common meeting point?

PA: Everyone reads a different book. That's what's interesting. Everyone sees a different film as well. We bring our pasts and our private experiences to whatever work of art we're engaged with. It's not mathematics. There are different answers for different people. But talking with another person about something you've both seen or read can often sharpen your thoughts about that work and help you think more clearly about it.

AVC: Does that happen for you when you're talking about your own work?

PA: No, it's completely different. To tell you the truth, I don't like talking about my work at all. I find it very difficult. I never know what to say. It's too close to me, and so many things happen unconsciously while I'm working, things I'm not even aware of, that when people point these things out to me, I'll say, "That's interesting." But I don't know what to make of them.

AVC: Do you ever learn anything about your own work from what other people say about it?

PA: No, I don't think so. [Laughs.]

AVC: In *Man in the Dark*, when Katya and her grandfather are discussing the films *Grand Illusion*, *The Bicycle Thief*, and *The World of Apu*, she comes up with this theory of the object—

PA: Yes, about inanimate objects as a means of expressing human emotion. I think it's important that you hear this conversation about the first three films—there's the fourth film that Brill speaks about later [*Tokyo Story*], but the first three films are discussed early in the book. Each one of these films and the themes in the films are very intimate. Three stories about men and women, husbands and wives. And because the story Brill is thinking about is so huge and apocalyptic, the counterweight to that is the intimacy of the stories in these films. Then, as the book moves on, about two-thirds of the way through, three-quarters of the way through, it takes a very sharp turn. Brill and his granddaughter are suddenly together in the dark talking about the family and his marriage to her grandmother. It becomes an extremely intimate story at that point.

AVC: Yeah, you sort of expect the story he's concocting for himself in bed to deliver the climactic moment of the novel as a whole, but there's a shift.
PA: From the big to the small, from the imagined to the real. The story that Brill thinks up is as much about Brill's state of mind as anything else. It can be read as a psychological portrait of a man through the medium of a story.

AVC: There's also the character of Katya's mother, Brill's daughter, Miriam. She's working on a book about Nathaniel Hawthorne's daughter Rose, which leads Brill to abandon work on his own memoirs. He makes the excuse that "one writer in the house is enough." Seeing as how you're married to a novelist [Siri Hustvedt], it's hard not to interpret that as an inside joke.
PA: Actually, I wasn't thinking about that at all. I project myself so deeply into the characters in my novels that I'm not thinking about my own life. It really isn't a reference. I mean, if you want to see it as a joke, that's fine. [Laughs.] But it wasn't intended that way, for the fact is that there are two writers in our house, and neither one of us has ever had any problems with that.

AVC: In Brill's alternate reality, he mentions how the new Independent States of America have a foreign policy of "no meddling anywhere" and a domestic policy of "universal health insurance, no more oil, no more cars or planes," etc. But he also states that these things are "a dream of the future, since the war drags on." Will these perfect things or ideas always be off in some unattainable distance, as our own war drags on?
PA: I don't think of them as "perfect things." Medical care for everyone in the country seems to me a basic right. If every other country in the West can do it, why can't we? It's not some starry-eyed vision of a utopian future, it's something we could easily do right now. I think the Independent States

of America in the book fully intend to do it, but they're fighting a war, their backs are against the wall, and they haven't worked it through yet.

AVC: There's a line in the book about how we all go about our regular lives until "an unexpected event comes crashing down on us to jolt us out of our torpor." September 11 jolted us, but was eventually exploited to achieve mostly negative things. Can we be jolted into something positive?

PA: It all depends. I remember those days vividly. It's just seven years ago now. I can remember doing quite a few interviews at the time, interviews with foreign journalists. Right here, in Brooklyn, the smoke was coming into our house, and I was not fit for writing anything at that point. I had just finished *The Book of Illusions*, in fact, so I wasn't doing much of anything, and people kept calling me from all these different radio and TV stations in Europe and Japan to comment. And for once, I did it. I went out and talked. I can remember saying again and again and again, "A terrible thing has happened, *but* this should be a wake-up call for our country, and we have a great opportunity now to reinvent ourselves. To rethink our position about oil and energy, to rethink our relationships with other cultures and countries, and to examine why there are other people out there who want to attack us." I still believe we wasted a golden opportunity to make significant changes in our country. I think people in America would have been ready and willing to do it, but the Bush administration took a simplistic, moronic approach to it, playing on peoples' fears rather than their hopes. It's only now that the public seems to have woken up and is ready to boot him out of office, even though he's leaving anyway. He's done. I look at him on TV now, when he's giving a speech, and he looks like a ghost. He doesn't exist anymore. He's finished. Defunct.

AVC: Brill looks at Miriam's manuscript and fixates on a line of Rose Hawthorne's poetry: "As the weird world rolls on. . . ." Throughout the book, there's this sense of life just happening to us, with or without our input. Are we all just stumbling toward some gloomy fate?

PA: No! It's just the opposite. "The weird world rolls on . . ." meaning that through all the ups and downs, all the travails we go through, all the horrors, all the wars, all the deaths, all the cruelties, there's still something that keeps us wanting to wake up in the morning and go on with our lives—to make children, to fall in love, to continue the enormous adventure of being alive.

A Connoisseur of Clouds, a Meteorologist of Whims: *The Rumpus* Interview with Paul Auster

Juliet Linderman/2009

From *The Rumpus.net* 16 Nov. 2009. Reproduced with permission of Juliet Linderman

Rumpus: What were you doing before we met today? What is a typical day in the life of Paul Auster?

Paul Auster: There are two kinds of typical days. There's the typical day when I'm writing a novel, and there's the typical day when I'm not. I just finished something new, so I'm unemployed again, which means that I had a pretty lackadaisical day. When I'm writing a novel, I stick to a rigid routine. I get up between seven and eight, I have orange juice and tea, read the paper, and then go off to a little apartment I have in the neighborhood where I work. I stay there until five or six. It's a very spartan environment. I don't even own a computer. I write by hand and then I type it up on an old manual typewriter. But I cross out a lot—I'm not writing on stone tablets, it's just ink on paper. I don't feel comfortable without a pen or a pencil in my hand. I can't think with my fingers on a keyboard. Words are generated for me by gripping the pen, and pressing the point onto the paper.

Rumpus: You're a very prolific writer. You've published works of fiction, nonfiction, poetry, translation, critical essays and screenplays. When and how did you decide that you wanted to be a writer, and what do you recall as your earliest formative reading experience?

Auster: For one reason or another, I became a passionate reader when I was very little. By the age of nine or so, I was writing little poems—don't ask me why, they were wretched, wretched, awful little things—but I enjoyed doing it, and eventually I graduated to writing short stories. When I was twelve years old, in the sixth grade, I wrote a long short story, and the teacher let me read it out loud to the other students at the end of school each day. My public debut as a writer! If I'm not mistaken, it was a story about someone hiding stolen pearls in a typewriter. I don't know where I came up with the idea, I probably stole it. I remember doing drawings of all the faces of the characters too . . . ridiculous. But as I got older and entered my adolescence, I got more serious about all this. The turning point for me was *Crime and Punishment*, which I read in a kind of fever at fifteen. When I put it down, I thought, if this is what novels are, then I want to be a novelist.

Rumpus: You've got a new novel out, *Invisible*. In part two of *Invisible*, one character says to another, "Fear is a good thing. Fear is what drives us to take risks and extend ourselves beyond our normal limits. Any writer who feels he is standing on safe ground is unlikely to produce anything of value." What kinds of risks do you take as a writer, and when is the last time you truly felt you were not standing on solid ground?

Auster: I never feel I'm standing on solid ground, and I do write with a certain kind of trembling fear. As a poet or a novelist or a painter, you are pushing yourself all the time, always looking for a new way to approach things, challenging yourself and never, never trying to write the same book twice. You challenge yourself aesthetically, morally, psychologically. You go into terrain that can be very uncomfortable, and you have to do it with a certain boldness. You can't shrink from the task, but that's what makes it all so interesting. Otherwise, better to do another job. With *Invisible*, the structure is very strange, it's very risky, as was *Man in the Dark*. That one loops in on itself, then takes a sudden right-turn about two-thirds through. As does this new one; it breaks into pieces by the end. There are two male narrators, and a female narrator in the last chapter as well. The story seemed to demand to be written that way. Then there's the business that takes place in part 2 . . . which was utterly new territory for me, and it was difficult to write. I wanted to do it in a very open and honest way, which was demanding emotionally. I don't even know where it came from—but there it was, and I went with it.

Rumpus: Do you have a particular process, or do you find that you invent a new process with each new book you write?

Auster: It's new, it's always new. I'm scared at the beginning of each book, because I've never written it before. I feel I have to teach myself how to do it. The tone of every book is slightly different; there's a music in each that is distinct from all the others, and even the new book that I've just finished

[*Sunset Park*]—is shaped differently from anything I've tried before. It contains some very long sentences, sentences that are three pages long, but there was some sort of inner cadence I was trying to create, and I felt that by using long, rolling, run-on sentences, the book had more propulsion.

Rumpus: You seem to have a fascination with writers, and they tend to play very central roles in your novels. Sometimes it seems that you explore the act of writing as a form of therapy, as if writing about something somehow makes it more real, gives it more meaning. But you also write about writing as a compulsion, as a tool that can unlock dark, difficult parts of the unconscious that you might not even know exist. Aside from a career, what role does writing play in your life? In short, why write?

Auster: I don't know why I write. If I knew the answer, I probably wouldn't have to do it. But it is a compulsion. You don't choose it, it chooses you. And I wouldn't recommend it to anyone. When young people tell me they want to write, I say: Think very carefully about it. There will be few rewards, you probably won't make any money, you probably won't become famous, and you will spend your whole life locked up in a room by yourself worrying about how to survive. You have to have a tremendous taste for solitude. I think all writers are a bit crazy. Damaged souls, incapable of doing anything else. On the other hand, when I'm writing, even though it's hard and often a struggle, I'm happier than when I'm not writing. I feel alive. Whereas when I'm not writing, I'm nothing more than your common everyday neurotic. I feel that the act of writing, in and of itself, is a tool for probing the world in ways that wouldn't be possible without a pen in your hand. It's a strange, almost neurological phenomenon, and the words seem to generate more words—but only when you're writing. You can't do it in your head. It's only in the heat of composition that these things occur to you.

Rumpus: So solitude is healthy for you?

Auster: Up to a point. I wouldn't want to live alone. How grim things would be if I didn't have Siri to talk to and share things with. But our days are spent apart, each one alone in a room.

Rumpus: You've worked as a translator, and you are obviously very sensitive to language, and you do often write about words themselves as being particularly important in and of themselves. Are words simply a vehicle for expression, or can they be the inspiration?

Auster: It can be both, and it shifts. I sometimes feel that my goal as a novelist is to write a novel in which the language is so transparent that the reader will forget that language is the medium of communication. To see right through the words into the story itself. At other times, the materiality of the words themselves is the essence of the story. In *Timbuktu*, for example. It's all about the language, the careening mayhem of free association. So it depends on what book we're talking about.

Rumpus: I've read in several places that you are heavily influenced by Herman Melville. In *Moby-Dick*, the narrator Ishmael is decidedly unreliable. As readers, we don't know who he is, or where he came from, and are given nearly no history of him at all. Similarly, in *Invisible*, and in some of your earlier work, your narrators are unreliable as well, playing with the notion of what truth is, and whether or not it can be qualified. When you craft your characters, do you endow them with histories? Do you always know exactly what forces drive them? Do you have emotional relationships with them, and why are some of them so opaque?

Auster: I find my characters as I'm writing. It's quite incredible how fully realized they are in my mind, how many details I know about each of them. Even after a book is finished, they seem to live on, as if they were as real as I am or you are. About a year ago, I was in Denmark, out by the water in Elsinore, and I was very moved to see that the name of one of the ferry boats was *Hamlet*. An imaginary character becomes so important to people that we name a ship after him. The imaginary lives on in the real. *Invisible* is the most complex book of mine in terms of narration. But as August Brill says at one point in *Man in the Dark*, "the real and the imagined are one. Thoughts are real, even thoughts of unreal things."

Rumpus: What now, what's next?
Auster: I'm not sure. For now, I'm still ruminating on the novel I just finished, *Sunset Park*. I'm still under the spell of it. I wrote the last pages at the end of August, but then there was the typing and correcting to do, and I didn't let go of it until a couple of weeks ago. I seem to have a new rhythm now. Up until *The Brooklyn Follies*, I always knew what I wanted to write next—I had a backlog of books in my head. But after that, the drawer was empty. It is as if these last four books have been plucked out of thin air, with long gaps after writing, five, six, seven months. But after something crystallizes, I can write ferociously and finish a novel in six months, which

in the past would have taken me two years or longer. When I start, I have a feeling for the characters, and maybe the shape of the story. Sometimes I might even have the last sentence in mind. But no book I've written has ever ended the way I thought it would when I started. Characters disappear, others come forward. Once you start writing, everything changes.

Paul Auster on His New Novel, *Invisible*

Nick Obourn/2009

This interview first appeared in October 2009 on "The Culture Spoke" blog on the website *True/Slant.com*. It is reprinted with permission of Nick Obourn.

Nick Obourn: Why choose the Vietnam era to open this book?

Paul Auster: I can never say "why" about anything I do. I suppose I can say "how" and "when" and "what." But "why" is impenetrable to me. Stories surge up out of nowhere, and if they feel compelling, you follow them. You let them unfold inside you and see where they are going to lead. This one fascinated me. I think I was interested in exploring youth again. My previous three books had all been about older people. I thought maybe I had explored that enough for a while. There were anniversaries coming up too—many fortieth anniversaries were looming as I finished the book in '08.

'07 had been the fortieth anniversary of the Newark riots, which I had seen. Many pivotal things from my youth are being reexamined now. I was thinking a lot about them as well, and maybe the book came out of that— forty years later.

NO: A lot of *Invisible* is based on memory, on what people remember about the way certain events happened, which, as the story unfolds, has its faults. Memory can have its faults. If you want to speak to it, I'd like to know a little bit about how memory relates to narrative and fiction for you.

PA: Let me give you a memory story. It's not connected to the book, but it's connected to that time, so it is relevant. One of my teachers at Columbia was Edward Said, who died a few years ago. He was the advisor for my master's thesis, which was the last step in my formal education. I didn't go any farther than that.

A posthumous book by Edward has recently been published, *On Late*

203

Style. It was put together by another old professor of mine from Columbia, Michael Wood, who is now at Princeton and remains a good friend. In fact, Michael is the person who interviewed me for the *Paris Review* about five or six years ago. So it's a friendship that has continued. In the book, there is an essay about Jean Genet. I can't remember what year it was, it might have been '69, but Genet came to the Columbia campus in support of the Black Panthers. He gave a talk at the Sundial, right in the middle of the campus. Since I knew French, some people who knew about this event asked me if I would be his interpreter for the day, which I gladly agreed to do. I remember walking around with him, and he was in very good spirits. He had a little flower behind his ear, spoke softly, and kept smiling. It was a beautiful spring day.

Edward writes in his essay that he recalls Genet's visit to the Columbia campus. He wrote that he ran into one of his students, who said, "Genet is indeed coming, and in fact, I'm interpreting for him." I don't remember running into Said and saying this. Then he said Genet got up and spoke, and his remarks were very simple and very much in support of the Black Panthers and against racism in the United States, but that the student interpreter elaborated all his remarks and made all sorts of accusations against American imperialism and capitalism. I have no memory of whether or not I was the one interpreting for him when he gave his speech. I was very shy then and had great difficulty standing up and speaking in public. If I had been that person interpreting that particular speech of Genet's, I know for a fact that I would not have added anything of my own.

When I saw Michael Wood recently, we talked about this. He said, "You know, it's quite possible that Edward misremembered everything." And so we have this giant memory hole: I can't remember if I did it or not, and he couldn't remember what actually happened. I've been puzzling over this now for the past several weeks. I can't get a grip on it. *Invisible* functions a little like this episode.

NO: The book is very much about the idea of the narrative, and the various shapes that it can take, the various voices that it can have, and the various approaches that an author and a reader can have to a story. For you, in creating this book, what were some of the most important parts of the narrative?
PA: It's hard to say, everything is important.

NO: Were there certain parts that came to you right away and certain parts that took a little work to get out?

PA: The central motivating force that drove me into the book was the Born/Walker relation. That was the thing that came first. The book becomes more than that, of course. But it is a constant drum beat in the book as well. I think it had to do with the way young people, even very bright young people, and Walker is nothing if not very bright, are too naive and have too little experience to understand certain kinds of people they run into.

Most people that age have similar kinds of experiences, maybe not as dramatic, but the general idea is: falling in with people and being out of your depth. It's a fascinating moment in life, I think, because at thirty you don't make those mistakes. You can read people more quickly. You can sniff out danger, but at twenty, everything is an adventure and everything is new and happening for the first time. You don't want to block yourself off from experiences. So Walker is open enough to allow Born to befriend him but also stupid enough to think that strangers just walk around giving you money to start a magazine.

NO: That's one of the things that I liked about their relationship in that first section. There is a romantic optimism and excitement behind starting a magazine at that time.

PA: All young poets wanted to have magazines then. And many of them were doing it. Some were very cheaply produced—printed by mimeograph machines. Before the explosion of off-set printing, mimeo magazines were all over the place.

NO: Do you remember any from that era then that you particularly liked?

PA: Let's see. *Adventures in Poetry*, edited by Lewis Warsh and Anne Waldman on the Lower East Side. There was also a small publisher with the bizarre name of Siamese Banana Press—which published my first book, *A Little Anthology of Surrealist Poems, Translations*—run by a prose writer named Johnny Stanton. Mimeo books, with covers by Joe Brainard and George Schneeman. Then, of course, there were prettier magazines, just as Walker describes. *Evergreen Review* was very important then. The *New Directions Annual* and the *Paris Review* were among the most important periodicals at the time. Along with some beautiful magazines like *Art and Literature*, which was short-lived. It was a very fertile period for poetry and little magazines. So Walker jumps—because it's just too irresistible.

NO: Your last book had a lot to do with war.

PA: Yes.

NO: And war plays a part in this book too.
PA: Yes.

NO: I'll steer clear of why, but how does war end up being part of your writing process?
PA: We're surrounded by it now, aren't we? We're so immersed in it that it's hard to think about anything else. We've been in Iraq longer than we fought in World War II, and it's been the same kind of disaster on a much smaller scale that Vietnam was. Now there is Afghanistan, which never goes away. Everybody seems to be trying to blow everybody up all over the world. Every day I open the paper and somebody is shooting at somebody else or bombing somebody else, or threatening to do it. In this book, I'm talking about Vietnam. It would be difficult to explain to you what that war did to American society, how deeply it tore us to pieces. I don't think we've ever recovered. The fact that we went into Iraq for no earthly reason seems to me doubly tragic because it proves that we learn nothing from the past. There's no end to such a war except humiliation, defeat, and the deaths of untold numbers of innocent people.

I've been banging my head against the wall out of frustration. Born is French and therefore someone who has experienced the French debacles: namely Algeria and Indochina, which became our Vietnam. Those two things ruined France also. France has never been the same.

The violence of imperial wars erodes the fabric of the society waging the war. Both of my recent books explore that. As for Born, the curious thing is that I did not name him after the Provençal poet, Bertran de Born. Born was Born, and then I remembered the poet. For some reason, all my characters come to me with their names attached to them. I never have to search for the names.

NO: So they come to you rather finished?
PA: Yes, for one reason or another, they're just there. So Born was born, so to speak, and then I began delving into his namesake poet, whose work I had not read since I was a student—since I was Walker's age. Brutal, brilliant, utterly shocking poetry. And yes, he is indeed in Dante's *Inferno*—walking around in the 28th Canto with his severed head in his hands.

The poem in the book I translated is a real Bertran de Born poem from around 1185. I don't know Provençal, but I used a literal French translation to produce my English version.

NO: And that is the translation that appears in the book?

PA: Yes. Bertran is the poet of war. Born, the twentieth-century character in my book, is someone who has been ruined by war and is also, in some sense, an advocate of war.

NO: Do you think that there is no end to the ways that you can explore, in your writing, the ideas of war or the idea of what happens to people who are involved in war?

PA: It's interesting that you should mention this because I recently finished another book—a new novel that is about the same length as *Invisible*. It takes place now (2008 and 2009) with quite a few characters. Most of the people in the book are in their late twenties, and one of these people is a graduate student writing her dissertation on the immediate aftermath of World War II and the effect it had on American society ('45-'47) as reflected in books, crime novels, films, and other pop culture manifestations. One of the things she writes about is *The Best Years of Our Lives*, a film I like very much.

Part of the novel, then, explores the young generation of that period, which is to say, my parents' generation. My mother was born in 1925, which means she was sixteen when America entered the war. In other words, her late adolescence and early adulthood were lived in the shadow of the war.

Everyone from that generation is completely marked by World War II. The effect of war on soldiers is sometimes swept under the rug. People were ruined. Lives were absolutely destroyed. My wife's father was a nineteen-year-old draftee in World War II. He became a 1st Sgt. in the Pacific. He never got rid of it. Siri used some of the things he wrote about that time in her most recent novel, *The Sorrows of an American*.

I am talking about the extracts from her father's memoir, which he wrote for the family. He served in the occupation army in Japan and was discharged in '46. That's when he was finally demobilized and sent home. He was the most sane, rational, earnest, moral person I've ever known. A good, good man, but he came home crazy. He went back to the farm in Minnesota—the poor, broken-down farm that had been mostly lost during the Depression—and spent the whole summer chopping down trees. One after the other after the other. This was a young man out of his mind with trauma. Again, in the new book, I do touch on war. It is only one sliver of the novel, which is mostly about other things, but I can't stop thinking about it.

NO: A couple of reviews of *Invisible* in the trades (*Kirkus* and *Publishers Weekly*), draw a comparison to *Heart of Darkness*, the ending specifically. When you are writing a book, how aware are you of other works of literature? Are you aware of them or are you trying to push everything else away and concentrate on that only?

PA: I'm not thinking about it. I can see why people would say that, although it's really quite different. I certainly wasn't thinking of Conrad while I was writing.

NO: This book is written in several defining parts. When you got to the end of a part, did you know that was the end of that part?

PA: Yes. It's funny because the book is written in the first person, the second person, and the third person. It's written in the past tense and the present tense. In terms of the narrative, the Walker story ends after Part 3. Part 4 is a kind of coda, but without Part 4, the book wouldn't have the effect it does.

NO: Right. We learn what happens to Born.

PA: Yes. It's a funny thing, structure in a narrative. This book does not have a traditional "arc." Little of my work does. I remember when I was making the film *Smoke* with Wayne Wang. That was back in the '90s as well. The story jumps among a number of characters. I think the film is divided into five parts, each one with a name of a character. Again, the whole gist of the story is told in the first four parts. Then there is a fifth part in which someone tells someone else a story. That part is ostensibly unrelated to everything that has happened before, and yet, deeply connected, but only in the most oblique, subterranean ways. The whole emotional payoff of the film is in that final part, even though it doesn't serve the so-called plot in any obvious way. It helps finish the story off and give it some kind of conclusion. In *Invisible*, Cécile's diary functions more or less in this way. It's disconnected from the rest of the story so far, and yet it is important to have it there.

NO: So there is always a story standing next to a story, standing next to a story. It could go on like that for infinity?

PA: I think that in the previous book, *Man in the Dark*, I took what is probably the greatest risk I have ever taken in terms of narrative structure. For the first two thirds of the book, Brill is alone in his room thinking up his story. Then he comes to the end. Then he starts thinking about other things. Suddenly, there's a knock on the door, and his granddaughter enters. At that point, we make a sharp, right turn into something else. It turns into the story of Brill's marriage and the story of young Katya's grandmother. It felt right to me. I can't justify it in any way, but there it is. Another unorthodox approach.

NO: You write from several different points of view in *Invisible*. Did you connect more with any specific characters while you were writing?
PA: The truth is that I feel close to all my characters. I can't describe how deeply I love them all, even monsters like Born. I felt very close to him as well. In a funny way, I feel the most tenderness toward Margot—the lost and confused Margot.

NO: Margot's is quite a sad story.
PA: Terribly sad. But there's also Cécile—the brilliant, gawky girl who turns into a rather formidable scholar.

NO: These are the women in Adam's life, aside from his sister Gwyn, whom the reader is fully introduced to in the second part. This is also the section where the reader encounters an event that Adam and his sister are involved in. It's an event that is hard for a lot of people to understand and hard to read in some ways. Yet we also sympathize with Adam. How did you make sure that sympathy was the thing that people felt in light of what happened? Or was it a conscious balancing out of those two things?
PA: No, it's just something that happened. Adam doesn't feel guilty. Gwyn doesn't feel guilty either, and therefore neither one is traumatized by what they do. I'm talking about the incest that might or might not have occurred between them. Everyone passes over it in silence.

NO: Writing about your work in the *New York Review of Books* last December, Michael Dirda said that your characters have a habit of escaping into stories. What is it about this escaping that is so fascinating to you and to your characters?
PA: I've written several novels that are linear stories that go from A to B to C all the way to Z, quite a few actually. Other books are more complex. I think it has to do with the mood I'm in, the kind of story I want to write or that seems to be asking to be written. I really do feel at the mercy of the material. I don't try to manipulate what I have been given. I listen, and I follow.

NO: Down the rabbit hole essentially.
PA: At times. I do feel that there can be interesting effects in what I call

"collage." When you have two or three or four things in the frame or canvas with spaces in between them, there can be a kind of energy that's created in the spaces between the different elements of the collage. If any one of those objects is put alone on the wall, it wouldn't have the same effect that the grouping does. So I guess I'm interested in the energy created *between* stories. I can't justify this philosophically. It's simply an emotional position.

NO: This is your fifteenth novel, and you said you just completed another one. Over the span of your writing these novels, has your approach changed? Has there been any sort of marked difference in the way that you begin and end?

PA: Things have changed in the last few years. For a long time I had a backlog of ideas, and so I pretty much knew when I was writing a novel what the next one would be or what I hoped it would be. I would often think about the next as I was writing the present book. I had a little pact with myself. It's very hard to explain how obsessive writing a novel can be, how it takes over all your waking thoughts. I'm a great believer in the unconscious. When I stop working for the day, I try to push the book out of my head. It's not easy to do. The danger zone, the most risky moment is lying in bed about to go to sleep. For years I would say, "Push the book out of your head, think about the next one." I would think about the next story or the next book. Up until *The Brooklyn Follies*, that's how I functioned. I knew, more or less, what the next thing was that I wanted to do. Then, suddenly, the drawers were empty. I've written four books since then, two short ones and two longer ones, with great gaps in between the finishing of one and the starting of another. I think after *Invisible* I went six or seven months before I started writing the new book. Each of these four books has been written in a fury.

NO: Really?

PA: In a matter of months, whereas in the past it would take me two or three years to write a book. *Invisible* was written in about six months.

NO: Interesting.

PA: This new forthcoming book was written in six months. They're both around three hundred pages. I don't understand it. My daily output seems to have increased, but my times of inactivity have increased as well. These stretches of unemployment are not very happy ones. I'm trying to relax, but you don't want it to go on too long.

NO: Right. So what do you do with the time?

PA: You begin to feel useless. I've been doing a lot of little things in the past two months or so, just to keep myself busy.

NO: One last question about *Invisible*: the title is not something that, at first, strikes the reader as very connected to the material in the book. It's connected, but it's not obvious. Where did it come from?

PA: I used the word "invisible" several times in the book, always very consciously. The first time is when Born's face is described. Walker says, "It was the kind of face that would become invisible in any crowd." He talks about the downtrodden in America, particularly poor black people as being invisible. When Freeman is flying back home in the dark from California to New York, he says, "there's an invisible America lying beneath me." In the very last pages of the book, as Cécile is walking down the hill, she hears something but can't see it. And because she can't see it, she has no idea what she's hearing.

I think, in a sense, that's how the whole book functions. We hear things, but we can't always see them, or, even if we do see them, we're not sure that we're seeing correctly. Hence: *Invisible*.

Index

Printed in the United States
By Bookmasters